An Introduction to
Sociology in Ireland

THIRD EDITION

An Introduction to Sociology in Ireland

THIRD EDITION

Bernadette McDonald

Gill & Macmillan

Gill & Macmillan
Hume Avenue
Park West
Dublin 12
www.gillmacmillan.ie

© Bernadette McDonald 2014

978 07171 5622 1

Print origination by Síofra Murphy
Printed by GraphyCems, Spain

This book is dedicated to my parents, Mary and Peter

Contents

Preface

The third edition of this text maintains the aim of the earlier editions – to introduce students to the world of sociology. It introduces students to key sociological concepts in the hope of enabling them to apply these concepts to themselves in the context of their family setting, community and wider society.

This text, which is suitable for students studying for FETAC (level 5 and level 6), BTEC and HETAC qualifications in the caring fields, aims to increase the student's understanding of social, economic and political arrangements in an unequal society. The text is learner-friendly and will provide the student with an up-to-date knowledge of the sociological context of social studies.

The book is organised into twelve chapters providing information to familiarise the student with the distinct discipline of sociology, with the major theoretical perspectives and methods used to produce sociological knowledge, and with key sociological concepts and topics.

When working with individuals and groups, it is important that social carers and students develop an awareness of, and respect for, the variety of human experiences in our society today. By writing this book, I hope to provide an introduction to issues that have become and continue to be increasingly critical as we go through the twenty-first century, and to encourage students to develop an attitude of critical reflection and thought.

1

Introduction to Sociology

CHAPTER OBJECTIVES

After reading this chapter you should be able to:

- define sociology
- understand sociology as a perspective
- distinguish between sociology and common sense
- trace the origins of sociology
- define key sociological terms and concepts: culture, status, roles, social group, social institution, social stratification and social control.

SOCIOLOGY DEFINED

'Sociology is concerned with the study of society and specifically with key issues such as explaining change and the distribution of power between different social groups' (Barry and Yuill 2002:1). According to Matthewman *et al.* (2007:14) 'Sociology is a form of consciousness, a way of thinking. Of particular concern are the often inarticulated or hidden connections within society, the figurations that help shape our fate.' The task of sociology is to reveal to us the unseen connections that determine our lives.

This chapter begins with an examination of what is meant by the term 'sociology'. The authors of *Sociology – A Global Introduction* (2nd edition), by John Macionis and Ken Plummer, have defined sociology as 'the systematic study of human society' (2002:4). The word 'systematic' implies that sociology is a social scientific discipline that studies society, and as a discipline it offers its students specific methods of investigating, explaining and understanding how patterns in society are created and how they change over time. Society shapes what we do, how we do it, and how we understand what others do.

The definition given by Restivo (cited in Tovey and Share 2003:16) describes sociology as 'a field of inquiry simultaneously concerned with understanding, explaining, criticising and improving the human condition'. When attempting to answer the question 'What is sociology?' Osborne and Loon (1999) say that 'sociology is about explaining what seems obvious – like how our society works, to people who don't understand just how complicated it really is'.

Sociologists (people who study sociology) attempt to:

1. understand how society works, and
2. explain why people do the things they do, in the way that they do them. (Marsh 2002)

A central concern of this discipline of sociology is the study of the relationship between individuals and society, i.e. how people act and impact on the society they live in and vice versa (Hyde *et al.* 2004:5). 'While we are all different and while we are independent actors, we are shaped by long-term processes of social change and by social structures such as class, religion, gender, ethnicity and so forth' (www.sociology.ie).

, For Donohoe and Gaynor, sociology is 'the scientific study of society that aims to look at the causes and consequences of social change and the principles of social order and stability' (1999:149).

These definitions show that:

- sociology is the study of human beings
- sociology is the study of interactions and relations among human beings
- sociology is a form of enquiry
- sociology is a science that requires the gathering of evidence
- sociology is a distinct academic discipline.

Sociology occurs when people start to address and question what goes on between individuals – how they relate and interact with each other. According to Babbie, 'Sociology addresses simple, face-to-face interactions such as conversations, dating behaviour, and students asking a professor to delay the term paper deadline' (1988:3). Not only does sociology study how humans relate to one another at an individual level, it also looks at how institutions and formal organisations function. It looks at how whole societies function and the relationships (or non-relationships) between and among societies.

Sociology requires us to study how people live together, how we co-operate or compete when times are good or when times get tough. 'Sociology enables us, then, to develop self-awareness and self-understanding, facilitating an increased recognition of what enables and constrains our, and others' actions' (McIntosh and Punch 2005:10). Because human needs and wants sometimes result in situations that put humans in conflict with each other, there is a need to create rules. The creation of rules is an attempt to help humans live together, an attempt to help establish some order in a world that would otherwise be chaotic.

Babbie in his 1988 work *The Sociological Spirit* also states that 'sociology is also the study of how rules are organised and perpetuated' (1988:4). While it is important to examine the rules that govern how people live together, we need to examine how they arise and how they change over time. For Babbie, sociology is also the study of how we break rules and why at times this is not always a bad thing. 'A sociological understanding of the world . . . enables us to consider how our lives are intertwined with others. This enhances our ability to see the world from other viewpoints and to engage with people from different backgrounds. It encourages us to become more tolerant and sensitive to cultural differences' (McIntosh and Punch 2005:10). Sociology as a subject appeals to those who wish to challenge their assumptions and to go beyond common-sense explanations. Those interested in sociology are being asked to look at the familiar with fresh eyes, 'to question accepted understandings of the world and to critically evaluate widely held ideas that might otherwise go unquestioned' (www. sociology.ie).

While the above section outlines briefly what sociology is, the next touches on the approach we must take if we are to develop a sociological perspective.

THE SOCIOLOGICAL PERSPECTIVE

'Each discipline within the social sciences has its own unique viewpoint' (Curry *et al*. 2005:4). The sociological perspective offers us a way to view, understand and affect the world we live in. It requires sociologists to take a broad view, to stand back and start to question all that we have taken for granted. To 'do' sociology, we need to think outside our own experiences and to start looking at what seems ordinary or 'mundane' to us in a new light. For Macionis and Plummer, 'using the sociological perspective amounts to seeing the strange in the familiar' (2002:4). According to Peter Berger (1967) 'The fascination of sociology lies in the fact that its perspective makes us see in a new light the very world in which we have lived all our lives (cited in Marsh 2000:8).

Sociology is not just about human societies, it is also a way of thinking about human societies (Hyde *et al.* 2004:6). The American sociologist C. Wright Mills emphasised the importance of developing 'the sociological imagination' and of using it within sociology. Failure to use this sociological imagination would mean that the discipline would lack a critical and questioning edge and sociology would be reduced to a discipline that lacked any 'real purpose other than to describe, to provide background detail and a social context' (Barry and Yuill 2002:9). Most simply put, 'the sociological imagination requires us, above all, to "think ourselves away" from the familiar routines of our daily lives in order to look at them anew' (Giddens 2001:2).

To really be a proponent of this perspective we must give up the idea that the way humans behave is simply a result of their deciding to behave that way and accepting instead the notion that society guides our thoughts and actions. Many sociologists today believe that we must combine the study of major changes in society and individual lives and by doing so, sociologists can develop their understanding of social life (Haralambos and Holborn 2004:xxv). While this may initially seem strange and difficult to do, it is a skill we need to master in order to view the world sociologically.

Thinking sociologically requires us to see society as much more than a collection of human beings. Failure to do so and to recognise the power of social institutions that outlive humans means we will be unable to deal with important problems and opportunities in our lives and in the world. An understanding of the power that society has on influencing our thoughts and actions can empower us to deal with the problems of the world. Mills' work on 'the sociological imagination' showed the ability to study the structure of society at the same time as individuals' lives. Mills 'held up sociology as an escape from the "traps" of our lives because it can show us that society – not our own foibles or failings – is responsible for many of our problems' (Macionis and Plummer 2005:10). He argued that the sociological imagination allowed people to understand their 'private troubles' in terms of 'public issues' (Haralambos and Holborn 2004:xxv). An example of this can be seen when we look at problems such as marital breakdown, unemployment and war. Although these are problems that are all experienced by people, due maybe to problems in their own personal lives, individuals need to react to them differently and the way they do so impacts on society as a whole. However, Mills argues that these issues need to be examined and can only be fully understood in the context of wider social forces. 'For example, very specific circumstances might lead to one person becoming unemployed, but when unemployment rates in society as a whole rise, it becomes a public issue that needs to be explained' (*Ibid.*: xxv). Mills maintains that sociology transforms personal problems into public and political issues. His work describes 'both the power of society to shape our individual lives, and the importance of connecting our lives (biographies) to history and society' (Macionis and Plummer 2005:10).

Grasping the sociological perspective requires us to grasp the idea that 'who we are' is a function of the society we live in. By doing so, we will see how it can help us deal with the constraints of society. This can set us on a quest for answers that may prove invaluable.

Developing a sociological perspective will enable us to:

1. develop a new way of thinking; one that questions our familiar way of understanding ourselves
2. critically assess commonly held truths and allow us to see opportunities or constraints that affect our lives
3. empower us to become active participants in our society
4. recognise human differences and suffering that may influence our decisions to confront problems of living in a diverse world. (Macionis and Plummer 2002:9)

Where there are clear benefits (mentioned briefly above), there are certain pitfalls and problems associated with the perspective that we must try to avoid. Because we are part of a rapidly changing world, it sometimes becomes difficult to study society as it too changes. Becoming aware of this will enable us to question research findings and statistics that might have been reflective of a particular society at a particular time but that may be out-of-date or invalid today. Because we are part of the world we study, it is important that we try to maintain some distance from it and not develop a view that holds our society's practices or our cultural views superior or inferior to another's. We must also be aware that the information we produce as sociologists, and the findings we present, become part of a society's knowledge and that too can shape the working of that society. Overall what is being highlighted is the impact of sociology on society. To help us understand the perspective, it is necessary to examine it at the time and in the context it first emerged. To do so, a historical account of the development of the subject is necessary. However, prior to discussing the origins of sociology as an academic discipline, it is important to highlight the differences between sociology and a commonsense approach to society.

SOCIOLOGY AND COMMON SENSE

Some may argue that since sociology focuses on issues, problems or challenges we encounter in our everyday lives, it is difficult to distinguish it from commonsense theories of everyday life. Sociology is concerned with studying many things most people already know something about. Everyone will have some form of knowledge, information and understanding on areas such as family life, work, the education system and the health system. 'This leads many people to assume that the topics studied by sociologists and the explanations sociologists produce are really just common sense: what "everyone knows"' (Browne 2005). This is a very mistaken assumption. Sociology does not see society as operating on commonsense lines because 'In the world of common sense there is also little requirement to be "scientific"' (McIntosh and Punch 2005:27). Sociology sees society as consisting of 'often complex social patterns which needed to be uncovered and analysed, just as a physical scientist would study a chemical compound or the laws of motion. If evidence was gathered through rigorous empirical ways then theories could be seen as true and valid' (Scott, cited in Marsh 2002:9). Research carried out by sociologists has shown many widely held common-sense ideas and explanations to be false. According to Browne (2005), 'Ideas such as that the poor and unemployed are inadequate and lazy, that everyone has equal chances in life, that men are "naturally" superior to women . . . these have all been questioned by sociological research. Much of the concern of sociology lies in re-examination of such common-sense views.'

Sociological explanations of the social world differ to commonsense explanations in the following ways:

1. Sociology, like other social sciences such as psychology, uses methods of research to obtain information and knowledge about the social world.
2. 'Sociological studies seek to move beyond individual subjective understanding in order to ask how others might understand the same processes differently' (Hyde et al. 2004:6). Sociologists are required to adopt a sceptical attitude and as a result depart from limited observations of the commonsense explanations of the social world.
3. Sociology teaches us to critically assess and evaluate commonly held assumptions by gathering evidence as a result of rigorous research. On the basis of such evidence we should construct logical arguments and then 'attempt to relate what we have learned to a wider social context' (McIntosh and Punch 2005:29).

Sociologists look at and examine evidence on issues before making up their minds. 'The explanations and conclusions of sociologists are based on precise evidence which has been collected through painstaking research using established research procedures' (Browne 2005:2).

THE ORIGINS OF SOCIOLOGY

'The discipline of sociology is fundamentally a "modern" one, bound up with attempts to explain, anticipate and alter a rapidly changing world' (Barry and Yuill 2002:7).

Sociology, the science of social life, is a discipline of relatively recent origin. It was so named by the French writer Auguste Comte in 1838, making it a product of the early nineteenth century (Tovey and Share 2003). When Comte first used the term less than 200 years ago, he was interested in developing a new way of looking at the world. Unlike the great thinkers such as Aristotle (384–322 BC) and Plato (427–347 BC), who tended to focus their thinking on imagining the ideal society, Comte wanted to go a step further. For him, this involved analysing society as it really was and he believed that it was only by doing so that you could understand or try to understand how society actually operated. 'Comte was influenced by Enlightenment thinking as a new way of understanding the natural and social worlds. The new intelligentsia of the Enlightenment sought explanations for patterns in the natural and social worlds by rejecting religious (or supernatural) and metaphysical (or natural) explanations in favour of the development of scientific and rational explanations' (Hyde *et al.* 2004:3).

Unlike his predecessors and their approach to society, Comte's new approach was to be characterised by a buzzword – 'critical thinking'. Assertions about society must make sense, correspond to facts. Comte believed that in order to truly understand how a society actually operates there was a need to develop a scientific approach. Comte therefore was a proponent of 'Positivism' and saw it as 'the search for order and progress in the social world' (Marsh 2000:15). 'Positivism holds that science should be concerned only with observable entities that are known directly to experience' (Giddens 2001:8). To put it more simply, Positivism refers to using research methods of the natural sciences to carry out social enquiry and as a result produce a 'social science'.

Comte believed that when we were equipped with knowledge about how society operated, then people would be able to build themselves a better life and a better future. But why did this discipline emerge in that historical period? What was happening around Comte that resulted in his seeing a need for a new science?

By the time of the birth of sociology in the early nineteenth century, huge changes were taking place across Europe and North America that were having profound effects on the people of that time. These changes were a result of the industrial and democratic revolutions that occurred at the end of the eighteenth and beginning of the nineteenth centuries. These changes were rearranging society and changing the way people lived. Comte himself was one of those being affected by these social changes. He was born at the end of the democratic revolution in his own native France and grew up in the early years of the industrial revolution that first hit Britain before spreading to other areas of Europe. Society, as people knew it at that time, was undergoing massive transformations. The introduction of technology and the new economic processes associated with the industrial revolution were altering forever the organisation of societies. The democratic revolutions were raising issues about the proper relationship between the individual and society while debating human nature and authority. 'The changes occurring in society at this time provoked questions about how societies could or should be organised and how emerging forms of society affected relations between groups of individuals in society' (Hyde *et al.* 2004:4).

Social change was happening at a rate that had not been seen before and as a result people like Comte saw a need to identify these changes associated with modernity and to chart its likely path. By understanding what was happening one could build oneself a better future. Hence the emergence of the discipline of sociology (from the Greek and Latin words meaning the study of society) which Comte divided into two parts:

1. social statics, which looks at how society is held together, and
2. social dynamics, which looks at how society changes. (Macionis and Plummer 2002:12)

KEY SOCIOLOGICAL TERMS AND CONCEPTS

Culture

'Culture refers to the ways of life of the members of a society, or of groups within a society. It includes how they dress, their marriage customs and family life, their patterns of work, religious ceremonies and leisure pursuits'

(Giddens 2001:22). When people behave in a particular way, it is believed that their behaviour is determined by the culture they live in. Just as different individuals have different personalities, different societies have different cultures. For example, Irish culture is very different to Chinese culture.

Culture in its broadest sense is all the ways of behaving, interacting, thinking and communicating that are handed down from one generation to the next through language and all other modes of communicating which, according to Osborne and Loon, include 'gesture, painting, writing, architecture, music, fashion, food and so on' (1999:142). Although human culture is very recent, it is said to be the force that separates us from primitive ways of living. A society's culture is their way of behaving that allows them to make sense of the world. At the same time it makes sure everyone else knows what they are supposed to be doing. Cultures vary the world over, but despite huge differences they are found to be built on five major components:

1. symbols
2. language
3. values/beliefs
4. norms
5. material culture

Status

'Contrary to what people may believe, their social interactions are not always a matter of conscious choice. Each of us is linked to society, and whether we realise it or not, these linkages can determine how we interact with others. One of the most important linkages is status' (Curry *et al.* 2005:128). Status refers to the social positions a person can occupy within a society or within a small social grouping (Babbie 1988). For example, in society a person can occupy the status of mother, sister, student, doctor etc. Each of us in real life occupies numerous statuses and we act accordingly, because each status we occupy has certain kinds of behaviour associated with it. When you occupy the status of doctor there are certain kinds of behaviour expected of you that would not be expected of a disc jockey. Each status we occupy acts like a mask that we hold up when we interact with others, that determines our behaviour and the expected behaviour of another.

Throughout our lives we continue to learn the statuses we occupy, the behaviour expectations associated with those statuses and our relationships with people occupying other statuses. It is a process that continues right through our life cycle because during this time the statuses we occupy in society change. Our status as student ends when we finish study and enter the arena of work.

Sociologists distinguish between two types of statuses: ascribed and achieved. An ascribed status, such as race and sex, cannot be changed by individual effort whether we want to or not. An achieved status on the other hand is one that can be obtained through individual effort. For example, our occupational status can be achieved by our ability, how hard we work and an element of luck (Curry *et al.* 2005:129).

Roles

'Each status in society is accompanied by a number of norms that define how an individual occupying a particular status is expected to act. This group of norms is known as a role' (Haralambos and Holborn 2004:x). When we occupy a certain status in society we have functions to serve or roles to play. Social roles help us to organise and to regulate our behaviour. Teacher, dentist, waitress are all examples of occupational roles, while grandfather, aunt, daughter provide examples of family roles (Donohoe and Gaynor 1999). When we interact with other individuals in terms of their roles, we know what to do and how to do it. Knowing our role in society helps us to take part (in most cases) in 'pleasant and productive social interactions'. However, times or situations can arise that can result in role conflict – 'the incompatibility of the different roles played by a single person' (Turner 1990 cited in Curry *et al.* 2005:131). If we diverge too far from the social role we are expected to play in society, we can expect to be criticised or to experience some other form of social punishment.

Social group

Social gatherings of people such as an audience or a crowd do not constitute a sociologist's definition of a group. To be part of a group, members must agree on a number of characteristics springing from shared common interest or interaction with one another, and the group must have a sense of identity and some degree of structure.

Two types of groups have been distinguished by sociologists: primary groups and secondary groups (Marsh 2000:30). Primary groups are made up of people connected to one another through primary relationships; relationships we have with people closest to us, such as our family members or partner. On the other hand, the relationships we have within secondary groups are based on the statuses we occupy and the roles we expect of such statuses, such as that between a teacher and their student.

Sociologists are interested in how groups

1. contribute to our sense of identity, and
2. influence who people think we are.

Table 1:1 Primary and secondary group characteristics

Relationships	Kind	Length	Scope	Purpose	Typical examples
Primary Group	Personal orientation	Usually long-term	Broad – usually involving many activities	As an end in itself	Families, close friendships
Secondary Group	Goal orientation	Variable, often short-term	Narrow – usually involving few activities	As a means to an end	Co-workers, political organisations

(Source: Curry *et al.* 2005:138)

Social institution

Sociology is concerned with the study of social institutions. Institutions are various organised social arrangements which can be found in all societies. Sociologists speak of institutions when referring to the family, education, politics, religion and so forth. The concept can generally be applied to 'social aspects of social behaviour regulated by well established, easily recognised and relatively stable norms, values and law' (Mann 1983:172). These norms, values and laws lead to the establishment of agreements that govern broad aspects of social life. The main function of institutions is to support the survival of the group by firstly shaping individual experiences. According to Browne (2005:1), 'Sociology tries to understand how these various social institutions operate, and how they relate to one another, such as the influence the family might have on how well children perform in the education system'.

Institutional change does occur and is most likely to occur when the beliefs and values of one institution come into conflict with another. Change can also be a result of conflict within the same institution.

Social stratification

Social stratification refers to 'a system by which a society ranks categories of people in a hierarchy' (Macionis and Plummer 2002:178). Most societies the world over have some form of stratification that results in some groups of people being in superior positions. Such positioning in a 'hierarchy' allows certain groups to enjoy considerably more power, prestige or access to resources such as health, education etc. than others.

While every society (except the most technologically primitive) stratifies in some ways, four main systems of stratification have been identified by sociologists. These are slavery, estate, caste and class. Each of these systems is made up of its own strata or layers. Your life chances or opportunities are very much determined by the position you occupy on these social strata.

Some of these stratification systems are open and some are closed. In other words, when we speak of an open system of stratification we are referring to a system that allows people to change their position on the hierarchical structure throughout their life course. The class system that operates in Ireland is considered an open system. A closed system does not afford a person the same opportunity, and as a result a person's position in life is solely determined by the family group they are born into. The caste system that operates in parts of India provides a good example of a closed system of stratification.

Social control

'The processes of socialisation and social control are fundamental to the equilibrium of the social system and therefore to order in society' (Haralambos and Holborn 2004:940).

When people do not abide by the rules or behaviour expectations of a certain society they are disciplined. Social control aims to create social order. It can take many different forms but falls into two broad categories: informal and formal.

Informal social control can be expressed in disapproving looks by another if something is said or done out of context. In contrast more serious acts such as murder, theft or child abuse are disciplined by formal social control which is backed by the law, the Gardaí, the courts and the prison system. Other means of social control could possibly include psychiatrists and social workers.

The following chapters will deal with each of these concepts in greater detail, especially in relation to Irish society.

2

Concepts and Processes of Socialisation and the Acquisition of Culture

CHAPTER OBJECTIVES

After reading this chapter you should be able to:
- define socialisation
- distinguish between primary and secondary agents of socialisation
- briefly outline socialisation and the life course
- explain what is meant by 're-socialisation'
- define culture
- describe the components of culture: symbols, language, values, norms and material culture
- outline the causes of cultural change
- distinguish between ethnocentrism and cultural relativism.

SOCIALISATION DEFINED

'Socialisation refers to the preparation of newcomers to become members of an existing group and to think, feel, and act in ways the group considers appropriate' (www.nyu.edu 2012). 'Socialisation refers to the way in which we absorb the rules of behaviour which are common in our society' (Abbott 1998:10).

The process of socialisation involves learning the language, values, rules and knowledge of the culture into which we are born. Through socialisation we learn to live according to the expectations of the society in which we live through experience and through relationships. The process starts when we are babies and continues right throughout our lives. 'It is through the process of socialisation that a "raw" human infant develops into a social person, initiated into the beliefs and ways of life of his social group and able to play his own part in society' (Cox 1987:62). Contact with other people affects how our personalities are shaped and developed. 'We come to behave, to feel, to evaluate and to think similarly to those around us. Most societies tend to reproduce their social kind from generation to generation. However, the process is complex and not fully understood' (Clarke *et al.* 2000:150).

THE NATURE/NURTURE DEBATE

One of the big debates that has been going on for centuries is the nature/nurture debate. In this debate we are asked if the behaviour of people is due to their nature (or genetics) or to their nurture (or environment). Charles Darwin was one of the first who argued, during the nineteenth century, 'that each species evolves over thousands of generations as genetic variations enhance survival and reproduction. Biologically rooted traits that enhance survival emerge as a species' "nature"' (Macionis and Plummer 2002:152). This view enables us to exploit people. 'It is easy to exploit others if you think that they are not human in the same sense that you are' (www.usi.edu). However, these views were challenged by a psychologist, John B. Watson, in the twentieth century. He came up with the theory of behaviourism. His theory stated that human behaviour was not instinctive, but learned. Watson insisted that people differed only in their cultural surroundings, and from this theory we received the 'nurture' idea.

'In today's world, we do not say that our behaviours are instinctual, but rather they are learned. What we do with inherited potential depends on our social experiences' (Plomin *et al.* 1980, cited in www.usi.edu). Current thinking on this ongoing debate about the relative importance of nature versus nurture (or heredity and environment) in human development 'prefers to recognise the interdependence of the two, rather than the exclusive importance of either one' (Scott and Marshall 2005:621). According to Macionis and Plummer (2002:152) 'We should not think of nature as opposing nurture, though, since we express our human nature as we build culture. For humans, then, nature and nurture are inseparable.'

PRIMARY AND SECONDARY AGENTS OF SOCIALISATION

'Every society has individuals, groups, organisations and institutions that provide substantial amounts of socialisation during the life course. These are called agents of socialisation' (Curry *et al.* 2005:66).

Primary socialisation: First stage of socialisation. It occurs in infancy and childhood and is the 'intense period of cultural learning' (Giddens 2001:26). During this time children learn language, what constitutes acceptable behaviour and social skills which form the foundation for later learning. These are learned from those people who are closest to the child, that is, parents, near family and main carers. These are referred to as the primary agents of socialisation. Primary socialisation is characterised by 'close emotional ties, in which the child identifies with his significant others and, because he cares about them and for them, their influence is very strong and goes very deep' (Cox 1987:63).

Secondary socialisation: This stage of socialisation takes place in later childhood and maturity. At this stage, children adapt to the wider world and learn to relate to a variety of people in a variety of different ways. Peers, schools, clubs, churches, the media and eventually the workplace become socialising forces for individuals. 'Social interactions in these contexts help people to learn the values, norms and beliefs which make up the patterns of their culture' (Giddens 2001:28). Much secondary socialisation is less about emotional involvement and more concerned with learning appropriate knowledge, skills and attitudes.

The following settings have special significance in the socialisation process:

The family

'The home is the really important classroom in life . . . Schools teach you useful things but it is in the home you learn the important things' (Handy 2009:50).

Often seen as the agent that has the most impact on the socialisation process. For the first few years of life children are totally dependent on their parents. 'Within the family, the child first develops physical skills, such as walking, and the intellectual skills of counting and naming things' (Curry *et al.* 2005:75). During this time children are learning (consciously and unconsciously) from their parents. According to Macionis and Plummer (2002), 'The family also confers on children a social position, that is, parents not only bring children into the physical world, they also place them in society in terms of race, ethnicity, religion and class.' 'Parsons argued families "are factories" which produce human personalities' (Haralambos and Holborn 2004:469). Parsons believed that families are essential for this purpose, 'since primary socialisation requires a context which provides warmth, security and mutual support. He could conceive no institution other than the family that could provide this context' (*Ibid*.: 469). However, since family systems vary widely, the range of family contacts that the infant experiences is by no means standard across cultures (Giddens 2009:288).

Schooling

The school, which is a secondary agent of socialisation, differs from the family because instead of regarding the child as a unique individual, it expects the child as a student to meet standards, follow rules and behave like everyone else. The emphasis at school shifts from who the child is, to how well they perform. Apart from formal lessons that teach children how to read, write etc., it also teaches children the importance of punctuality and competition. When children go to school they meet other children from different backgrounds than their own. They tend to form play groups with children made up of one sex and race. According to Best (1983), 'boys engage in more physical activities and often spend more time outdoors while girls tend to be more sedentary, often helping the teacher with many housekeeping chores' (cited in www.usi.edu). The school is also a place for sharing informal knowledge. 'Simply listening to students as they talk over lunch will reveal the importance placed on movies, sex, sports, popular songs, proper dress and who likes whom' (Curry *et al*. 2005:74).

Peer groups

The peer group provides a great deal of informal socialisation, because children spend so much time with their peers. Peer groups allow children to escape the direct supervision of adults, allowing them greater independence and autonomy. 'Adolescent autonomy-seeking reduces emotional dependence on the parents and frees young people to explore other relationships, develop their independence and their identity' (Lalor *et al*. 2007:77). Topics such as girls/boys, music etc., can be discussed more freely. 'Peer groups aid in the socialisation process because children in certain groups conform to the ideals of that group while disliking other groups' (www.usi.edu). The influence of the peer group increases with age, peaking during adolescence. While there is a tendency to dwell on the negative aspects of peer groups, it has been shown that 'Positive peer relationships are associated with better physical and mental health and a lesser possibility of smoking and drunkenness' (Lalor *et al.* 2007:79). However, they go on to state that 'A major concern for adolescents is "fitting in" with their peers. Young people have to deal with contradictions between their developing individuality, their wanting to "fit in" with peers and their fear of sticking out' (*Ibid.*: 79).

Mass media

The mass media has an enormous influence on the process of socialisation. For example, children can become socialised through the programmes they are allowed to watch on the television. 'Because the media are so pervasive, many observers worry that both children and adults will be socialised into a world that does not exist. They say that the media are so simplistic, overly selective and distorting that a true picture of society never appears' (Curry *et al.* 2005:75). While the media includes newspapers, radio, magazines, the internet etc., some research states that 'television consumes as much of children's time as interacting with parents' (Macionis and Plummer 1997:141). A study entitled *Growing Up in Ireland* found that, when it came to computer and internet use in Ireland:

1. '86 per cent of all 9 year olds have a computer in their home.
2. 35 per cent of 9 to 12 year olds and 82 per cent of teenagers have a social networking profile.
3. Irish children spend at least one hour online per day and three quarters of 15 to 16 year olds use the internet every day' (cited in O'Neill and Dinh 2013).

The internet is mostly used for the World Wide Web, a global multimedia library, invented in 1990 by Tim Berners-Lee, a software engineer. An undergraduate student at the University of Illinois wrote the software that made it popular across the world (Giddens 2009:727). Despite its popularity and increased usage, some sociologists have expressed concerns with the spread of the internet. Among these are:

1. Increased social isolation and atomisation among its users. They argue that one effect of increasing internet access in households is that 'people are spending less quality time with their families and friends' (Giddens 2009:728).

2. The lines between work and home life are becoming blurred. Accessibility to the internet has meant that employees can finish work not completed during the day, check emails etc. The internet has encroached on domestic life.

Traditional forms of entertainment such as going to the cinema, library, music stores are falling by the wayside as is the human contact and social interaction often connected with these activities. According to Giddens, 'if current trends in TV watching continue, the average child born today will have spent more time watching television by the age of 18 than in any other activity except sleep' (2009:733).

SOCIALISATION AND THE LIFE COURSE

Socialisation is a life-long process. 'Because society deems it important that people learn certain essentials, socialisation is not left to chance, rather it is an integral part of our life course: the stages into which our life span is divided, such as adolescence and middle age' (Curry *et al.* 2005:66). It is important to note that cultural differences and also the material circumstances of people's lives in different types of societies will influence the stages of the life course. According to Macionis and Plummer (1997:141), 'our society organises human experience according to age, resulting in distinctive stages of life, i.e. (1) childhood, (2) adolescence, (3) Adulthood, (4) old age'.

Childhood: 'Childhood is both a biological reality and a social construct. It is defined not only in biology, but also by a particular society at a particular time in a particular way which represents the view that society has of childhood' (Hayes 2002 cited in CECDE 2004). The way a society conceptualises childhood can vary from society to society and from culture to culture. This conceptualisation can also vary as societies develop, meaning there is 'no one static universal conceptualisation of childhood' (*Ibid.*: 2004). Before the period of industrialisation, the concept of childhood had little meaning, as children worked alongside their parents (Aries 1973, cited in Hyde *et al.* 2004:163). Since then, childhood has been seen as a stage when children are said to be free from the responsibilities of adults. It is seen as a stage of playful innocence where children are exempt from legal, social and economic responsibilities. At the end of childhood, it is hoped that children have developed a level of maturity and self-esteem to enable them to take part in everyday activities with limited adult supervision (Curry *et al.* 2005:67).

Because of Ireland's late industrialisation, children were exploited for their labour up until the nineteenth century. Evidence provided by Kennedy (2001, cited in Hyde *et al.* 2004:163) suggests that:

1. Even by 1961, more people were employed in agriculture than in industry, which had implications for the role of children in Irish society.
2. Both girls and boys were an important source of labour on the family farm and this was reflected in statistics which showed that 'in 1964, almost two-thirds of sixteen-year-olds in Ireland were no longer in full-time education' (*Ibid.*: 163).

Cleary *et al.* (2001:XV) highlight a number of factors that may influence how we conceptualise childhood. Four key influences identified include:

1. The State – the legislation a state makes and the provision it makes for children and families by means of education, care and welfare, strongly impacts on our image of childhood.
2. The churches also play a role in the doctrines they espouse and the role children play within these institutions.
3. The media are also playing an increasing role in shaping society's image of childhood.
4. Finally, children are seen increasingly to be starting to influence their own role and position in society, through increasing consultation and prominence. (cited in CECDE 2004)

Buckingham, (2000 cited in Giddens 2009:298), has suggested that 'children now grow up so fast that the previously solid boundary between adults and children is rapidly diminishing, leading to the disappearance of childhood in the developed societies'.

Adolescence: 'Adolescence became a separate stage in the life course during the later part of the nineteenth century when the forces of industrialisation created a surplus of workers' (Skolnick 1986, cited in Curry *et al.* 2005:67). Some would say that this period was an 'invention of industrial western society' because prior to that time there was little opportunity or chance for a youth culture to emerge (Lalor *et al.* 2007:5). Adolescence is a less clearly defined period and refers to the stage of life between childhood and adulthood. While adolescence provides an opportunity for more socialisation it can also be a difficult time for teenagers as they struggle to develop identities separate from their parents.

While this period is meant to end when biological maturity brings adult status and an ability to be self-sufficient, in recent years it is a stage of the life course which has lengthened. Factors such as the recession have stretched adolescence from the teenage years to the mid-twenties and 'given rise to the demographic jokingly referred to as 'kippers' (kids in parents pockets eroding retirement savings)' (*Ibid.*: 2007).

Adulthood: Often seen as the period of life when most accomplishments occur. During this time most people begin careers, start families etc. 'During middle adulthood, between ages 40 and 60, people begin to sense that improvements in life circumstances are unlikely' (www.usi.edu).

Old age: This stage is defined as the final stage of life. The notion of old age, like childhood, is a social and cultural construct. According to Hyde *et al.* (2004:170) 'the norms associated with being older vary over time and in different socio-cultural contexts, and the nature of aging is influenced by how societies perceive ageing'. Because of retirement or because they may be too sick to care for themselves, people at this stage may begin to depend on others. 'The growth into old age in our society means leaving behind past roles and becoming dependent again' (www.usi.edu:9). The economic needs in a society appear to have influenced historical constructs of ageing.

RE-SOCIALISATION

This type of socialisation involves confinement in settings in which people are isolated from the rest of society and controlled by an administrative staff – often known as a total institution. Examples of these institutions include jails, psychiatric hospitals, nursing homes etc. The purpose of these institutions is often re-socialisation, or an attempt to change an inmate's behaviour and attitude in an environment that is carefully controlled. In some cases the reason for re-socialisation is 'because the people have done something wrong and need to be socialised in order to go back and be a productive member of society' (www.usi.edu). The staff who work in institutions whose goal is to re-socialise are involved in a two-part process:

1. eroding the inmate's identity and self-autonomy, and
2. building a 'new self' for the inmate through a system of rewards and punishments.

'By manipulating rewards and punishments and reducing or eliminating potentially conflicting influences from outside the institution, the staff hopes to produce lasting change – or at least obedience – in the inmate' (Curry *et al.* 2005:87).

CULTURE DEFINED

'In essence culture is the expression of group norms at the national, racial and ethnic level' (Hogg and Vaughan 2005:616).

Culture refers 'to the non-biological aspects of human societies – to the values, customs and modes of behaviour that are learned and internalised by people rather than being genetically transmitted from one generation to the next' (Marsh 2000:24). Sociologists divide culture into two basic types: (1) material culture, (2) non-material culture.

Material culture consists of the physical objects used by people to help them achieve their goals, such as machinery and technology. On the other hand non-material culture refers to the non-tangible element of a cultural system; the values, beliefs, language and other representations of the social and physical world.

Different societies have different cultures. We learn the culture of our society through the process of socialisation. Definitions of culture can vary, but they share the broad view 'that culture is an enduring product of and influence on human interaction' (Hogg and Vaughan 2005:616). Despite differences in the cultures found throughout the world, they all seem to be built on five major components: symbols, language, values, norms and material objects.

THE COMPONENTS OF CULTURE

Symbols

Symbols are tools that help shape commonly shared meanings of national identity. 'A symbol is anything that carries a particular meaning recognised by people who share a culture' (Macionis and Plummer 2002:100). Societies may develop their own symbols such as types of clothing, flags, logos, which will give particular coded meanings to other members of the culture. These symbols convey meaning to the people of a culture. For example, in Ireland,

- the tricolour is a symbol of our national identity
- the shamrock is a symbol of our Christian heritage
- it is customary to wear black at funerals.

The pint of Guinness, the bodhrán, the GAA etc., are all examples of symbols in Irish society. 'We "read" these symbols as signs which guide our behaviour in particular situations' (Abbott 1998:8).

Language

'Language contains the cultural deposit of centuries of a people living together in good times and bad. It also contains their prayers, songs and poetry. It is considered invaluable, totally unique and irreplaceable. It also provides a unique nuance on the world people live in and a link between past, present and future generations' (MacGréil and Rhatigan 2009:100).

The most obvious way in which members of a society share meanings is through using the same language. The modernisation perspective believes that 'modernising societies will become linguistically homogenous: within them everyone will eventually speak the same language, or at the very least, linguistic differences will decline as a significant source of division and conflict' (Tovey and Share 2003:332).

They go on to say that although this might be seen to have been the fate of the Irish language, as now the majority of the population of Ireland speak English, the Irish language is not dead. Evidence for this includes findings from Ó Riagáin (1997) which state that:

1. 'The number of families that use Irish as the main language in their family circle is roughly the same today outside as inside the Gaeltacht areas with a particularly high proportion living in the greater Dublin region.
2. Most English speakers in Ireland today know some Irish.
3. The Irish language is still regarded as a central element in Irish national identity by a large majority of the population' (Ó Riagáin 1998, cited in Tovey and Share 2003:333).

A study entitled 'The Irish language and the Irish people' carried out in 2007/08 by MacGréil and Rhatigan, found that 'positive attitudes and aspirations for Irish have been maintained at very high levels' (2009:4). The following statistics were presented in their study:

1. Of the Irish-born sample in 2007/08, over 40 per cent wish to see the Irish language revived, while over 52 per cent desire to see it preserved. Positive aspirations were held, therefore, by over 93 per cent.
2. Those who wish to see Irish 'discarded and forgotten' amounted to 7 per cent. (MacGréil and Rhatigan 2009:9)

Michel Peillon notes that for most people in Ireland, though broadly sympathetic towards the Irish language, 'the symbolic use of the language on official and state occasions is considered to be a sufficient expression of national identity' (Peillon 1982, cited in Moffatt 2008). An academic study undertaken by Moffatt in 2011 presents findings that show that 'though the Irish language is not heard at a conversational level in most people's environments, that at a personal symbolic level the Irish language and even speaking the Irish language remains firmly established within personal conceptions of Irish' (2011:149).

Table 2:1 Personal symbolic significance of the Irish language and speaking the Irish language

Symbols of Irishness	Very important	Important	Not important
		per cent	
Irish language	41.8	29	28.7
Speaking the Irish language	29.8	28.9	40

(Source: Moffatt 2011:149)

Figures from the 2006 census showed that 40.8 per cent of Irish people identify themselves as Irish speakers. More recent figures from the 2011 census showed that:

1. 'There were 77,185 persons speaking Irish on a daily basis outside of the education system in April 2011.
2. Twenty-three per cent of these were aged 5 to 18 (17,457 persons), a further 25,359 (30 per cent) were in the age group 25 to 44.
3. There were 42,157 females speaking Irish on a daily basis in 2011 compared with 35,028 males' (CSO.ie 2011).

'Groups of people with similar interests and outlooks often develop their own language. Examples would be people in the same job, followers of particular types of music, people from the same social class or people from a particular area in a country or city. The slang and jargon which such groups use can serve to identify the members to each other and help to reinforce their sense of identity. When we say that people will "know what we mean" we are saying that meanings are shared' (Abbott 1998:8).

Values

'Values are broad constructs used by individuals and societies to orient people's specific attitudes and behaviour in an integrated and meaningful manner. Values are tied to groups, social categories and cultures and are thus socially constructed and socially maintained' (Hogg and Vaughan 2005:624).

'Values are the standards people have about what is good and bad' (Macionis and Plummer 2002:104). Each society has its own set of values and norms. The values that a society holds in high esteem are reflected in the norms governing our everyday attitudes and behaviour. Values vary from culture to culture and they influence our behaviour, emotions and thoughts. 'Values are ideas that derive from beliefs that are about what is thought to be just, correct and proper. It is considered wrong to take another person's life but, in times of war and conflict, a person may be rewarded for killing people' (Donohoe and Gaynor 2003:239). In Irish society, areas given high value include:

- Christian values
- family values
- education
- work/status
- justice and fair play
- public safety.

'People who value learning will work hard in school, and people who value democracy may become angry if their views are not taken into account by elected officials' (Curry et al. 2005:35). According to Tovey and Share (2003:331), 'the values of this national culture then increasingly converge with those of the advanced societies and give rise to a shared "world culture" in which nationalism and national culture barriers are no longer significant'.

Norms

'Norms refer to common and agreed ways of behaviour in various social activities' (Abbott 1998:9).

According to Carr (2009:3), 'the manner in which the members of a society are expected to behave is encapsulated in the norms associated with their society'. Norms can be proscriptive or prescriptive. Proscriptive norms specify what we ought to avoid while prescriptive norms specify what we ought to do. Both sets of norms instruct us as to how we are to behave socially.

Some norms are formally established as laws. In Ireland we have laws prohibiting murder, robbery, rape, drink-driving, speed limits, abortion, underage drinking. A US sociologist, Sumner, recognised that some norms are more crucial to our lives than others. He referred to these as *mores* – 'a society's standards of proper moral conduct' (Macionis and Plummer 2002:107). He believed that

1. mores applied to everyone, everywhere, all the time
2. people developed an emotional attachment to these mores
3. people will defend them publicly (*Ibid.*: 107).

Our behaviour is also governed by the non-legal norms of our society. Norms provide us with guidelines that we can use as or when the situation demands. Not knowing them can cause feelings of anxiety. These non-legal norms 'are basically "social manners". It is the norm in Ireland to shake hands when introduced to someone' (Donohoe and Gaynor 2003:239). These norms can also include notes about proper dress, common courtesy etc. Sumner used the term 'folkways to designate a society's customs for routine, casual interaction. In short, while mores distinguish between right and wrong, folkways draw a line between right and rude' (Macionis and Plummer 2002:107). A society's particular norms are learnt by people from parents and peers through the processes of primary and secondary socialisation.

Material culture

An important component of any culture is the material culture or the tangible aspects. To help understand the culture of a society we must view the objects that culture produces, 'the material goods, products, and the tools that people use in their everyday lives, e.g. cars, computers, books, clothes, tools. These objects are sometimes called "material culture", and can be used to indicate status or to make cultural or social statements' (Abbott 1998:10). All these objects that we use in everyday life take on a symbolic meaning.

CULTURAL CHANGE

Cultural changes are set in motion in three ways:

1. The first is invention and involves combining known cultural elements in a way to produce a new product. Invention has given us the telephone, the television, the computer etc. All these inventions have had a major impact on our way of life. The process goes on constantly. However, it is important to note that 'the more knowledge, tools and technology a

society possesses, the more likely it is that some of those elements will be recombined into a new product' (Curry *et al.* 2005:54).

2. According to Macionis and Plummer (2002:110), the second cause of social change is discovery and 'it involves recognising and understanding something not fully understood before – from a distant star, to foods of another culture, etc.' Inventions and discoveries, major preoccupations of scientists, do not occur randomly. 'Unless the existing culture is ready, inventions and discoveries may lie dormant for centuries' (Curry *et al.* 2005:54).

3. Diffusion is the third cause of cultural change. Diffusion refers to the spread of cultural traits or elements from one group or society to another. 'The technological ability to send information around the globe in seconds – by means of radio, television, fax and computer – means that the level of cultural diffusion has never been greater than it is today' (Macionis and Plummer 2002:110). Through culture, we attempt to make sense of ourselves and the surrounding world. 'Culture can constrain human needs and ambitions, yet as cultural creatures we have the capacity to shape and reshape the world to meet our needs and pursue our dreams' (*Ibid.*: 120).

ETHNOCENTRISM AND CULTURAL RELATIVISM

'Ethnocentrism is a suspicion of outsiders combined with a tendency to evaluate the culture of others in terms of one's own culture' (Giddens 2009:641).

When we adopt a stance and view other cultures by the standards of our own, believing that our own culture is superior, our thinking is ethnocentric thinking. This negative thinking or ethnocentrism can and has caused great harm and suffering to millions worldwide.

The term multiculturalism refers to policies that encourage cultural or ethnic groups to live in harmony with each other. As society becomes more multicultural, we as individuals must become more accepting of different cultures; we must adopt an open mind. This view, called cultural relativism, 'recognises that each culture is unique and valid and judged on its own terms' (Curry *et al.* 2005:37).

An understanding of culture and its components can be enriching and beneficial and contact with different cultural and ethnic groups can dispel cultural myths and misconceptions that can lead to conflict. 'Culture pervades almost all aspects of our existence. Perhaps because of this, culture is often the taken-for-granted background to everyday life and we may only really become aware of the features of our culture when we encounter other cultures or when our own culture is threatened' (Hogg and Vaughan 2005:632).

3

Major Sociological Perspectives and Theories

CHAPTER OBJECTIVES

After reading this chapter you should be able to:

- explain what is meant by concepts
- talk about the founding of sociology
- describe the following sociological perspectives:
  - structural functionalism
  - conflict theory
  - social action theory
  - feminism
- explain briefly the main theories of
  - Durkheim
  - Marx
  - Weber.

'Sociological theories are necessary because without theory our understanding of social life would be very weak' (Giddens 2009:70). As a science, sociology is consciously committed to understanding how society operates. It is an attempt to understand the purpose and experiences of its members from a sociological perspective. In order for us to do this, a key component in our way of approaching sociology and to appreciate it as an area of study is the ability to think critically. To think critically requires that we give way to logical reasoning. How do we do that? In part, this involves the development of theories. 'Theory ➔ logical model specifying relationships among variables as an explanation for the way things are' (Babbie 1988). According to Giddens, 'good theories help us to arrive at a deeper understanding of societies and to explain the social changes that affect us all' (2009:70). To understand the true purpose of theory we need to consider a few of the basics, such as concepts and the relationships among variables.

CONCEPTS

'Concepts are mental images we use to bring order to the mass of specific experiences we have' (Babbie 1988:17).

By forming concepts we allow ourselves to group together similar things while at the same time to distinguish dissimilar ones. 'For example, the concept "human being" groups nearly 5 billion creatures into a single category and distinguishes them from billions and billions of other creatures. Male and female divide the 5 billion human beings into two categories' (*Ibid.*: 17).

Children, Asians, students, teachers are other examples of concepts that enable us to distinguish between different groups of humans. Concepts can also refer to ideas that do not always distinguish between groups of people. For example, when we speak of unemployment, depression, marriage, we are using concepts.

Along with carefully defining the concepts, sociologists seek to discover and establish order among concepts. The concepts Christian and Muslim are often referred to as attributes of individuals. The variable 'religion' is a concept bringing those two attributes together. Other examples of variables are gender, which is a concept that brings together attributes such as male and female, and nationality which brings together attributes such as Irish and French.

While sociology is committed to discovering relationships among the variables that distinguish different kinds of people, for example, by asking the question 'Are married men happier than single men?', it does not stop there. Upon identification of such relationships, sociological theory attempts to develop a more detailed picture of the interrelations among a great many variables. By doing so, it aims to provide a greater understanding of social life in general. Many of the questions and problems regarding sociologists' understanding of social life remain similar to those raised by the founders of sociology. The approaches they use to help them do so remain the three major models commonly used in modern sociology and they act very much as windows to our world.

THE FOUNDING OF SOCIOLOGY: MARX, DURKHEIM AND WEBER

'Sociology is a European invention. It is the academic discipline that specialises in understanding group life in modern society' (Matthewman *et al.* 2007:47).

Karl Marx (1818–83), Emile Durkheim (1858–1917) and Max Weber (1864–1920) were among the first to look at society in what we have come to think of as a specifically sociological way. Like Comte (who named the discipline) all three were interested in and wanted to understand the major changes that were occurring in Europe during their own time. Their attempts to do so were to have a major impact on the discipline of sociology. All three lived during the nineteenth century, which was a period of huge change. Revolutions such as the industrial and political revolutions were bringing huge changes to the society they knew. They were changing how their society operated and as a result were having a huge impact on the experiences of its members. The industrial revolution was transforming economic life while the French Revolution was seen to have 'invented modern political life – active citizenship replaced traditional patterns of kinship and monarchy' (Matthewman *et al.* 2007:50). The age of the 'Enlightenment' also had an important influence on the development of early sociology. According to Matthewman, 'thinkers of the Enlightenment assumed that applying scientific reason to human affairs would lead people steadily from darkness to light, freeing humankind from pre-modern ignorance and superstition' (2007:55). Marx, Durkheim and Weber wanted to understand and explain why such events and changes were taking place. To simply describe what was happening was not enough; they went deeper and by doing so they founded a new discipline – sociology. Durkheim, Marx and Weber had the common goal of examining society and trying to understand how it functioned and changed, but each one differed in his approach to doing so. Differences in their approaches led to their developing (separately) three different perspectives, all of which required a scientific approach.

SOCIOLOGICAL THEORY: STRUCTURAL PERSPECTIVES

'At this stage all that we mean by sociological theory is the body of ideas, tested and untested, making up sociological thought' (O'Donnell

1992:7). According to O'Donnell (1992), in order to construct an adequate sociological perspective we need to be able to examine and answer some basic questions of sociological theory. It was upon answering such questions that Marx, Durkheim and Weber helped to produce three distinct traditions of sociological thought or perspectives, namely:

- Structural Functionalism, which owes much to Durkheim
- Marxism, which is associated with Karl Marx
- Social Action Theory, which owes much to Weber.

For O'Donnell (1992:7), the seven key questions that need to be answered are:

1. How is society constructed?
2. How does society operate or function?
3. Why are some groups in society more powerful than others?
4. What causes social change?
5. Is society normally in orderly balance or in conflict?
6. What is the relationship of the individual to society?
7. What is the primary purpose of sociological study?

These three perspectives are structural in nature as they focus on how society affects individuals and groups, rather than on how individuals or groups create society.

Structural Functionalism: Durkheim

'Functionalism is a framework for building theory that envisages society as a complex system whose parts work together to promote solidarity and stability' (Macionis and Plummer 2002:22).

In other words, functionalists like Durkheim believed that for a society to survive, its various social processes must net smoothly together to meet the system's needs. Functionalism involves the study of society and the way its institutions connect together and change. According to Mann (1983:138), 'Functionalism's basic question is "How does society meet its needs?" Each process, institution and practice is seen as performing a function that meets a societal need and thereby helps to maintain the society's structure or equilibrium.' A more simple way to understand the basis of this perspective is to look at how it answered the seven basic questions highlighted by O'Donnell (1992).

1. How is society constructed?

Society is made up of various institutions which have specific purposes within society. These institutions perform certain functions which meet a need of that society, for example one of the functions of the family (which is a social institution) is the bearing and rearing of children. As societies develop, the number and complexity of social institutions increase. According to O'Donnell (1992:8), institutions are grouped together into four sub-systems:

(i)   economic (factories, offices)
(ii)   political (political parties)
(iii) kinship (families)
(iv)   cultural and community organisations (school, churches).

2. How does society operate or function?

Functionalists consider that societies 'can be most easily understood and analysed if they are compared to biological organisms' (Marsh 2000:56). Social institutions work with one another for the benefit of society as a whole, for example schools function in relation to work because they prepare people for work. According to Bilton *et al.*, the education system performs three vital functions on behalf of society, that is, it 'helps to develop the human resources of an industrial nation . . ., selects individuals according to their talents . . . and contributes to social cohesion by transmitting to new generations the central values of society' (2002:267).

3. Why are some groups in society more powerful than others?

Functionalists like Durkheim believe that it is necessary that some individuals and groups be more powerful than others, because only a limited number can make important decisions. Without leaders society would descend into chaos.

4. What causes social change?

Functionalists believe that social change occurs when it is functionally necessary for it to do so. 'For example, in modern societies, educational systems tend to expand because such societies require a more literate and numerate population than less "advanced" societies' (O'Donnell 1992:8). Society adapts its norms to meet changing needs, or to replace ones that have become dysfunctional. However, functionalists stress that change should be gradual because if it occurs too quickly it will result in confusion for members of that society.

5. Is society normally in orderly balance or in conflict?

Order is normal to society, but disorder can occur at times of war. Functionalists believe that order in society depends on the existence of 'moral consensus'. 'This means that everyone in society or nearly everyone shares the same values. . . . For them, they stress the importance of the effective teaching of social values in maintaining order and conformity' (O'Donnell 1992:8).

6. What is the relationship of the individual to society?

The individual is formed by society through influences such as the family, school, religion etc. Functionalists concentrate on how these institutions affect the individual.

7. What is the primary purpose of sociological study?

The purpose of sociology is to analyse and explain the functioning of society.

Marxism: Marx

Marxism, like functionalism, concentrates on 'the structure of society and explains individual actions in terms of the social structure in which they are located' (Marsh 2000:61). However, while the functionalist approach is based on solidarity, this approach is based on division or inequality in society. Marx's work looked at conflict in society.

1. How is society constructed?

According to Marx, society is made up of classes. He believed that the system of capitalism produced two major classes. For him, a person's position in the class structure is determined by their relationship to the means of production.

(i)   The most powerful class is the bourgeoisie – those who own the means of production, such as land and factories.

(ii)   The proletariat is the least powerful class. This group does not own the means of production. This group is forced to sell their labour (to the bourgeoisie) in order to make a living.

2.   How does society operate or function?

Marx argued that in capitalist society, the bourgeoisie and the proletariat are opposed. In his view society operates mainly through class and conflict. He used the term 'class conflict' to refer to conflict between entire classes over the distribution of wealth and power in society.

3.   Why are some groups in society more powerful than others?

Some classes are more powerful than others because they own more property and wealth. This power gives them the means to defend and keep what they hold.

4.   What causes social change?

Social change occurs as a result of class conflict.

5.   Is society normally in orderly balance or in conflict?

Marx concluded that societies throughout history have largely been characterised by conflict. While he did recognise that periods of social order can occur, they tended to benefit the rich and powerful more than others.

6.   What is the relationship of the individual to society?

According to O'Donnell (1992), there are two major schools of thought amongst Marxists about the relationship of an individual to society:
• one sees the individual as powerless to affect their own life or that of others, and
• the second school sees the individual having a much greater role in society.

7.   What is the primary purpose of sociological study?

The primary purpose of sociology is to describe, analyse and explain class conflict.

Social Action Theory: Weber

Max Weber (1864–1920), a German sociologist, was the founder of the Social Action perspective. Macionis and Plummer (2002:26) define this perspective as 'a micro theory that focuses on how actors assemble social meanings'. Weber was more interested in the way people behaved and in how their behaviour influenced the wider society, as well as in social structure. 'Social action lies at the heart of the sociological approach, and only by understanding the intentions, ideas, values and beliefs that motivate people can you really know anything' (Osborne and Loon 1996:56). It was Weber's focus on social interaction in specific situations that resulted in his approach being considered as a micro-level orientation. Macro-level orientations, which means 'a focus on broad social structures that characterise society as a whole' (Macionis and Plummer 2002:26), were shared by both the functionalist and conflict perspectives.

1.   How is society constructed?
For Weber, society is created through social interaction which involves people consciously relating to one another. People form institutions such as families and factories as a result of the process of interaction. Although people create institutions, institutions also influence people.

2.   How does society operate or function?
Weber believed that individuals influence society and society influences the individual. People's ideas and feelings can inspire action in society but these actions are limited by the society they live in.

3.   Why are some groups in society more powerful than others?
Weber agreed with the functionalists when he said it was necessary for some groups to have more power to ensure society functioned more efficiently. But he also accepted Marx's idea that those groups who do gain power in society use it primarily to protect their own interests.

4.   What causes social change?
Social change can occur for several reasons. 'Ideas, new inventions, war, the rise and fall of power groups, influential individuals and other factors all contribute to, and are part of, historical change' (O'Donnell 1992:11).

5.   Is society normally in orderly balance or in conflict?
Weber considered that society is normally either in balance or in conflict. He believed the state of society varies from case to case.

6. What is the relationship of the individual to society?

According to O'Donnell, Weber found it 'more important to understand the meanings that individuals experience in their own social lives than simply to analyse what "causes" or "influences" them to act as they do' (1992:12).

7. What is the primary purpose of sociological study?

The purpose of sociology is to understand and explain the meaning of social action and interaction.

Feminism

According to Ahmed *et al.* (cited in Marsh 2002:257), 'Feminism is not one set of struggles: it has mobilised different women in different times and places, who are all seeking transformations, but who are not necessarily seeking the same thing, nor even necessarily responding to the same situation.' While there is no single theory of feminism, while it does not fit neatly into one particular strand, 'a set of recurring themes and principles does emerge . . . which are of particular importance to feminist practice' (Kelly 1988, cited in Marsh 2000:257). Those listed are:

(i)   the centrality of women's experience
(ii)   research for women
(iii)   the rejection of hierarchy, and empowerment
(iv)   the critical reflexivity.

Feminism can be defined as being a critique of society based on the inequalities that exist through gender roles and assumptions. Feminism does not see women as being treated equally in terms of access to education, jobs, incomes, politics and power. According to Osborne and Loon (1996:122) 'the programme that feminism would advocate for a reconstructed sociology would look something like this . . .

(i)   placing gender at the heart of all analysis, on a par with class and race
(ii)   criticising all sociological theory for its male perspectives . . .
(iii)   analysing the relationship between the public and private spheres as being of central importance in understanding how society functions
(iv)   overhauling all of sociological theory'.

Because feminism is in a constant state of development and because it encompasses so many different strands, such as liberal feminism, radical feminism etc., it is difficult to pin down. According to Bell Hooks it 'is best described as a theory in the making' (cited in Marsh 2002:258).

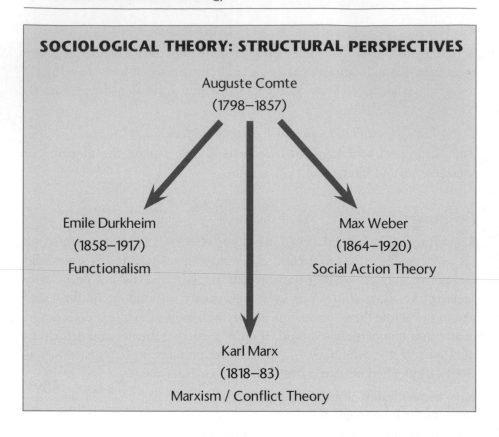

SOCIOLOGICAL THEORY: STRUCTURAL PERSPECTIVES

Auguste Comte
(1798–1857)

Emile Durkheim
(1858–1917)
Functionalism

Max Weber
(1864–1920)
Social Action Theory

Karl Marx
(1818–83)
Marxism / Conflict Theory

EMILE DURKHEIM (1858–1917)

One of the great names of sociology was Emile Durkheim, a French sociologist who lived during the nineteenth century. He became the world's first professor of sociology in 1896 (Cox 1987:9). At that time in Europe huge changes accelerated by the industrial revolution were under way. Transformations were occurring in the way people lived their lives, how they organised their work etc. Durkheim wanted to examine these changes and to try and understand what was happening. He wanted to understand how society functioned. Durkheim introduced the concepts of mechanical and organic solidarity and hence made a major contribution to the discipline of sociology. Areas discussed below in relation to Durkheim include:

- mechanical and organic solidarity
- anomie
- division of labour
- suicide
- religion.

Mechanical and organic solidarity

Durkheim developed an approach to help him try to understand society based on 'solidarity' and the different forms it takes. He argued that in pre-industrial societies, people were held together by a strong tradition (customs, values etc.) which acted like a 'social glue' and held everyone in that society together. He believed the system in operation in those societies was that of '*Mechanical solidarity* – meaning social bonds based on shared morality, that unite members of pre-industrial societies' (Giddens 2001). This solidarity comes from likeness and similarity and has been described as being mechanical because people feel a more or less automatic sense of belonging together. Durkheim believed that in such small-scale societies people developed *collective conscience* because they identified so much with other people in their community. Such a conscience would also allow them to punish anyone who challenged their way of life.

The advent of the industrial revolution meant the introduction of new machines, steam power, new ways in the production and transport of goods. Such developments brought huge changes to people's livelihoods and in the way work was organised. They also had a huge impact on the collective conscience of the group. As society became more complex due to an increase in the division of labour in society, mechanical solidarity began to break down and was replaced by a new type of solidarity, *organic solidarity*. This solidarity differed from mechanical solidarity because where people had once seen unity in likeness, solidarity was now based on differences among people. This type of solidarity emerged from the division of labour which now required each worker to specialise in a single activity that had to be complemented by other specialised workers. Social bonds were now based on the fact that people relied on others who followed specialised pursuits; they were dependent on them in order to secure the goals and services they needed every day.

Organic solidarity was a characteristic of industrial or modern societies. People now were dependent on the efforts of people they didn't know. Specialisation or the division of labour meant that the foundation of traditional society, moral consensus (moral agreement), was being replaced by functional interdependence. The emergence of industrial society in Europe in the nineteenth century did not extend equal rights to all its citizens. Such inequalities meant that some individuals and groups had restricted opportunities and unacceptable lifestyles. Instead of feeling a sense of unity or solidarity these people or groups experienced a sense of isolation or normlessness, which Durkheim termed 'anomie'.

Anomie

Durkheim believed that the social isolation or sense of meaninglessness associated with anomie occurred when society didn't make an adequate transition from mechanical to organic solidarity. He believed that the division of labour progressed to a far greater extent than the moral guidance people required to live in a more free, modern society. People did not have a clear idea of what is and what is not proper and acceptable behaviour. Individuals who experience anomie are not faced with sufficient moral constraint and hence feel isolated or meaningless. These feelings can impinge on their lives and their work. He also believed that such feelings can lead to suicide. 'As a society becomes more anomic, the suicide rate increases' (Mann 1983:12).

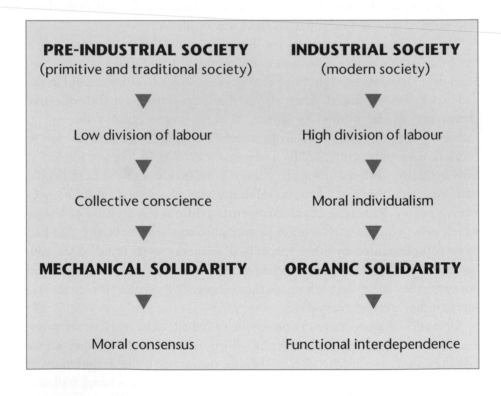

Division of labour

This is a very important term in sociology. Durkheim believed that many of the changes that came with industrialisation were a result of the division of labour in society. 'This concept refers to the organisation of work, the division of a particular task into a number of separate specialised jobs as a means to increasing productivity and efficiency' (Tovey and Share 2000:9).

Durkheim argued that in pre-industrial societies which had a low division of labour, one worker or workgroup (such as the family) did a range of different work tasks necessary to meet survival needs. Work was organised so that each stage in the production process was completed before the next was begun. This allowed a single worker to see the whole process through from beginning to end and to have a wide range of skills with limited specialisation. Modern society was characterised by a much greater division of labour. For Durkheim, 'the division of labour in society is a material social fact that involves the degree to which tasks or responsibilities are specialised' (Ritzer 1992:80). Ritzer goes on to say that 'People in primitive societies tend to occupy very general positions in which they perform a wide variety of tasks and handle a large number of responsibilities. In other words, a primitive person tended to be a jack-of-all-trades. In contrast, those who live in more modern societies occupy more specialised positions and have a much narrower range of tasks and responsibilities' (1992:80–81). According to Durkheim, this division of labour was more than just economic. Because work had become separate from the home and was extending rapidly into all areas of social life, a social division of labour was occurring. 'It is this wider fragmentation, this social division of labour, which has changed the relation of the individual to the moral order' (Lee and Newby 1986:216).

Suicide

In his famous work on suicide (1897), Durkheim 'attempted to link the personal act of suicide with social forces in operation which might encourage it' (IPA 1992:9). By comparing statistics from different societies, he analysed them in terms of categories such as age, sex, religion and family relationships. From evidence available he found 'that men, Protestants, wealthy people and the unmarried each had significantly higher suicide rates compared to women, Roman Catholics and Jews, the poor and married people' (Macionis and Plummer 1997:6). He believed that such differences between groups correspond to people's degree of social integration or strength of social ties. His work also highlighted the importance of social regulation in affecting suicide rates. According to Giddens (2001:10–11), 'Durkheim identified four types of suicide, in accordance with the relative presence or absence of integration and regulation':

1. egotistic suicide – too little integration
2. anomic suicide – too little regulation
3. altruistic suicide – too much integration
4. fatalistic suicide – too much regulation.

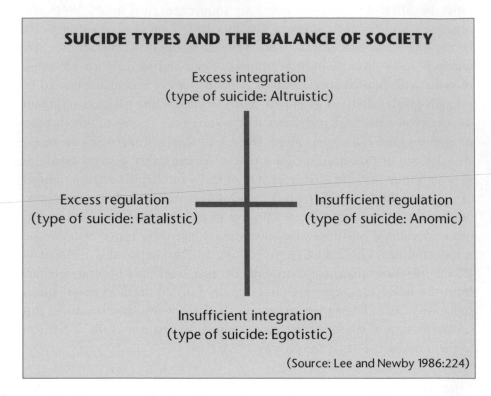

SUICIDE TYPES AND THE BALANCE OF SOCIETY

Excess integration
(type of suicide: Altruistic)

Excess regulation
(type of suicide: Fatalistic)

Insufficient regulation
(type of suicide: Anomic)

Insufficient integration
(type of suicide: Egotistic)

(Source: Lee and Newby 1986:224)

Egotistic suicide (too little integration): This occurs when there is insufficient integration in society. This type of suicide can occur when an individual feels isolated or when their ties to a group are weakened or broken. The extent of this suicide type can be shown by providing evidence of how suicide rates vary according to religion, marital status etc.

Anomic suicide (too little regulation): This is a modern type of suicide and is a result of inadequate social regulation. This type of suicide can occur when people feel lost or isolated, feel like they don't belong. It relates to Durkheim's concept of anomie, which means that people are without the norms or rules to guide them in their everyday life.

Altruistic suicide (too much integration): This type of suicide is a characteristic of traditional and primitive societies where mechanical solidarity prevails. It is said to occur when an individual is over-integrated and values the society in which they live as more important than themselves.

This type of suicide is found in the modern military context. Islamic suicide bombers are another example.

Fatalistic suicide (too much regulation): This type of suicide is a product of too much regulation and control and can, for example, be a characteristic of slave societies.

Durkheim believed that social factors could force an individual to take their own life when the state of society was not in orderly balance. According to Lee and Newby (1986:223), 'The state of balance is defined in terms of two dimensions:

1. Integration: the extent to which individuals experience a sense of belonging to the collectivity.
2. Regulation: the extent to which the actions and desires of individuals are kept in check by moral values'.

Different levels of the different types of suicide will be found in societies that display too much or too little of both integration and regulation.

Religion

Durkheim defined religion as 'a unified system of beliefs and practices relative to sacred things set apart and forbidden' (Selfe and Starbuck 1998:27). He saw religion as a necessary and essential feature of society. 'Religion served to integrate society together, produced shared values, justified the social order, produced opportunities for emotional expression, and gave an identity to individuals and groups' (Thompson 1986:4).

Durkheim was one of the first sociologists to describe the function of religion in binding communities together. 'His main emphasis was on the level of the social structure and how religious beliefs and rituals bring people together, giving them a sense of unity and shared values' (Giddens 2001:628).

Although there are many different religions, and the style and content of different religions may vary, they share the following characteristics:

1. They all act as a socialising agent – religion transmits norms and values that help to hold society together.
2. They share a 'coherent system of beliefs and practices serving universal human needs and purposes' (*Ibid.*: 629).

Durkheim made an analysis of the religious practices of Australian Aborigines, whom he took to be an example of the most primitive people of that time (Selfe and Starbuck 1998:27). While the initial purpose was to examine how social order was created and maintained in a society, his conclusion was that religion was the 'source of all harmonious social life' (*Ibid.*: 27).

For Durkheim religion is a universal human institution which permeates all aspects of life. However, he did not fail to observe that the effects of religion may vary between societies – in some it may influence the name a person is given, the diet that is followed, music, art, calendar and concepts of time.

Durkheim in his work *The Elementary Forms of the Religious Life* (1912) highlighted that regardless of what people believe about sacred matters, all religions have certain elements in common. 'The presence of these common elements makes different religions similar and enables sociologists to recognise, categorise and analyse the relationships between religious systems and society' (Curry *et al.* 2005:375).

These common elements or characteristics of religion include:

1. beliefs
2. the sacred and the profane
3. rituals and ceremonies
4. moral communities
5. personal experiences. (Curry *et al.* 2005:375–6)

   According to Durkheim, the functions of religion include:

1. stability and cohesion
2. social identity
3. collective conscience
4. socialisation and social control
5. meaning and purpose. (Selfe and Starbuck 1998:27)

KARL MARX (1818–83)

Marx spent most of his adult life in London and while living there witnessed the growth of factories and industrial production. Although societies were producing more goods than ever before, he was awed by the inequalities that persisted between segments of society. Capitalism, an economic system 'which involves the production of goods and services sold to a wide range of consumers' (Giddens 2001:11) was dividing the population into two major classes:

1. bourgeoisie – owners of property and factories, and
2. the proletariat – people who provide labour necessary to operate factories and other productive enterprises.

Marx used the term 'class conflict' to refer to conflict between entire classes over the distribution of wealth and power in society. 'Although owners of capital and workers are each dependent on the other – the capitalists need labour and the workers need wages – the dependency is highly unbalanced. The relationship between classes is an exploitative one since workers have little or no control over their labour and employers are able to generate profit by appropriating the product of workers' labour' (Giddens 2001:12).

Marx believed that the working class would become conscious of their exploitation (develop a class consciousness) and as a result they would act to produce social change which would bring about a fairer society (Harvey *et al.* 2000:23).

Capitalism and alienation

Marx also criticised capitalism for producing alienation. He used it to 'refer to the situation, whereby because of the unequal relationships of capitalism workers cannot achieve their full autonomy and potential' (IPA 1992:12). 'The tragedy of capitalism, Marx believed, lies in the way that the system transforms work from something that is meaningful to something that is meaningless. Because the system is relentlessly driven by profits, workers become mere machines in human form' (Curry *et al.* 2005:10). Alienation refers to the separation of individuals from themselves and others. 'At its simplest, alienation means that people are unable to find satisfaction and fulfilment in performing their labour or in the products of their labour' (Haralambos and Holborn 2000:68).

Marx looked at four ways in which capitalism alienates workers:

1. Alienation from the act of working – workers are denied a say in what they produce and how they produce it. This leads to monotony, repetition, lack of meaning and a lack of control over the job.
2. Alienation from the product of work.
3. Alienation from other workers.
4. Alienation from human potential. (Macionis and Plummer 1997:81)

For Marx, 'Religion emerges as a product of alienation, in which people endeavour to regain some illusory purpose and an acceptance of their lot' (Selfe and Starbuck 1998:22).

Marx and religion

Marx viewed religion as 'an illusion which eases the pain produced by exploitation and oppression. It is a series of myths that justify and legitimate the subordination of the subject class and the domination and privilege of the ruling class' (Haralambos and Holborn 2004:409). Religion for him was a product of a class society because not only did it aim to dull or ease the pain of oppression, it also acted as an instrument of that oppression. He saw religion as having two key functions – maintaining social control and keeping people in their place. 'The reality is that religion is a drug to make their unhappy lot bearable. They are unable to see the disturbing realities of the deceptions which control their lives' (Selfe and Starbuck 1998:32).

From a Marxist viewpoint, religion discourages people from attempting to change their situation in life by making life more bearable in the following ways:

1. 'It promises a paradise of eternal bliss in life after death. The Christian vision of heaven can make life on earth more bearable by giving people something to look forward to.
2. Some religions make a virtue of the suffering produced by oppression. Religion can make poverty more bearable by promising some form of compensation and reward for their injustices in the afterlife.
3. Religion can offer the hope of supernatural intervention to solve problems on earth, and
4. Religion often justifies the social order and a person's position within it' (Haralambos and Holborn 2004:410).

MAX WEBER (1864–1920)

Weber developed an approach 'that social behaviour is best understood by examining the meaning which people as social actors place on events and ideas. People can establish and justify reasons for actions and so make sense of the world' (Selfe and Starbuck 1998:32).

The sociology of action

According to Weber pre-industrial societies cling to tradition while people in industrial-capitalist societies embrace rationality. Actions of people in traditional societies are guided by the past, by beliefs about what is considered right and proper, because that is the way it has always been done. People in modern society take a different view of the world. They have a new way of thinking, they tend to choose to think and act on the basis of present and future consequences. For example, people in industrial society evaluate jobs, schools etc., in terms of what we put into them and what we expect to receive in return. Weber presents four types of action:

1. **Traditional action:** Action carried out under the influence of custom or habit. A great deal of everyday activity comes under this heading.
2. **Affective action:** The action of the individual is guided by emotions, for instance, it may involve seeking revenge.
3. **Value-rational action or *wertrational*:** The individual follows strongly held values and morals. Behaviour is guided by ideals. It is rational action because it involves the setting of objectives to which the person orients their activities. (Giddens 2001:74)
4. **Technical-rational action or *zweckrational*:** Here the individual rationally calculates the probable result of a given act on the attainment of a particular goal (Lee and Newby 1986:176).

For Weber, whole societies could be characterised by these forms of action.

The Protestant ethic and the spirit of capitalism

The core of Weber's theory is that attitudes involved in the spirit of capitalism derived from religion. Weber showed how different religious ethics led to different economic outcomes. He showed that some world religions were not suited to the development of capitalism. 'Buddhism, Hinduism, Islam and Catholicism did not develop the necessary economic rational values to promote skills in financial occupations in the way that Calvinistic Protestantism did' (Selfe and Starbuck 1998:32). In his work *The Protestant Ethic and the Spirit of Capitalism* (1904), Weber was not saying that capitalism was caused by the rise of Protestantism but that the beliefs it provided were significant contributory factors. Calvinism did not teach that people must stay in the social class into which they were born. According to Weber, Calvinists approached life in a highly disciplined and rational way. He believed that industrial capitalism became established primarily in areas of Europe where Calvinism had a strong hold. The religious doctrine of John Calvin

1. placed stress upon thrift and saving
2. encouraged reinvestment of capital into further economic activity
3. was based on a belief that it was divine will that the individual Christian should serve his God through hard work

4. stated that rewards from work matched effort expanded (Pryke 2002:133).

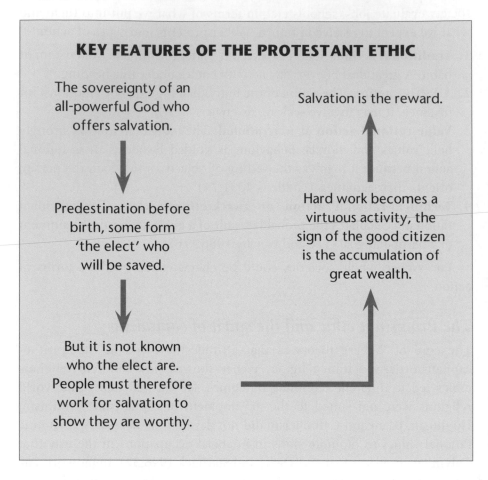

KEY FEATURES OF THE PROTESTANT ETHIC

The sovereignty of an all-powerful God who offers salvation.

Salvation is the reward.

Predestination before birth, some form 'the elect' who will be saved.

Hard work becomes a virtuous activity, the sign of the good citizen is the accumulation of great wealth.

But it is not known who the elect are. People must therefore work for salvation to show they are worthy.

Several movements have recently influenced the development of sociology. These include anti-racism, environmentalism and internationalism. These movements and their perspectives can be viewed as attempts to understand the developments that have taken place in society. 'Sociology has always sought to explain and make sense of change and is increasingly impelled to do so in the context of an interdependent world' (O'Donnell 1992:17).

4

Methods of Research and Social Investigation

CHAPTER OBJECTIVES

After reading this chapter you should be able to:

- define research
  - outline the stages/steps in the research process
  - review the literature
- distinguish between quantitative and qualitative research, primary and secondary methods
- select and describe appropriate survey methods, e.g.
  - questionnaires
  - interviews: structured, semi-structured and unstructured
  - participant observation
  - experiments
  - case studies
  - action research
  - secondary/historical analysis
  - the internet
- explain what is meant by 'sampling'
- discuss the importance of ethical issues and considerations in research
- write a report
- document and acknowledge sources consulted using the Harvard system of referencing

RESEARCH DEFINED

'Research includes the ability to ask questions, to listen, to make notes and to think' (Blaxter *et al.* 2001:4).

According to Clarke and Hockey, research can be defined as 'an attempt to increase available knowledge by the discovery of new facts through systematic scientific enquiry' (cited in Clarke *et al*. 2000:254). The idea of undertaking research may seem difficult or irrelevant to some students but once they are made aware of the steps to be taken when carrying out a piece of research they can see how it contributes to deepening understanding of social issues.

Carefully planned and well conducted social research contributes by:

- attempting to resolve problems, and
- helping us to understand why events happen as they do.

According to Hall and Hall (1996:10), 'Research answers such questions as:

- What is happening?
- Why is that happening?
- How does that affect people?'

Students who engage in sociological research can investigate anything that is linked to society or people but before embarking on this 'journey of adventure, they must have a genuine interest in that area, an interest that will carry them through the research process' (Miller and Crabtree 1992:3, cited in Hall and Hall 1996:9). 'Research is the investigation of a topic for a purpose' (Green 2000:2). Once an area has been selected for research, for example Depression, you must then narrow it down to a specific topic. A simple way to do this is to ensure that your research topic statement has three points: a general area of study, a people point and a place point. So instead of having a broad subject area such as Depression, you would now have a more manageable topic, for example:

Depression among secondary school males in the Cavan area

Area under investigation	People point	Place point

It is important to remember that there are a number of factors at play when deciding on a topic for research. According to Scott (cited in Marsh 2002:27), the three most important factors are:

1. Professional factors: How will the research meet the assessment criteria of a particular course? Does it clearly state the aims and objectives?
2. Personal factors: How interested is the researcher in the topic? Can the researcher remain open-minded and self-reflective?
3. Feasibility factors: What limitations are imposed on the investigation? How much time or money is needed to carry out the research?

The research process needs to be planned, systematic and structured and the researcher needs to ensure that the investigation is carried out in a coherent way. While there is not one perfect way to conduct a research investigation there is 'a broadly accepted series of stages that should be a part of a process of research inquiry' (Walsh 2001:2).

Steps/stages in the research process

Define the problem: Select a topic for research.

Review the literature: Familiarise yourself with existing research on the topic.

Select a research design: Choose one or more research methods: experiment, survey, observation, etc.

Carry out the research: Collect your data, record information.

Interpret your results

↓

Report the research findings: What is their significance? How do they relate to previous findings?

(Giddens 2001:643)

According to Walliman, the answers to the following four important questions 'underpin the framework of any research project' (2005:24). These are:

1. What are you going to do?
2. Why are you going to do it?
3. How are you going to do it?
4. When are you going to do it?

Aims and objectives of research

'The purpose of the research is something that needs to be understood concisely, precisely and right from the beginning' (Denscombe 2002:29). Identifying the purpose of the research at the start of a project is important because it will have a major impact on the overall design of the investigation from methodology to the types of data collection techniques used, for example, questionnaires, observations etc. Kumar (1996, cited in Walsh 2001:5) 'suggests that research can broadly do one or more of four different things'. Research can be:

1. Descriptive: this type of research simply outlines or describes what is happening. It describes the problem or situation and does not go on to ask the questions of 'how' or 'why' the problem or situation has arisen.
2. Exploratory: researchers in this instance strive to find or discover information that did not exist before.
3. Explanatory: this type of research often looks for 'causes' or seeks to understand the relationship between events and phenomena. Researchers here try to explain a link between a number of factors and then hopefully arrive at theories with the objective of 'improving our understanding of why things happen as they do' (Denscombe 2002:26).
4. Correlational: seeks to establish whether links exist between a number of factors. Correlational research identifies and establishes links if they exist but does not try to explain them.

Ragin (1994, cited in Matthewman 2007:39), identified distinct goals of sociological inquiry and matched these to quantitative and qualitative research. These are as follows:

Table 4:1 Quantitative and qualitative research

Goal of inquiry	Quantitative research	Qualitative research
Identifying patterns	Used mainly	Used rarely
Making predictions	Used mainly	Used rarely
Testing theories	Used mainly	Used occasionally
Developing theories	Used occasionally	Used mainly
Interpreting events	Used rarely	Used mainly
Giving advice	Used rarely	Used mainly

(Source: Ragin 1994:32 in Matthewman 2007:39)

Selecting a research topic

The first step/stage in the research process involves selecting a topic for research. This involves identifying a subject/topic that you want to gather information about. If you have some say in your choice of topic for a research project, one key factor that you must take into account is your interest in the proposed topic. According to Robson (2002:49), 'all enquiry involves drudgery and frustration, and you need to have a strong interest in the topic to keep you going through the bad times'.

On selection of a topic, the researcher formulates a hypothesis. 'A hypothesis is an idea which the sociologist guesses might be true, but which has to be tested against evidence' (Browne 2005:420).

Having decided on a topic, there are a number of issues that should always be considered when carrying out or assessing research. The 'main task in this situation is clarificatory: translating the problem presented into something researchable and, moreover, 'do-able' within the limits of the time, resources and finance that can be made available' (Robson 2002:48). Other factors that need careful consideration include reliability, validity and ethics. To help researchers focus and consider these areas they are often requested to submit a research proposal. A good research proposal should include the following:

1. 'Relevance, either to the student's course or the funding body
2. The research is unique or offers new insight or development
3. The title, aims and objectives are all clear and succinct
4. Comprehensive and thorough background research and literature review has been undertaken

5. There is a good match between the issues to be addressed and the approach being adopted
6. The researcher demonstrates relevant background knowledge and/or experience
7. Timetable, resources and budget have all been worked out, thoroughly, with most eventualities covered, and
8. Useful policy and practice implications'. (Dawson 2009:63)

Literature review

'If you try to produce a project purely from your own knowledge and experience without supporting it with references to literature, your research is likely to become too personal, anecdotal or subjective' (Green 2000:43).

Having selected a topic for research the next step in the process is usually to review the available literature in the field. This is a very important part of the research process because researchers need to know what has already been written on their selected area. The literature review puts the research in context. Carrying out a literature review is very important because it allows the researcher to:

1. show a familiarity and a good understanding of the topic being investigated
2. identify the gaps that exist in the literature available – to identify areas that have been overlooked and to show how their research proposes to fill these gaps
3. see if previous research has identified a similar problem
4. see how other researchers have gone about resolving the problem
5. refine their research question/topic and develop ideas about how to carry out the research.

A well conducted literature review could take several months or even years but it can provide invaluable information that adds to our knowledge base. Scott (cited in Marsh 2002:28) highlights that the main reasons for carrying out a literature review on the topic include:

• 'to avoid repeating work already done
• to try and build on existing work
• to seek out the gaps in the existing literature to produce something new and original'.

Literature on a topic can originate from many sources but for Benton *et al.* (cited in Cormack 2000:89), the following are the most common formats (see diagram). Some of these formats may be of greater value than others.

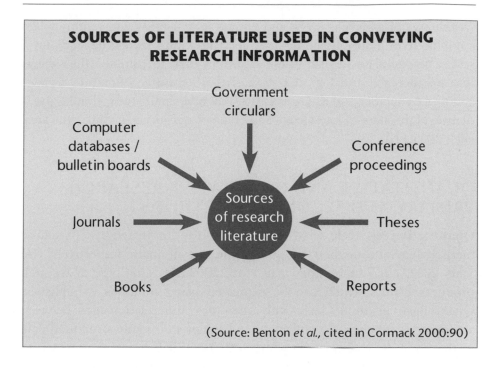

SOURCES OF LITERATURE USED IN CONVEYING RESEARCH INFORMATION

Government circulars

Computer databases / bulletin boards

Conference proceedings

Journals

Sources of research literature

Theses

Books

Reports

(Source: Benton *et al.*, cited in Cormack 2000:90)

Researchers must also be selective in the material they consult because of the huge volume of material available on all topics. To help ensure you gather relevant information and to make the task more manageable, Scott (cited in Marsh 2002:19) suggests you take some of the following steps:

1. See who are the key writers and theorists on your topic by looking through general introductory textbooks in the area.
2. Prepare keywords or phrases to use in catalogue and internet searches.
3. When reading the literature you should keep the following questions in mind and try to answer them:
    - Who is/are the author(s) of the piece of work, what is the title, date of publication etc.? This information is needed when writing up your research.
    - What research methods were used to collect the data?
    - What results did the research generate? What conclusions did the researcher draw?
    - How would you evaluate the research?

To carry out an effective literature review, researchers need to do more than just identify the literature that is relevant to the topic of investigation. They need to develop skills to enable them to assess and to critically evaluate what they are reading. They need to be able to identify the strengths and weaknesses of a piece of work and discuss its reliability and validity when applying it to a specific context. A good literature review depends on a researcher's skill to identify these areas and then to combine their views into a structured and logical review of the literature. 'Literature reviews should be succinct and as far as is possible in a small study, should give a picture of the state of knowledge and of major questions in your topic area' (Bell 2005:110).

QUANTITATIVE AND QUALITATIVE RESEARCH, PRIMARY AND SECONDARY METHODS

Quantitative research: relates to quantity. 'It is dominated by a particular methodology and method; the survey and questionnaire respectively' (De Vaus 2002, cited in Matthewman *et al.* 2007:27). This type of research produces results which can be expressed using numbers or statistics. Quantitative research 'deals with quantities and relationships between attributes. It involves the collection and analysis of highly structured data in the positivist tradition' (Bowling 2007:194). It is a useful approach to use if the focus of your inquiry is exploring 'How many . . .? How often . . .?'. Quantitative research always involves measuring in some way. This research involves the use of statistical analysis for which there are now dedicated software packages.

Qualitative research: relates to quality. This type of research seeks to gain understanding through the study of individuals; it seeks to obtain viewpoints and personal feelings from the participants of the study. Qualitative research aims to study people in their natural social settings and to focus on people's experiences. Such an approach produces non-numerical data, which can be difficult to measure. Qualitative research describes in words rather than numbers and is concerned more with questions like 'why?' and 'what?' rather than 'how many?'. 'Researchers who use a naturalistic approach to investigate people's feelings and beliefs, or ways of life, find qualitative data in a variety of sources and are interested in appreciating the "meanings" attached to them' (Walsh 2001:7). This type of research is most closely associated with participant observation and the collection of data by means of interviews, personal journals etc. According to Haralambos and Holborn (1991) 'compared to quantitative data, qualitative data are usually seen as richer, more vital, as having greater depth and as more likely to present a true picture of a way of life, of people's experiences, attitudes and beliefs' (cited in Matthewman *et al.* 2007:27).

While there are advantages and disadvantages associated with each approach, the general consensus is that the use of both in a research project (if possible and/or appropriate) can enhance the area under study and provide 'maximum opportunity for exploration' (Bowling 2007:352). For Bowling, 'Qualitative research can also enhance quantitative research by placing quantitative data into meaningful social contexts' (*Ibid.*: 352). In order for researchers to collect data in a systematic way, they need to employ a method. Methods of research can be divided into two broad types:

- 'Primary methods involve researchers collecting their own data . . . The data they collect is new', and
- Secondary methods involve reanalysing information that 'has already been used as part of a research study' (Harvey *et al.* 2000:17).

Examples of primary and secondary research methods

Primary
- Questionnaires
- Interviews
- Observation
- Experiments
- Case studies
- Action research

Secondary
- Literature searches
- Case studies
- Technology-based research
- Statistical analysis
- Media analysis

(Green 2000:3)

QUESTIONNAIRES

Questionnaires are a primary method of data collection and are one of the most commonly used instruments for collecting information. The aim of the questionnaire is to gain information from the research population to enable the researcher to answer their overall research question.

'The ability of surveys to produce accurate data concerning behaviour, attitudes, conditions and opinions ensured that the survey became a central method within social science research' (Scott, cited in Marsh 2002:54).

However, despite its usefulness as a research instrument, careful consideration must be given to the preparation and design of the questionnaire. After all, answers obtained are only as good as the questions asked. The following are some of the advantages and disadvantages associated with using questionnaires.

Advantages of using postal questionnaires
1. They can be distributed to large numbers of people.
2. They tend to be cheaper than other methods of data collection.
3. If designed properly, their analysis can be easier than other methods of data collection.
4. Persons completing the questionnaire can remain anonymous.
5. Administration is straightforward, especially when the questionnaire is distributed to a group or by post.

Disadvantages of using postal questionnaires
1. There can be a low response rate.
2. Some people or groups may have difficulty or be unable to complete the questionnaire. For example, the illiterate, young children, the visually impaired or non-native speakers may understand the spoken but not the written word.
3. The absence of an interviewer may mean it is impossible to clarify or rephrase certain questions.
4. There is a lack of personal contact between the researcher and respondent (Murphy-Black, cited in Cormack 2000:302).

Administration
Questionnaires can be administered in three different ways: postal surveys, face-to-face interviews and telephone surveys. Factors such as your research topic, time and travel will greatly influence the type you decide to use.

Designing a questionnaire
The design of a good questionnaire requires considerable preparation. Attention should be paid to the following:

1. What type of questionnaire are you going to use?
2. How long is the questionnaire going to be? (Researchers are generally advised to keep questionnaires short. By doing so it is hoped that they will maintain the interest and co-operation of the respondent.)
3. What types of questions will you ask and how will they be worded?
4. What format will questions take?

Types of question

There are a number of different types of question that can appear on questionnaires:

1. **Closed question:** This type of question requires the respondent to answer simply 'yes' or 'no'. They are not required to expand on answers. This may be seen as an advantage as it allows respondents to complete the questionnaire quickly but it also means that individuals cannot offer any variation in their answers. An example of a closed question would be:

    Have you studied sociology before?   Yes ☐   No ☐

2. **Forced question:** This type of question is very similar to a closed question in that answer categories are provided but they require more than a simple yes / no answer. The most commonly asked forced choice question to appear on questionnaires is that relating to gender, i.e.

    Are you   Male ☐   Female ☐

3. **Multiple choice question:** This type of question provides the respondent with a list of possible answers and asks them to choose one or many from that list, for example

    Which of the following modules do you like studying? (please tick two)

    Applying psychology   ☐
    Health promotion   ☐
    Project   ☐
    Social studies   ☐

    With this type of question it is important to add 'Other, please specify' at the end in case you have omitted something from the list.

4. **Ranking question:** This type of question requests respondents to 'state their preference'. Researchers could provide respondents with a list of possible responses and ask them the following:

From this list of modules, please rank according to usefulness to your work placement, where 1 is most useful and 4 the least useful.

Applying sociology □

Equality, diversity and rights □

Care services □

Welfare rights □

Another way of approaching this type of question is to ask respondents to provide their own list and to rank them in order of importance, for example:

Please list the three modules you consider most useful to your course, with 1 being most useful and 3 least useful.

1. _____

2. _____

3. _____

5. **Filter question:** This allows individuals who answer 'no' to a particular question to be directed to the next relevant question, for example:

1. Do you smoke?   Yes □

                          No □

If No, go to Question 5.

6. **Likert Scale:** This scale was devised by Likert in order to measure the attitudes and opinions of respondents. The main characteristic of this method is that statements are provided and, on the basis of a five-point scale, respondents are asked whether they strongly agree, agree, neither agree nor disagree, disagree or strongly disagree, for example:

	SA	A	NA/D	D	SD
All Irish people are racist	1	2	3	4	5

There a number of important points to keep in mind when devising a Likert scale:

• Scales should consist of an equal number of positive and negative statements (this reduces researcher bias).

• Format of scales should ensure that negative and positive statements are adequately dispersed.

7. **Open question:** These allow respondents to give more detailed responses to questions, to comment in their own words and allow for individual variation. Researchers should provide enough space to allow respondents to do so. Leaving a number of lines etc. also makes clear to respondents exactly how much detail is requested from them, for example:

How do you feel about refugees in Ireland?

_____

_____

_____

These questions can generate very useful information but too many of them in one questionnaire could deter a potential respondent. They are also more difficult to code and increase the work of analysis for the researcher.

Wording of questions

Careful consideration must also be given to the wording of questions. The general rule is to keep questions (1) short, and (2) simple and straightforward. If questions are unclear, respondents may provide useless or irrelevant data that when collected will be of no benefit to the area under investigation. Use language appropriate to the population you are studying and when necessary define terms that need explanation (Cormack 2000:304).

Questionnaire format

Attention to layout or format of a questionnaire is also very important. The following pointers will act as a guide to ensure the questionnaire is structured in a logical, coherent way.

1. **Title:** Always provide a title for your questionnaire.

2. **Introduction:** An introduction or an introductory letter is an important part of the questionnaire as it outlines to the respondent the purpose of the study, provides information on the researcher and most importantly offers them a guarantee of confidentiality.

Sample introduction

My name is _____. I am a second-year student in CCFS studying for a BTEC Diploma in Social Care. As part of the course we are required to undertake a piece of research on a topic of our choice. The topic I plan to investigate is 'Discrimination experienced by members of the Travelling Community in Cavan town'. Your name has been selected as part of a random sample. The information you provide will be treated in the strictest of confidence. The questionnaire will take (approx.) 10–15 minutes to complete. Your help and co-operation is greatly appreciated. Thank you.

3. **Instructions:** Researchers must give clear instructions on how to complete the questionnaire, for example 'Tick boxes provided', 'Circle numbers' etc. If a question is not applicable, give instructions to 'Write N/A in the space provided'.

4. **Question order:** According to Kane (1983:75), 'the usual practice is to place the questions in this order':

   (i)   broader, impersonal, easy-to-answer questions which enlist the respondent's co-operation and interest
   (ii)   less interesting questions
   (iii) sensitive or personal questions and open-ended questions.

   Maintaining order ensures that you are aware of your respondent's feelings and gives them a chance to ease into the questionnaire (Kane 1983).

Problem questions

Kane in her work *Doing Your Own Research* (1983:78–9) points out a number of traps to avoid when writing your questions. These are as follows:

1. **The double question:** 'Do you cycle to college or have lunch in the canteen?' A question like this is confusing for the respondent as it contains two unrelated parts.

2. **The wrong-choice question:** It is important to ensure that you give respondents appropriate questions and all the relevant choices of answers. For example, a question like 'Are you married, separated, divorced or widowed?' doesn't allow single people or people who never married a chance to reply.

3. **The kitchen-sink question:** This question type asks several things in one question, for example, 'Please list all the clubs you have joined in

the past three years, activities taken, prices to join and reasons why you joined.' To ensure that a response will be in any way useful, ask each part of the question separately.

4. **The fuzzy-word question:** 'Should middle-aged people live it up?' There are two problems here: 'middle-aged people does not mean the same age group to everyone' (Kane 1983:78) and 'living it up' could mean anything from a fancy meal once a month to a night on the beer every week!

5. **The cover-the-world question:** 'What do you think of Bob Geldof?' A question like this could cause problems as it doesn't specify to the respondent what exactly they are to answer on, for example are they to refer to his music, his work for Live Aid/Live 8 or to him personally?

6. **Dream questions:** 'What kind of job would you like for your child when they finish school?' A question like this could produce hugely different responses from different individuals. For example, one parent might give an answer that states their absolute ideal, while another parent might provide an answer that is in line with their child's capabilities and talents.

7. **Leading questions:** 'Why are you happy in Cavan?' This type of question assumes people are happy in that area and doesn't give them the chance to say they are unhappy there if that is the case.

8. **Hearsay questions:** Avoid asking people the opinions of others. Asking the settled community about how Travellers feel about their new halting site does not provide an accurate picture of how the Traveller Community actually does feel (Kane 1983).

Other issues concerning questionnaires
1. Use good quality paper.
2. Use the same font size throughout.
3. Clearly number questions.
4. Provide enough space for answers.
5. Carefully code each question to facilitate the analysis process.

Pilot study

Having designed the questionnaire, the next stage in the process is a pilot study or what Robson (2002:383) refers to as a 'dummy run'. 'The pilot study is a small version of the main study and is useful to test all the procedures and the feasibility of the study' (Murphy-Black, cited in Cormack 2000:311).

INTERVIEWS

'An interview is a series of questions a researcher addresses personally to respondents' (Macionis and Plummer 2002:50). This is also a primary method of data collection. There are many different types of interview, such as:

1. structured interview
2. semi-structured interview
3. unstructured interview.

The type you decide to use in your research will depend on the research topic, your research population, the kind of information you need etc. You might find that your research topic justifies the use of all interview types.

1. Structured interview

With this type of interview you are asking each person the exact same question in the same order. The only difference between this and a questionnaire is that in an interview the researchers complete the form for the respondents as opposed to their doing so themselves, as they would for a questionnaire. It is a useful type to use when:

(i) you are interviewing a large number of people
(ii) you are interviewing people who share similar characteristics and outlooks
(iii) you have good background knowledge of your subject area, so that you know what is important to ask and how to ask it (Kane 1983).

This type of interview produces quantitative data: information that can be neatly coded and analysed. This interview type does not leave much room for interviewees to expand on their answers or to offer variations on responses.

2. Semi-structured interview

Researchers who employ this interview type realise that it may take different questions, maybe put in a different order, to get the same information from different people. For example, if you want to get attitudes on current childcare provision you must take into account that care providers, childcare workers and parents of those in childcare may focus on different aspects. The childcare provider may focus on quality of service.

This interview type may be more difficult or time-consuming to code as the answers provided may not fall into such neat categories as in the structured interview.

3. Unstructured interview

This type of interview produces qualitative or in-depth data. Instead of approaching the interviewee with a set of questions, the interviewer has a list of topics which they want the respondent to talk about. During the interview, the interviewer uses this list or topic guide to phrase questions in any order they want, at a time when it suits. It is a useful technique to use at the beginning of a research project, when you know very little on the research topic or when you are looking for a more in-depth sense of what people are thinking or feeling. Because this interview is more like a conversation, the interviewer must be experienced in order to manage it and to ensure the respondent does not go off on a tangent.

Advantages and disadvantages of interviews

According to Clarke *et al.* (2000:266), the following are some of the advantages and disadvantages of interviews.

Advantages
1. The interviewer may get all the sample to respond to the questions.
2. The interviewer can ask the respondents to explain their answers.
3. The interviewer can see if the respondents understood the questions.

Disadvantages
1. They are time-consuming and may cost a lot if you have to pay the interviewers, travel distances to conduct interviews etc.
2. It can be difficult to interpret the data.
3. Interviewers have to be trained.
4. Personal interviews may intrude unnecessarily into people's lives.

Interviewer skills and techniques
1. Introduce yourself to the interviewee and explain the purpose and nature of the study to the respondent. Explain how they came to be selected.

2. Guarantee anonymity and confidentiality if appropriate.
3. Keep your objective in mind and do not deviate too far in an unstructured situation.
4. Explain to the respondent or interviewee that they are free to interrupt or seek clarification when needed.
5. Use probes to generate information, but be sensitive when doing so!
6. Ensure your tone of voice, manner, gestures etc. do not suggest a particular response.
7. Do not judge respondents by expressing approval or disapproval during the interview.
8. Be aware that the environment where an interview takes place can influence the quality of an interview. Where possible make sure the location is free from distractions (e.g. radio) or interruptions (e.g. telephones). Because information provided can be of a sensitive nature it is important that interviewees are in a place where they feel safe, for example, where they are free of the fear of being overheard.
9. Ask for permission to record the interview and explain why you wish to do so.

PARTICIPANT OBSERVATION

Participant observation is 'a method by which researchers systematically observe people while joining in their routine activities (Macionis and Plummer 2002:51). Researchers who use this method do so in order to gain an inside look at social life in a wide variety of settings. These settings could range from a more informal setting such as a shop or a night club to observation carried out in a laboratory. For participant observation the researcher is required to become some kind of member of the observed group. The researchers themselves become the research instruments and unlike other research methods, participant observation may require the researcher to become immersed in the setting for weeks, months or even years. 'The proponents of participant observation argue that it provides a depth of insight and penetration into social settings which other methods cannot match' (Mann 1983:278). Participant observation tells you what people do in situations where you get an opportunity to observe. As Kane (1983:54) points out, 'Participant observation is a technique to use when you wish to learn from people's actions what they do, as opposed to what they say they do'.

Role of observer

As the name Participant Observation suggests, the information the observer gets will depend on their ability to become a participant in a particular setting. Gaining an 'insider's look' depends on the observer – '"hanging out" with others, attempting to act, think and even feel the way they do' (Macionis and Plummer 2002:51). This job of participant observer is not an easy one; in order to ensure that valuable, useful data is produced, 'the observer has to remain neutral while at the same time being closely involved with those being studied' (Marsh 2000:149). During the study the researcher must maintain some distance as an 'observer'. To ensure worthwhile data is collected great sensitivity and personal skills are required from the observer, their ability to mentally step back to record field notes and eventually to make sense of action. These roles of 'insider' participant and 'outsider' observer can cause a number of problems for the researcher, for example:

1. It can place physical and emotional demands on them.
2. It can result in both roles becoming blurred, i.e. role of observer with role of participant, which according to Marsh (2002:144) can cause 'role crisis'.

The above problems have resulted in participant observation being criticised as a research method. Questions have arisen regarding its validity especially as a method of data collection. 'Observation research is part craft and part art. Anyone can observe, but it takes practice and careful planning to observe and record a scene accurately and then to analyse perceptively anything of significance that happened' (Clarke et al. 2000:256).

After you observe you still have to make sense of what you saw. Kane believes that this requires much more than the observation tells you. You may also need to know:

1. how representative your observation is
2. how often this kind of thing occurs
3. what people say about it.

You may also need to know if they would behave differently if you or other observers were not present (Kane 1983:53). Kane believes that the role of researcher involves:

1. observing and hearing with as much attention to detail as possible
2. recording, to the extent that is humanly possible, everything you see and hear in a situation

3. making no judgments about what is significant or irrelevant
4. recording any questions or comments which you make in the course of an observation, because they may have affected the situation.

When participant observation might be useful in a small project

Participant observation can prove useful when:

1. working with small groups
2. activities are accessible to observers
3. your prime motivation is to find out what is going on, and
4. you are not short of time. (Robson 2002:316)

Advantages and disadvantages of participant observation

According to O'Donnell, the following are some of the advantages and disadvantages of participant observation:

Advantages

1. Some groups may have a lifestyle which makes it difficult to study them in any other way.
2. Researcher can fully understand relationships within the group being studied and therefore can understand why people behave in a particular way (and appreciate their point of view).
3. It is possible to study everyday routines and spot factors which might not appear important to the group members and which would not occur to them to mention in other circumstances.
4. Unexpected factors may emerge which the researcher might not have thought of.
5. The observer may not influence the group's behaviour if unrecognised as a researcher.
6. It is possible to record non-verbal communication.

Disadvantages

1. It may be difficult to control personal bias.
2. The presence of the observer may influence the behaviour of the group.
3. It may be difficult to gain acceptance by the group being studied.
4. It may be difficult to record information as it occurs, and important details may be forgotten.

5. There may be legal or moral problems. For example, a delinquent group may expect behaviour which is either illegal or contrary to the values of the observer.
6. There may be ethical implications. For example, 'undercover' operations tend to require the observer to lie in order to maintain 'cover'.
7. Participant observation is very time-consuming, it can create problems of cost and disrupt the 'normal' lifestyle of the researcher. (O'Donnell 2002:14)

FOCUS GROUPS

Focus groups are sometimes referred to as group interviews or discussion groups. A number of people are brought together to discuss a specific topic or issue. A moderator or facilitator leads the discussion by asking specific questions about the topic under discussion. They also stop any break-away conversations from taking place. According to Dawson, the following are some of the advantages and disadvantages of focus groups:

Advantages
1. 'Can receive a wide range of responses during one meeting
2. Participants can ask questions of each other, lessening impact of researcher bias
3. Helps people to remember issues they might otherwise have forgotten
4. Helps participants to overcome inhibitions especially if they know other people in the group
5. The group effect is a useful resource in data analysis
6. Participant interaction is useful to analyse'. (Dawson 2009:30)

Disadvantages
1. 'Some people may be uncomfortable in a group setting and nervous about speaking in front of others
2. Not everyone may contribute
3. Other people may contaminate an individual's views
4. Some researchers may find it difficult or intimidating to moderate a focus group
5. Venues and equipment can be expensive
6. Difficult to extract individual views during the analysis'. (Ibid. 2009:30)

EXPERIMENTS

'An experiment can be defined as an attempt to test a hypothesis under highly controlled conditions established by an investigator' (Giddens 2001:649). This method is rarely used by sociologists because it is impractical and can involve too great a restriction on human rights. For this method to work the researcher needs to directly control the circumstances being studied. Despite its limitations in social research this method is mentioned as 'its classic experimental design helps us to understand the logic of all research designs' (Clarke *et al.* 2000:262). The experiment is seen as a pure form of research as it asks not just what happens but why. It is for reasons such as this that the experiment is treated as a model against which other designs can be evaluated.

Advantages

1. The experiment, because of its nature, can usually be repeated and as a result can build up a body of data.
2. Experimenter bias is reduced, making this method the most objective.

Disadvantage

This method is difficult to use by sociologists as it is difficult to select and keep two similar group contexts.

CASE STUDIES

'Case studies focus on one (or just a few) instances of a particular phenomenon with a view to providing an in-depth account of events, relationships, experiences or processes occurring in that particular instance' (Denscombe 2007:35).

In-depth studies of single cases are known as case studies. The case chosen by the researcher can be a person, group or a situation and it is usually selected because of its 'uniqueness and rarity value' (Walsh 2001:52). On the other hand it could be chosen 'because it's a typical example of a type of person, group or situation' (*Ibid.*: 52). Case studies have become a popular strategy within social research and especially for students carrying out small-scale research projects. When a researcher is selecting a 'case' to study they must make sure that it is:

1. not randomly selected

2. the most suitable strategy for your research investigation. You must be able to justify your selection of a particular case.

Advantages and disadvantages of case studies

Advantages

According to Cohen and Manion (1995:123) advantages of case studies are as follows:

1. The information drawn from case studies is based on people's experiences and practices in their 'natural settings' and as a result is seen to be strong in reality.
2. They allow for generalisations from a specific instance to a more general issue.
3. They show the complexities of social life.
4. They can provide a data source from which further analysis can be made.
5. They build on people's experiences and practices, so their insights can be linked to action and can contribute to changing practice.
6. Because they are built on such practices and experiences of people, the data they contain is seen as being 'more persuasive and more accessible'. (Cited in Blaxter *et al.* 2001:73)

Disadvantages

1. The fact that generalisations can be made from specific instances often leads to criticism regarding the credibility of these generalisations made from its findings.
2. Gaining access to the 'natural' setting of the case study may be difficult or withheld. Gaining access to certain situations or documents could raise ethical issues such as confidentiality.
3. Despite the fact that case study researchers can use whatever research methods seem most appropriate in a situation, case studies are often 'perceived as producing "soft" data. The approach gets accused of lacking the degree of rigour expected of social science research' (Denscombe 2007:45).
4. The presence of the researcher in the case study setting may influence those being researched. According to Denscombe, 'those being researched might behave differently from normal owing to the knowledge that they are "under the microscope" and being observed in some way' (*Ibid.*: 46).

ACTION RESEARCH

'The purpose of action research is always and explicitly to improve practice' (Griffiths 1998:21, cited in Blaxter *et al.* 2001:67).

Action research is a relatively new form of research strategy and has become an approach used by researchers in the social sciences. 'Action research, from the start was involved with practical issues – the kind of issues and problems, concerns and needs that arose as a routine part of activity in the real world' (Denscombe 2007:122). Because it is an applied approach it is particularly suited to the needs of researchers conducting research in their workplaces or in areas such as education, health and social care. With this approach researchers can 'focus on improving aspects of their own and their colleagues' practice' (Blaxter *et al.* 2001:67). Because it is focused on problems, it involves a change intervention with the aim of improvement and involvement. Action research is really based on a cyclical process that could go on for quite a long time. For example:

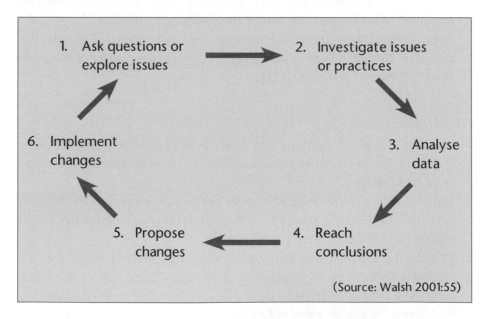

(Source: Walsh 2001:55)

Advantages

1. It requires the researcher to look at practical problems and feeds the results directly back into the process with the aim of finding solutions and making changes.

2. The researcher is able to develop their own practice, contributing to their own self-development.
3. It can provide benefits to participants and organisations because of the continuous cycle of development and change which aims to solve problems and improve practice.
4. It involves participation in the research for practitioners. (Denscombe 2007:130, Walsh 2001:55)

Disadvantages

1. Action research is ethically constrained. Researchers must be aware of what is permissible and ethical within the workplace setting. It usually affects people's lives, so the researcher has the responsibility to limit any risks to those affected.
2. Action research can involve extra work for the practitioners, especially at the early stages.
3. Action researchers are not detached or impartial in their approach to the research. (Denscombe 2007:131, Walsh 2001:55)

SECONDARY/HISTORICAL ANALYSIS AND CONTENT ANALYSIS

'Secondary data – data often in the form of official statistics from other printed sources that have not been generated by the present researcher' (Bilton *et al.* 2002:444).

The sociologist who uses this research method does not collect their own data personally; instead they use data collected by others. 'Secondary sources of information are records made or collected by others, and cover a wide range of material' (Hall and Hall 1996:212).

These sources may include:

1. official statistics
2. published studies
3. other people's diaries and personal documents
4. public records
5. mass media reports
6. books
7. electronic media (O'Donnell 2002:13)

Secondary sources

Official statistics	**Other research**	**Mass media**	**Other sources**
Census	By sociologists	Newspapers	Diaries and letters
Crime statistics	By journalists	Magazines	Historical documents
Health statistics	By government	TV and radio	Photographs
Suicide statistics	Reports and surveys	Film and videos	Autobiographies
Employment statistics			

(Browne 2005:418)

Advantages

1. It is cheap to use.
2. It is more quickly available than primary sources.
3. Data usually exists in considerable quantities.
4. It allows historical research.
5. It allows the researcher to compare one period with another.

Disadvantages

Despite its advantages, secondary research has inherent problems, for example:

1. The data available may not exist in the form one might wish.
2. There could be problems with the accuracy of work done by others.
3. How objective is the data? It can be difficult to account for researcher bias.
4. The researcher may not be able to check the purpose for which the data was originally collected.

   Before you use a secondary source you must evaluate how reliable the information contained in it is. To enable you to do so Clarke *et al.* (2000:273) recommend that you should ask the following:

1. Who collected the data?
2. For what purpose was the data collected?
3. How was it collected?

4. Was the sample size large enough for the results to apply to your research?

'Content analysis is a way of trying to analyse the content of documents and other qualitative material by quantifying it' (Browne 2005:417).

THE INTERNET

'The internet can also be highly productive, opening up access to relevant literature on a global scale and including the latest research from a huge variety of sources' (Denscombe 2002:56).

In recent years the internet has become a valuable source for students when trying to gain background information for assignments, projects etc. This can cause problems. According to Walsh (2001:29), 'You cannot rely on websites to be reliable sources of valid and objective information. Anyone can publish anything on the internet.' Walsh provides the following guidelines for doing research online:

1. Don't use online resources only; make use of library resources too.
2. 'Cross-check any information obtained from the internet with authoritative library resources' (2001:29).
3. Make sure you evaluate the internet sites you use. For Walsh, the following questions need to be asked:

   - 'Can you identify the author(s) of the web pages or websites?
   - Are the author(s) well known in the area you are researching?
   - Do the authors give their credentials and their reasons for publishing the information?
   - Is the site linked to other authoritative and reputable sites?
   - Where did the author(s) gather the information from?
   - Is the information based on original research or secondary sources?
   - When was the information published? (Many websites are never updated or properly maintained.)
   - Is the information academic (produced by researchers), popular (produced for the general public), governmental or commercial (produced by a business for commercial reasons)?
   - Does the information express an opinion or claim to be factual?
   - How does the information compare with what you already know?
   - Does it add anything to your understanding of the topic?' (Walsh 2001:291)

'Internet sources come with no guarantees about the accuracy of their arguments or research findings' (Denscombe 2002:56).

Table 4:2 Four classic research methods: a summary

Method	Application	Advantages	Limitations
1. Experiment	For explanatory research that specifies relationships among variables, generates quantitative data.	Provides greatest ability to specify cause and effect relationships; replication of research is relatively easy.	Laboratory settings have artificial quality unless research environment is carefully controlled.
2. Survey	For gathering information about issues that cannot be directly observed, such as attitudes and values; useful for descriptive and explanatory research, generates qualitative or quantitative data.	Sampling allows surveys of large populations using questionnaires, interviews. Provides in-depth response.	Questionnaires must be carefully prepared and may produce a low return rate. Interviews are expensive and time consuming.
3. Participant observation	For exploratory and descriptive study of people in a natural setting. Generates qualitative data.	Allows study of natural behaviour, usually inexpensive.	Time consuming. Replication of research is difficult. Researcher must balance roles of observer and participant.
4. Secondary analysis	For exploratory, descriptive or explanatory research whenever suitable data is available.	Saves time and expense of data collection, makes historical research possible.	Researcher has no control over possible bias in data. Data may not be suitable for current research needs.

(Source: Macionis and Plummer 2002:52)

SAMPLING

'A sample: the numbers of people/groups about whom facts are gathered' (Donohoe and Gaynor 2003:282).

The term 'population' refers to all those people that researchers have singled out for study. 'The term "population" is used here in a restricted sense, not of the population of a country but all the individuals who fall into the category of interest' (de Vaus 1991:60, cited in Hall and Hall 1996:106). These could be the employees of a factory, the students in a college etc. Most surveys are of groups too large for everyone to be questioned individually. Because of this, researchers must select or 'sample' some individuals for questioning rather than others. According to O'Donnell (2002:18), researchers should ensure that:

1. the numbers are large enough to fairly represent the group
2. the number selected is reasonably easy and economic to handle.

'A sample is a portion of the universe and ideally it reflects with reasonable accuracy the opinions, attitudes or behaviour of the entire group' (Kane 1983:90).

One key problem for the researcher with taking a sample is making it representative. 'Sampling is essentially the process of selecting people or information to represent a wider population' (Marsh 2000:143). In order to ensure that the sample is representative, sociologists 'incorporate a system of randomness into the selection procedure' (Cormack 2000:26). For Cormack, 'The term random does not mean haphazard or careless but refers to a precise method of selection where all individuals in a defined population stand an equal chance of being selected for inclusion in the study sample' (Ibid.).

Different methods of sampling are available to the sociologist, including probability (or random samples) and non-probability (or purposive samples).

The most common types of sampling are:

1. Random or probability sampling, which includes:
    (i)   simple random sampling
    (ii)   quasi-random sampling (systematic sampling)
    (iii)   stratified sampling
    (iv)   multi-stage cluster sampling.

2. Purposive or non-probability sampling, which includes:
    (i)   quota sampling
    (ii)   snowball sampling
    (iii)   judgmental sampling
    (iv)   accidental or convenience sampling. (Hall and Hall 1996:109)

Probability sampling

1. Simple random sampling

With this sampling technique each member of the population has an equal chance of being selected for the sample. In order to use simple random sampling, you first need a list of all the people who could be selected (the sampling frame). The choice of who is actually included in the sample is made objectively by random means. Random numbers that are computer-generated can be used to select a sample (de Vaus 1991:63, cited in Hall and Hall 1996:109).

2. Quasi-random sampling (systematic sampling)

This sampling method requires you to:

(i)   firstly decide how many you want in your sample, and
(ii) then divide this number into the total in the sampling frame to give the sampling fraction.

For example, say you have a population of eighty and need a sample of ten. To calculate your sampling fraction divide eighty by ten; your sampling fraction would be eight (or the nearest whole number). Using a list of names or numbered items, pick the first name/item at random (say the second name on the list) and then every eighth name after that until ten are drawn. This is a fairly easy and cheap method but it is important to make sure lists themselves are not ordered or patterned in a way that could result in certain groups being overlooked (Kane 1983:92).

3. Stratified random sampling

This sampling type requires you to order the population into different groups or strata such as gender, age or social class, and then select informants randomly within each stratum, usually by quasi-random sampling. For example, if you were studying the job concerns of all the employees within a VEC, and the teachers, admin. staff, cleaners etc., had very different needs and interests. These groups could also differ very much in size. So in this method, you first divide the employees into strata (four in this case) and take a random sample from each stratum. The numbers in the strata are drawn to reflect their proportions in the study population. Thus if our employees fell into the following numbers:

Teachers	80
Principals	20
Admin. staff	80
Cleaners	20
	200

We see that the teachers represent 40 per cent of the total number, so in the sample they will also form 40 per cent. If our sample is going to be sixty people, we will need twenty-four teachers (40 per cent of sixty), six principals, twenty-four admin. staff and six cleaners. These are selected by random sampling within each group (Kane 1983:92).

4. Multi-stage cluster sampling

This is a good method to use when you have a large area to cover. For example, if you wanted to study how people in a city might feel about a new law, it would be too difficult and expensive to assign every voter a number and start from there. Instead, this method would permit you to:

1. divide the city into appropriate areas or regions and draw a sample of areas, and
2. take each sample area selected and draw a sample of voters from each.

However, to ensure your sample is representative of the entire population, this sampling technique would require you to have a good knowledge of the area and to make sure that no group had been omitted from the study.

Non-probability sampling

1. Quota sampling

'Quota sampling – where interviewers are instructed to find people to interview who meet the target numbers for the relevant characteristics of gender, age and social class (the "quota")' (Hall and Hall 1996:112).

This type of sampling is often used in taking public opinion polls and the final selection of informants is left in the hands of the interviewer. This technique is often questioned by social scientists because those interviewed are quite literally those who were available, for example those in the street at that time. Such a method can exclude a large number of the population whose attitude and behaviour could be quite different from those asked.

However, as this technique may be the only choice available to you due to limited finances, time etc., be sure to make this clear in your study. Try to make sure that your quota reflects the proportion of each group or category in the area selected, for example, if 2 per cent of the study population are Travellers, 2 per cent of your sample should be Travellers.

2. Snowball sampling

Sometimes in research it is impossible to identify beforehand all those who might fall into your category of interest. A sampling frame, or list of the population, may not be available. For example, if you were conducting research on deviance, you may not find accessible a list of 'deviants' who can be surveyed. In this situation you can use snowball sampling, where the researcher begins with one or a few contacts who then help to find others, and so on. 'Like rolling a snowball, the sample gets bigger the more interviewing you do' (Hall and Hall 1996:113).

3. Judgmental sampling

This type of sampling is similar to quota sampling but less detailed. According to Hall and Hall, 'a judgment sample relies on the researcher to try to obtain as wide a representation of individuals as possible, taking account of likely sources of difference in their views and experiences' (1996:115).

4. Accidental or convenience sampling

This is a quick and cheap way of sampling that involves simply asking anyone who happens to be around and available. Because of this we do not know how representative the results are of the relevant population.

A good sample is not solely dependent on size. Researchers must also:

1. avoid bias in the selection procedure
2. aim to achieve maximum precision for the resources available.

'A poor sample can be disastrous – it can provide misleading information and result in errors' (Clarke *et al.* 2000:268).

ETHICAL ISSUES AND CONSIDERATIONS IN RESEARCH

'Research ethics refers to the standards of behaviour and the practical procedures that researchers are expected to follow' (Walsh 2001:70). As a researcher you have a responsibility to ensure that no harm comes to any of the participants (those taking part) in your study, that you do not invade their privacy unnecessarily, and that you respect their confidentiality and get their permission or consent before the research begins. The researcher must be open and honest with the participants about the purpose of the research. Findings of the research must be reported honestly and researchers never make fake claims or falsify their data. Ethics in research require that those taking part in the study:

1. are free from harm, and
2. that their privacy and confidentiality are protected.

Confidentiality can be safeguarded by anonymity. Participants in the study have the right to remain anonymous and to withdraw from the research investigation at any stage if they wish to do so.

Informed consent

'In more complex forms of data gathering, e.g. experiments, extended interviews etc., it is good practice to get written confirmation from the participants that they understand what is required and agree to take part' (Walliman 2005:347).

As a student you will need to get written confirmation from your tutor 'that you are legitimately carrying out research' (Green 2000:73).

If children are part of the study, parents must provide written confirmation on their behalf. If research is being carried out in a school, the principal needs to give their written consent to allow you to be where you need to be. According to Walliman (2005:347) 'getting consent from vulnerable people (this includes children, some old people, the illiterate, foreign language speakers, those that are ill, and even the deceased) requires particular consideration, depending on the circumstances'. This may involve assessing their level of understanding or consulting with those who are responsible for them. The following is a sample letter that could be used when seeking permission to carry out a piece of research.

Sample letter

The letter should be printed out on the headed paper of the school or organisation from which you are carrying out the research.

Date:

> Your name
> Address of home
> College or school
> Telephone no. (if appropriate)

Dear _____

I am a student at _____ College, studying the _____ course. I have been asked to carry out a piece of small-scale research and have chosen to explore the subject of _____.

As part of my research I would like to conduct a survey of people working in this field, and am seeking permission to involve members of your staff. Between six and ten participants would be ideal. Response can be made anonymously and no names will be used when I write up my research.

I have enclosed a copy of my questionnaire together with the aims and objectives of my study for you to view.

I do hope you will feel able to assist me. I have enclosed a s.a.e. for your reply, or alternatively you can contact me on the above telephone number.

I look forward to hearing from you.

Yours sincerely

_____

(Source: Green 2000:73)

WRITING A REPORT

Most research ends with the production of a text of some sort. It is this stage in the research process that can cause many problems for students. It is important to plan your work, to work through drafts and to always proofread them. The following checklist provided by Marsh acts as a guide for students writing up a piece of work. He believes the more 'yes' answers, the more chance you have of your finished text being up to assessment standard.

Table 4:3 Writing a checklist

	Yes (please ✓)	No (please ✓)
Do I fully understand what I am being asked to do?		
Do I fully understand my assessment criteria?		
Do I have sufficient literature review?		
Do I need to include an abstract?		
Have I included transcripts if required?		
Do I need to include a discussion of timescale and planning?		
Do I need to include a discussion on budget?		
Have I reviewed methodological issues and shown where my research fits?		
Have I discussed my choice of research techniques fully and clearly?		
Is my data clearly presented?		
Have I discussed ethics?		
Do I analyse my data sensitively and as accurately as possible?		
Do I place my research and data in the wider sociological context?		
Do I offer suggestions for improving future research?		
Do I incorporate the work of others in my data analysis?		
Do I evaluate my research in relation to the work of others?		
Do I offer a critical awareness of my research?		
Do I have a clear and well-organised structure to the text?		
Are sentences short and snappy?		
Have I used subtitles and headings to make the text clearer?		
Do sections link well together?		
Have I used the correct referencing system?		
Have I included a correctly constructed bibliography?		
Is it word-processed?		
Have I done a spell check?		
Have I read through a draft to check grammar and spelling?		
Have I asked someone else to read through a draft to check grammar and spelling?		

(Source: Marsh 2002:67)

There is no one way to organise a report. The following headlines are provided as guidelines:

1. **Title:** The title of your report should summarise the main topic of the report. The title deserves considerable attention as it is this that 'sells' the report. Your title can change during the course of the work; do not be afraid to change it. 'A two-part title structure is common: something capturing the essence of the study followed by a more descriptive subtitle' (Robson 2002:509). The title page should also include:

    (i)   name of report writer
    (ii)   date of submission
    (iii) organisation name (if appropriate).

2. **Summary/abstract:** A concise summary (typically 100–150 words) allows other readers to quickly see if the research is of interest to them before they read the main body. The summary or abstract should explain what you did, the methods you used and the results.

3. **Introduction:** This should provide the reader with a general description of the research problem. It should also:

    (i)   Explain why you undertook the work
    (ii)   state your hypothesis
    (iii) state the aims of your research. (Clarke *et al.* 2000:302)

4. **Review of literature:** The purpose of the review is to inform the reader of relevant literature you have read directly relating to your research. The review should provide the reader with an overview of the field you are studying, and should also include:

    (i)   an evaluation of this previous work
    (ii)   the relationship of your work to these earlier studies.

    According to Cormack (2000:449), 'Literature which is supportive of, and which disagrees with, the research being reported is also included.'

5. **Methodology:** Robson in *Real World Research* lists the following as areas that need to be dealt with in the methodology chapter:

    (i)   the kinds of data you have obtained
    (ii)   why this data was selected
    (iii) how the data was obtained, including issues of access and consent
    (iv)   the methods used to collect the data
    (v)   why these methods were used
    (vi)   the approach taken to data analysis

(vii) discussion of the reliability, validity and generalisability of the data

(viii) the decisions made during the course of the study, including change of focus and directions

(ix) ethical issues raised by the study and the procedures followed to address them. (Robson 2002:510)

6. **Results:** This section gives you the opportunity to present your results. Collected data should be clearly described, analysed and presented. Tables, graphs etc., can be used to present data.

7. **Analysis and discussion:** 'The discussion will enable speculation about the meaning of the findings, recognition of the limitations of the study and suggestions for future research in the subject area' (Cormack 2000:451). This section enables you to discuss to what extent your results support or do not support your original hypothesis. Do not introduce new research data in this section.

8. **Conclusions:** The major aim of the closing section, according to Donohoe and Gaynor (2003:287), is to 'Summarise, clarify, evaluate and recommend'. Present any conclusions you have drawn from your results and on the basis of these make recommendations.

9. **Appendices:** In this section include material that is not suitable for the main part of your study, for example newspaper cuttings, maps, a copy of the questionnaire you used etc. It is important to label them clearly so that the reader can refer to them in the main text. The last few pages of your appendices should be your bibliography – a detailed list of all the references and sources you have used in your report.

Presentation and organisation of a report

1. Use language that is clear and understandable.
2. Be honest and accurate.
3. Organise the parts of the paper. According to Kane, a paper may have any of the following.

Table 4:4 Organisation of a Report

Preliminary material	Main body	Reference materials
1. Title	7. Introduction	12. Appendix
2. Abstract	8. Methodology	13. Footnotes
3. Preface	9. (The paper proper)	14. Glossary
4. Table of contents	10. Conclusions	15. Bibliography
5. List of tables	11. Suggestions for future research	16. Index
6. List of illustrations (pictures, charts, diagrams, maps etc.)		

(Source: Kane 1983:177–8)

THE HARVARD SYSTEM OF REFERENCING

Why *reference?*

'It is to acknowledge the work of other writers, to demonstrate the body of knowledge on which you have based your work, to enable other researchers to trace your sources and lead them on to further information' (www.lmu.ac.uk).

A number of referencing systems are used by researchers when acknowledging the work of authors, for example the Harvard system and the footnote system.

According to Cormack (2000:110), the Harvard system of referencing is 'perhaps the most widely used system for citing references within scientific publications'. When you use this system you cite the surname of the author and the year of publication of the work within parentheses. If readers need to find out more information regarding the material being cited, such as the title of the work, the name of the publishing company etc., they must consult the bibliography at the end of your report. This is an ordered list of all the references you have used in your work. References are organised alphabetically, in order of author's surname.

The Harvard system: According to the web page www.lmu.ac.uk, the Harvard system was developed in the USA in the 1950s and 60s and has 'become the most common system internationally'. It is considered a flexible, simple, clear and easy-to-use system for both reader and author.

Donohoe and Gaynor (2003:291) highlight the following points that a researcher should follow when referencing work:

1. Quotations must be taken word-for-word from the original text.
2. Quotations of three lines or less should begin and end with a single inverted comma.
3. When quotations are longer than three lines, omit inverted commas and indent the quotation. Along with author's surname and year of publication of the work, give the page number, so that the reader can check the accuracy of the statement.
4. If you do not quote a sentence in full, indicate omitted text by use of an ellipsis, i.e. '...'
5. When there are multiple authors, cite only the first, followed by 'et al.' meaning 'and others'.

Bibliography: list of references

A bibliography is an alphabetically ordered list of the references you have referred to in the body of your work. When arranging this list there is no need to separate books from journals or any other type of material. However, it is important that you provide the following information when referring to:

Books

1. Author(s) or the institution responsible for writing the document
2. Date of publication
3. Title (and subtitle if any) (underlined)
4. Series and volume number (if applicable)
5. Edition (if not the first)
6. Publisher
7. Place of publication.

For example:

Kane, E. (1983) *Doing Your Own Research*, Turoe Press Ltd, Dublin.

Journal articles

1. Author's surname, followed by initials
2. Year of publication in brackets
3. Title of article in quotes
4. Title of journal (underlined)
5. Volume and part number, month or season of the year
6. Page numbers of article.

For example:
Gaffney, C. (2003) 'Social Research', *Irish Journal of Sociology* No. 3, Spring, pp. 90–95.

If the article is anonymous:
Social Research ? (2003) *Irish Journal of Sociology* No. 3, Spring, pp. 90–95.

Newspaper articles
1. Author of article
2. Year of publication in brackets
3. Title of article
4. Title of newspaper (underlined)
5. Date of publication
6. Page number(s) of article.

For example:
McDonald, D. (2004) 'Rise in Crime Rate', *The Anglo-Celt*, 15th September, p.3.

Theses and dissertations
1. Author's name
2. Year of publication (in brackets)
3. Title (and subtitle if any) (underlined)
4. Type of document (e.g. M.A., Ph.D. etc.)
5. Place of publication
6. Awarding institution.

For example:
Elsadig, O. (2004) *Ethics in Research*, Ph.D. thesis, University College Dublin.

Films
1. Film title (underlined)
2. Date of release (in brackets)
3. Director's name
4. Place of publication
5. Production company name
6. Medium and format (in square brackets).

For example:
Dreams (2002) Directed by Ciara Gaffney. New York, Warner [Film: 35mm]

Video / documentary

1. Series title
2. Year
3. Programme title (underlined)
4. Place of publication
5. Publisher
6. Date of transmission
7. Medium and format (in square brackets).

For example:

Questions and Answers. (2000) *Crime Rates in Ireland.* Dublin, RTE, 2 March [Video: VHS]
(Adapted from www.lmu.ac.uk)

Electronic journal articles

1. Author(s) or editor(s)
2. Year
3. Title of article
4. Title of journal (underlined)
5. Type of medium
6. Date of publication
7. Volume no. (issue no.) pages etc.
8. Availability statement
9. Date accessed (in square brackets).

For example:

Walsh, P. (1999) Sociology in Ireland, *Journal of Sociology* [Internet] 6 March, 2 (4), pp. 122–4. Available from: http://lmc.ac.irl [Accessed 1 June 2001]

World Wide Web documents

1. Author or editor
2. Year
3. Title (underlined)
4. Internet (in square brackets)
5. Edition
6. Place of publication
7. Publisher (if ascertainable)
8. Available from: URL
9. Date accessed (in square brackets).

For example:
Smith, S. (2000) *Law Reform* [Internet] Dublin City University. Available from: http://www.dublincity.ac.irl/service.depts_Pub.lawreform.html [Accessed 22 July 2002]

Blog
1. Author(s) surname, first name
2. Year site published/last updated in brackets
3. Title of message
4. Title of internet site
5. Day, month of posted message
6. Available at: URL
7. Accessed day, month, year in brackets

For example:
Sweeney, Hannah (2012) 'Hard-work', *Mary Higgin Blog*, 13th March. Available at: http://maryhigginblog.com/blogs/archive/2011/02/14/15/aspx [Accessed 13th May 2012]

Email communication
1. Sender's last name, initials
2. Year of message in brackets
3. Medium of communication, receiver of communication
4. Day, month of communication

For example:
McKenna, M. (2013) Email to Mary McDonald, 22nd January.

Interviews:
1. Last name, initials of person interviewed
2. Year of interview in brackets
3. Title of interview (if any)
4. Interviewed by/with, interviewer's first name and last name
5. Title of publication
6. Medium in which interview appeared (journal, radio, video etc.)
7. Publication details

For example:
Kenny, E. (2013) Interviewed by Noel Ryan, *Six One News*, T.V., RTE Two, 16th July (www.ucd.ie)

Twitter:
1. Author of tweet
2. Year of publication in brackets
3. Full tweet
4. Date of tweet
5. [online]
6. Available at: URL
7. Accessed: date in brackets

For example:
@science (2012) *dogs have two brains, http://sic./y/w5cclx* 16th June [online], Available at http://twitter.com/#/worldview14/status/34523672, [Accessed 7th July 2012]
(http://Library.open.ac.uk)

Other issues concerning bibliographies
1. When a web page does not give an author, use the title as the main reference point as you would do with any anonymous work.
2. 'Second and subsequent author's initials come before the surname' (Donohoe and Gaynor 2003:293).
3. The abbreviation '*ibid.*' Can be used when you refer to the same author and book twice (or more) in a row and when there is no other reference between them. '*Ibid.*' (*ibidem*) means 'the work referred to above' (Donohoe and Gaynor 2003:293).

PLAGIARISM

'The worst offence against honesty in research is called plagiarism: directly copying someone else's work into your report, thesis etc., and letting it be assumed that is your own' (Walliman 2005:336). When you use other people's ideas or work in your assignments etc., and do not acknowledge them, that is plagiarism. Green provides the following checklist to help students avoid plagiarism.

- 'Write in your own words.
- Never put a direct quote into your notes without recording where it was found.
- Put all direct quotations in quotation marks.
- Ensure all references are included in your bibliography.
- Read and re-read your work before submitting it.' (2000:68)

5

Sociology of the Family

CHAPTER OBJECTIVES

After reading this chapter you should be able to:

- define what is meant by the family
- talk about the changing structure of the family – range and cultural diversity
- outline the perspectives on the family – functionalist, class-based and feminist
- describe the changing family patterns in Irish society
  - divorce in Ireland
- discuss family disintegration and breakdown – patterns and reasons
  - violence
  - child abuse
- outline family and social care legislation protecting the family.

THE FAMILY DEFINED

'Any combination of two or more persons who are bound together by ties of mutual consent, birth and/or adoption or placement and who, together, assume responsibility for, *inter alia*, the care and maintenance of group members through procreation or adoption, the socialisation of children and the social control of members' (UN, cited in Donohoe and Gaynor 2003:242). To put it more simply, a family is a group of individuals who are related in some way, usually live together, engage in sex, have responsibility for rearing children and function as an economic unit.

The family is regarded as one of the most basic and important institutions in society because it is where society is reproduced in its most basic form – the individual. Defining 'family' is not simple as it takes many forms. 'There is no such thing as the family – only families' (Gittins 1993, cited in Macionis and Plummer 2002:436). Sociologists say that there is no such thing as the family, 'no single definition that can encompass the myriad of domestic and kinship arrangements that characterise contemporary social life' (Sclater 2000:6). The family is an area of great interest to sociologists especially when set in a comparative context over time and culture.

All societies contain some form of family arrangement. Several decades of research, inquiry and discussion have enabled sociologists to increase our understanding of the family, its changing patterns over time and its role within the wider society.

For sociologists, the family is not a stable or unchanging universal phenomenon. According to Lunn *et al.* (2009:iii), 'Families, as the bedrock of our society, are ever changing and evolving. Knowing the extent and nature of the shifts in family life is vital if we are to cater for the needs of families'.

THE CHANGING STRUCTURE OF THE FAMILY – RANGE AND CULTURAL DIVERSITY

'For many years a great transformation has been taking place both in the structure of the family as a social institution and in the nature of relationships among family members' (Curry *et al.* 2005:312).

The great diversity of family and household forms has become an everyday feature of our age. Family patterns have undergone rapid change over the past several decades. 'The major difference which engaged sociological research and debate concerns the transition from a predominantly extended family form in pre-industrial times to the nuclear or conjugal family more typical in modern industrial society' (IPA 1992:34). Sociologists have identified the following family types:

- **The extended family:** Consists of parent(s) and their children plus other relatives such as grandparents, aunts, uncles etc., living with them or very close to each other. The extended family is composed of two or more generations of kin who function as an independent social and economic unit. This family type was the basic social unit in traditional or pre-industrial families. Religion played a key role in influencing the values that were central in regulating conduct between individuals in this family unit. According to Bilton *et al.* (1996), 'People worked on the land, and while inheritance of property was a concern for property-owning groups, for all classes the family operated as an economic unit and depended on producing its own goods and services' (cited in Hyde *et al.* 2004:166). The Irish extended family was also referred to as the 'stem' family. It usually consisted of two generations – the parents, the son and his wife and their children and the unmarried brothers and sisters (IPA 1992:34).

- **The nuclear family:** This type of family is the most common type found in industrialised societies. It consists of two adults living together in a household with their own or adopted children. The nuclear family lives in a unit that is separate from the wider family. This modern type of family, for most purposes, acts as an independent decision-making unit. In circumstances where the family cannot be self-supporting, 'help may come from other individuals or from government welfare agencies, but this help is meant to be temporary' (Curry *et al.* 2005:313). According to Donohoe and Gaynor (2003:247), this family type also includes one-parent families which consist of one parent and a child or children living together. One-parent families occur because the parent has never lived in a partnership or because of death, separation or divorce.

- **The reconstructed family or step-family:** Often known as the blended or reconstituted family, this family type is comprised of two people who have had children in previous relationships and who are now married or live together and each bring their children to live together with the new children they may decide to have.

Families are linked by kin connections. Kinship ties are 'connections between individuals through marriage or through lines of descent that connect blood relatives' (Giddens 2001:173). Marriage can be defined as 'legally sanctioned relationships involving economic co-operation as well as normative sexual activity and child-bearing, that people expect to be enduring' (Macionis and Plummer 2002:436). Every society has rituals and laws that define a valid marriage. According to Curry *et al.* (2005:316), 'In most societies, people marry for pragmatic reasons such as wealth or power. In a minority of societies, however, people are expected to marry for love.' They go on to suggest that marriage based on romantic love is more highly valued in societies that have weak extended family ties and vice versa. 'Romantic love and the increase in the numbers of marriages based on it has been linked to the rise of industrialisation and the growth of the nuclear family.' Why is this the case? According to Curry *et al.*, the following reasons can be given:

1. 'In industrial societies romantic love provides an incentive to marry and form families.

2. Romantic love is more highly valued in industrial societies because it provides a source of support in times of stress, and

3. When spouses are in love they become committed primarily to each other rather than to their families of orientation'. (2005:317)

There are three basic ways in which a family may be constituted:

1. Monogamy – one man married to one woman
2. Polygyny – one man married to several women
3. Polyandry – one woman married to several men (O'Donnell 2002:36). This is rare and is found in only about 1 per cent of all societies. 'It appears to arise where living standards are so low that a man can only afford to support a wife and child by sharing the responsibility with other men' (Browne 2005:230).

Polygamy is the term used to cover both polygyny and polyandry. Economic, social and sexual reasons influence the existence of any particular family pattern, for example in societies where polygyny is practised there are usually more girls than boys.

Table 5:1 Differing family patterns

Types	Examples
1. **Polygyny:** one man and more than one woman. Surplus of women, sometimes artificially increased by early marriage for girls and late marriage for men, or by acceptance of homosexuality. Also men more likely to be killed, e.g. in war. (Note: only the rich and/or powerful may have more than one wife.)	Saudi Arabia, Masaí and Yoruloa in East Africa. (The Koran permits Moslem men to have up to four wives.)
2. **Polyandry:** one woman and more than one man. Surplus of men (rare). May be enforced in order to limit children born and reduce pressure on scarce resources.	Tibet, some Eskimos.
3. **Monogamy:** one man and one woman. Roughly equal balance between sexes. Tends to occur as hygiene and medical care reduce imbalance between sexes (i.e. greater infant mortality among males) and/or modern wage economy makes additional wives/children economic liability rather than economic asset.	Modern Europe, USA.

(Source: adapted from O'Donnell 2002:41)

Families can also be classified by power and on lines of descent.

Power

Patriarchal: Wealth and power come from the father and he controls the family.

Matriarchal: Mother controls the family.

Egalitarian: Authority in the family is more or less equal.

Descent

Patrilineal: Descent through the father – takes father's surname, sons inherit.

Matrilineal: Descent through the mother.

Bilineal: Descent through both mother and father. (O'Donnell 2002:37)

Exogamous marriage permits individuals to marry someone from outside the group to which they belong. Endogamy, on the other hand, means that individuals are normally restricted to marrying someone of their own social group (Haralambos and Holborn 2000:180).

PERSPECTIVES ON THE FAMILY

Functionalist perspective on the family

This approach believes that families perform vital functions for their members and for society. These functions include:

1. **Socialisation:** According to sociologist Talcott Parsons, the family's 'main functions are primary socialisation and personality stabilisation' (Parsons and Bales 1956, cited in Giddens 2001:175). When children learn the cultural norms of the society into which they are born, the process is referred to as primary socialisation. Because this process happens during a child's early years, the family is considered a hugely important setting for the development of the human personality. For Giddens, 'Personality stabilisation refers to the role that the family plays in assisting adult family members emotionally' (2001:175). According to Shaw ' As a social grouping and institution, the family reproduces the kind of order people feel they need to anchor them to the world and to give them a sense of place relative to those things around them that are constantly changing' (2007:378).

2. **Regulation of sexual activity:** 'Every culture regulates sexual activity in the interest of maintaining kinship organisation and property rights.

One universal regulation is the incest taboo; a cultural norm forbidding sexual relations or marriage between certain kin' (Macionis and Plummer 2002:440). Different societies have rules regarding who can marry who but they usually apply the incest taboo to close relatives. Apart from the fact that reproduction between close relatives could have negative effects on the mental and physical health of offspring, Macionis and Plummer highlight the social reasons for its existence:

(i)   It minimises sexual competition within families by restricting sexual relations to spouses.

(ii)   It forces people to marry outside their immediate families to form border alliances.

(iii) It keeps kinship intact. (2002:440)

3. **Social placement:** A child's identity based on race, ethnicity, religion and social class is ascribed at birth through the family. Families permit the transmission of wealth and status from parents to children.

4. **Material and emotional security:** Family members are dependent on each other economically and emotionally. This was especially the case when there was no social welfare system and when the state did not provide support. According to Parsons 'men performed an instrumental role, that of economic provider (or 'breadwinner') whilst women's role was an expressive one, as nurturer and emotional provider' (cited in Sclater 2000:22).

Criticisms of functionalist perspective

This perspective has been criticised for a number of reasons, as follows:

1. Children are socialised outside the traditional family.
2. People have sexual relations outside the family.
3. Increasing evidence of violence and abuse within families suggests that the family can be a dysfunctional place.
4. This perspective minimises the problems of family life.
5. Family plays a part in reproducing and maintaining the capitalist system.
6. This perspective pays little attention to how other social institutions meet some human needs.
7. The anti-psychiatry movement in the 1960s and 1970s 'pointed to the demands and tensions of ordinary family life as instrumental in the production of mental illness' (Sclater 2000:25).

Class-based analysis of family: conflict theory

This perspective on the family views it as another institution that is involved in 'promoting dominant societal values and perpetuating the exploitation of subordinate groups by upholding the norms and values of capitalist society' (Marsh 2000:554).

Marx and Engels looked at the role of families in the social reproduction of inequality. The contribution of Marxism to the sociology of the family can be summarised in the following points:

1. Through the socialisation of children, the family reproduces both labour power and a false ideology which keeps the capitalist system going. 'Families thus support the concentration of wealth and reproduce the class structure in each succeeding generation' (Macionis and Plummer 2002:440).
2. Patriarchy: Engels stated that families transform women into the sexual and economic property of men. Women perform unpaid labour in the home that would otherwise cost a lot to those who benefit from it. By controlling the sexuality of women, men know who their heirs are. Women also make up a 'reverse army' of labour that can be called on, such as in times of war.
3. Race and ethnicity: As people continue to marry others like themselves (endogamy), racial and ethnic categories will continue to persist.

Critical comments on conflict theory

This perspective has been criticised because though Engels condemned the family as part of capitalism, non-capitalist societies also have families and family problems.

Feminist approaches to the study of the family

Much research on the family carried out in the 1970s and 1980s was dominated by different feminist perspectives. In looking at the family they focused on the presence of unequal power relationships within the family and on showing that certain family members tend to benefit more than others. They argued that men generally benefit greatly from families whilst women often do not. 'Feminists highlight the continuing exploitation of women in capitalist societies, not least in terms of the way in which their contribution to the bulk of private domestic work remains unrecognised, unrewarded and undervalued labour' (Marsh 2000:552).

Feminists argue that within the family, the woman:

(i)   has little decision-making autonomy

(ii)   has to do more housework than men, and still spends more time looking after the children, the sick and the elderly (Finch 1989, cited in Macionis and Plummer 2002:441).

Feminists claim that despite the fact that violence and abuse that occurs within some families has received much more public attention, problems such as 'wife battering, marital rape, sexual abuse of children have long been ignored in both academic contexts and legal and policy circles' (Giddens 2001:177). For many feminists, 'the private isolated nuclear family is seen not as a functional unit, but as dysfunctional, particularly for women and children' (Sclater 2000:27). A feminist perspective has significance in the sociology of the family as it highlights:

1. The importance of women within the core of the domestic unit.
2. The changing attitudes to and roles of women in the areas of marriage, divorce and cohabitation.
3. The increasing significance of women's role as carers within the community. (Marsh 2000:554)

A critic of this perspective suggests that feminists fail to take into account the growing trends towards equality in decision-making between women and men.

CHANGING FAMILY PATTERNS IN IRISH SOCIETY

'The family, in Ireland as elsewhere, has been identified as an important symbol of collective identity, unity and security' (O'Connor, cited in Tovey and Share 2003:89).

The nature and structure of the family unit in Ireland has undergone major changes over the years. 'As in other societies modernisation and industrialisation have had an enormous impact upon the traditional Irish family including family relationship patterns, kinship and the conjugal relationship itself' (IPA 1992:35). Two studies carried out by Arensberg and Kimball in the 1930s and Hannon in 1976 provide profiles of family life and family relations that are very different from each other and provide some evidence of the major changes that have occurred. The typical family described by Arensberg and Kimball was characterised by:

1. a strong localised community and kinship network
2. a domestic subsistence economy
3. clearly and sharply defined roles according to age, sex and relative status.
   These family roles were also work roles.

At the time of this study, the Irish traditional family was structured around the domestic economy of the farm and household. The family was primarily a unit of production and reproduction. The success of this economy base required full commitment from family members and as a result rigid roles emerged that reflected the work roles of its individual members. The father's role was that of provider and as owner-director of the family farm he was the 'object of obedience and respect from his children and wife' (*Ibid.*: 36). The wife/mother dominated within the household as she was responsible for the care of the children, housekeeping duties and some areas of farm work. The clear distinction in the roles of husband and wife meant that family roles were more formal and lacked emotional depth. Arranged marriages or 'matchmaking' was also common in 1930s Ireland and was a matter for the couple's parents and kinsfolk. 'Marriage was essentially understood in terms of its role in transmitting property and creating new kin networks of co-operation' (IPA 1992:36). In a study of the Irish family entitled *Cottage to Crèche* (2001) carried out by Finola Kennedy, she writes that 'until 1980 marriage rates in Ireland were relatively low and there were huge numbers of bachelors and spinsters' (cited in Bacik 2004:60). She attributes these marriage patterns to the following factors:

The legacy of the famine: The fact that land was so scarce and family life was so tied up with land ownership led to a system where one child from each family (usually the eldest son) would inherit the land, marry and produce the next generation. Because this was a widespread practice throughout Ireland at that time it had implications for other family members; 'the others had to emigrate, enter religious orders, or remain single' (*Ibid.*: 60–61).

Economic conditions: Because of economic conditions at that time, people waited and didn't marry until they could afford to do so. Once married, fertility rates were high, and this continues to be the case today. According to the International Reform Monitor (2004, cited in Hyde *et al.* 2004:167) 'Ireland continues to have the highest fertility rate among countries in the EU.' These high fertility rates could be linked to the unavailability of contraception until relatively recently and also to the role of the Catholic Church in influencing decisions and 'operating social control mechanisms over the number of children a person had, their sexual practices . . . and matters of mind such as self-control, contrition and conscience' (Hyde *et al.* 2004:166). It is only since 1979 that contraception has been legally available in Ireland for married people 'and for single people (with age restrictions) since 1985' (*Ibid.*: 167).

Anne Byrne, a feminist academic, confirms that 'historically, Ireland has had an exceptionally high proportion of people who remained single' (1997, cited in Bacik 2004:60). Women, as a result, moved out of the family home, leading to high numbers of men remaining in rural areas while women moved to urban areas. 'Even in the 1940s Ireland had one of the highest rates of female migration and emigration in the western world' (Byrne 1997, cited in Bacik 2004:62).

Hannan's 1976 survey of farm families found greater diversity in family relationships ranging from 'the rigidly traditional patterns to patterns more characteristic of modern urban middle class families' (IPA 1992:37). The results of this survey presented the following findings:

• One-third of this sample displayed traditional sex roles and decision-making patterns similar to those of the traditional family in the 1920s. This pattern was reflected more in the older age groups.
• One-quarter of the sample had what 'Hannan described as a very modern pattern of interaction involving joint decision-making, more sharing of tasks especially childcare tasks' (*Ibid.*: 37).

Despite change, Galligan (1998, cited in Tovey and Share 2003:244), states that 'At the same time the more limited notions of the "traditional" family continue to receive active support from many if not the majority in Irish society. In particular, most men and women that are not working outside the home tend to have more traditional views in relation to the family.' In modern society, the traditional functions of the family have been transferred to other social institutions, for example:

• Crèches, nurseries and pre-schools can provide full day care from the age of three months, and later on schools provide education.
• The social service system can provide children with the basic necessities such as food, shelter etc., should the need arise.

The following is evidence that reflects the shift in the structure of the family in Irish society today:

Marriage patterns

'A marriage is a multifaceted bond based on commitment, love, intimacy. Yet while this relationship is an intensely private affair, it is also shaped by macro forces, such as the law, economics, religion, and gender expectations' (Zinn *et al.* 2011:254). Relationships and marriages are driven on the 'relatively modern westernised notion of romantic love' (Donohoe and Gaynor 2003:243). This concept sees individuals as free to choose their own spouse. Bacik (2004:62–3) provides the following statistics reflecting changes in attitudes and changing patterns in marriage that have occurred in recent decades:

- By the mid-1970s marriage rates peaked at a level that has not been surpassed yet. 'In 1974, the peak year, a grand total of 22,833 marriages was recorded' (Bacik 2004:63).
- In the 1980s early marriages and large families began to decline due to economic recession. The numbers of single people began to increase once again.
- Better economic times in the 1990s saw an increase in marriage rates and in the numbers of couples cohabiting. 'However, the figure of 20,047 marriages recorded in 2002, while it marked an increase from previous years, is still well below the sort of figures seen in the 1970s' (*Ibid.*: 63).

Hyde *et al.* (2004:167) provide figures for the year 1996 which show 'that the average age at marriage for men was recorded as 30.2 years and for women 28.4 years'. Figures from the *Statistical Yearbook of Ireland* (2006:57) state that the 'average age of marriage increased by two years between 1996 and 2002 for both brides and grooms'. It also highlighted that in 2005, 20,723 marriages were registered (*Ibid.*: 57).

A study carried out by Lunn, Fahey and Hannan in 2009 entitled 'Family dynamics and family types in Ireland' presented the following key findings:

1. 'A trend away from marriage among young adults that is partly due to a large rise in cohabitation.
2. In 2006, for those aged 25, twice as many cohabitated as married. Cohabitation peaks at 28 years, after which marriage becomes more popular.
3. Later age of marriage is more common across all the classes.
4. Those in lower social classes are more likely to marry young.
5. Travellers are particularly likely to get married young.
6. Non-Irish nationals are more likely to be married.
7. Irish are more likely to be unmarried at all ages' (2009:8).

Table 5:2 Summary data for marriages 1996, 2006, 2009

	1996	*2006*	*2009*
State	16,174	22,089	21,627
Marriages per 1,000 population	4.5	5.2	4.8
Average age of groom	30.2	33.2	34
Average age of bride	28.4	31.2	31.8

(Source: adapted from CSO Statistical Yearbook 2012:69)

Statistics provided by Lalor *et al.* (2007:63) show that the figure of 5.1 marriages per 1,000 in 2003 is relatively high by European standards. Recent demographic data from *Eurostat* (2012) shows that the number of marriages per 1,000 inhabitants has decreased within the EU27 in recent years, while the number of divorces has increased. 'The crude marriage rate was highest, among EU member states, in Cyprus (7.3 marriages per 1,000), Lithuania (6.3) and Turkey (8). The lowest rates were in Slovenia (3.2), Bulgaria (2.9) and Luxembourg (3.3)'.

Fluctuating marriage rates in Irish society seem to be influenced by factors such as modernisation, economic conditions and changing attitudes. 'While positive evaluation of the family as such is unwavering, the picture for marriage is more mixed. Marriage was formerly seen as the only legitimate avenue to sexual relations but that attitude is now rare' (Fahey *et al.* 2005:119).

Births outside marriage

Births outside marriage are also on the increase. According to Tovey and Share (2003:246), 'these births made up nearly a third of all births in Ireland. This increase reflects a change in attitudes about our ideas about the family and in social values'. Bacik (2004:65) states that 'the percentage of births outside marriage now (2002) stands at just over 31 per cent, that is almost one-third of births, compared with just over one quarter (25.3 per cent) in 1996'. Along with an increase in births outside of marriage, the demographic profile of non-married mothers is also changing, with an increase in the number of births taking place for women in the age group from twenty-five to forty-four. According to Rush *et al.* (2006:143, cited in Fanning 2006), 'Mothers aged 40 and over had 6 times more children outside marriage than young mothers.' In 2011, 'just over a third of births, 25,190, were outside marriage. This compares with 19,210 (31 per cent) births outside marriage in 2003'. (CSO 2012:63) The following statistics presented by Treoir in 2013 state that:

1. '6,543 or 34 per cent of all registered births were outside marriage
2. 54 per cent of births outside marriage were to unmarried parents with the same address (3,556)
3. Waterford City had the highest percentage of births outside marriage at 50 per cent
4. Roscommon had the lowest percentage of births outside marriage at 22 per cent (Treoir 2013).

Table 5:3 Births outside marriage classified by age of mother at maternity

Age	2006	2009	2011
15 and under	48	45	40
16–19	2,121	2,031	1,525
20–24	6,522	6,834	5,987
25–29	6,311	7,890	7,876
30–34	3,883	5,049	6,001
35–39	1,999	2,692	2,948
40–44	488	657	776
45 and over	14	42	31
Age not stated	11	12	6
All ages	**21,397**	**25,252**	**25,190**

(Source: adapted from CSO Statistical Yearbook 2012:66)

'The introduction of the Unmarried Mother's Allowance in 1973 gave a means of supporting children outside of marriage without family approval or support' (Donohoe and Gaynor 2003:247). Fahey *et al.* (2005:114) refer to a study carried out in 1976 surveying moral attitudes in the Republic of Ireland. The findings of that study 'showed strong disapproval of sex before marrying – in 1973 almost 3 out of 4 Irish people aged 31–50 felt that it was "always wrong".' Fahey (1999:62, cited in Fahey *et al.* 2005), in the early 1990s, almost twenty years later, found 'that the proportion of 31–50-year olds who felt that way had plummeted to one in five'. The concept of illegitimacy was in effect abolished in 1987 with the Status of Children Act of that year, and according to Kennedy (2001) 'it ensured children born outside marriage were afforded the same legal standing as other children' (cited in Lalor *et al.* 2007:63). However, despite changing attitudes and economic assistance from the state, lone parents constitute a large number of the population who experience poverty and discrimination in society.

Increase in number of one-parent families

'Significant transformations in the structure of the Irish family have characterised modernity with a distinct trend towards lone-parent and other alternative family arrangements emerging in recent decades' (Healy 2009:18). There has also been an increase in the number of one-parent families. According to the CSO (2009), 'lone parents accounted for 18 per cent of families in the state; an increase of 80 per cent over the past two decades'. Apart from people who never married or lived in a partnership, this group includes a parent on their own as a result of death, separation or divorce. According to statistics from the 2006 census:

* 'There were approximately 189,200 lone parent families in 2006, an increase of 23 per cent on 2002. This figure for 2011 is 211,315.
* Nearly 86 per cent of lone-parent families were headed by females. In 2011, lone mother with children made up 186,284 of all family units.
* Single parents accounted for 36 per cent of all lone families in 2006 while in 29 per cent of families the lone parent was a widow.
* In a further 30 per cent of families the lone parent was separated or divorced.

(*Ibid.*: 20–21)

Table 5:4 Types of family in Ireland, 2002 and 2011

Family categories	2002	2011
Husband and wife without children	184,950	261,652
Cohabiting couple without children	47,907	83,292
Married couple with children	508,035	588,682
Cohabiting couple with children	29,709	60,269
Lone mother with children	130,364	186,284
Lone father with children	23,499	29,031

(CSO Statistical Yearbook 2012:20)

Other features of the family in Irish society include:

- Smaller completed family size: 'Although Irish birth rates have fallen considerably in recent years, they are still the highest in the EU25. For example, in 2004 Ireland had 15.2 live births per 1,000 inhabitants compared to 12 in the UK and 8.6 in Germany' (*Eurostat* 2006, cited in Lalor *et al.* 2007:62).

  Recent data presented by www.thejournal.ie based on the 2011 census shows that 'the average size of families in Ireland is continuing to decline but at a slower pace than previous years'. It also highlights that:

  1. 'The average number of children in each family is now 1.38 – a drop from 1.41 in 2006
  2. The number of one-child families increased by 13 per cent
  3. Data showed there were 1,592 families with seven or more children in Ireland'. (www.thejournal.ie)

- According to CSO (2006:17) the number of single persons grew by 138,600 (10.5 per cent) between 2002 and 2006. Between 2006 and 2011, the percentage of single people in Ireland fell slightly. At present, 'about 37 per cent of the Irish population is married . . . overall, there are 1.5 million single people in Ireland' (www.thejournal.ie).

- Change in female employment patterns: 'Changes in the family in Ireland are matched by changes in the labour market where women, including married women, are increasingly active, giving occupational status a new significance to Irish attitudes' (Richardson 2003, cited in Rush *et al.* 2006:150). Figures presented by Lalor *et al.* (2007:61) citing www.worklifebalance.ie suggest that 'Women's participation in the workplace is the highest amongst younger women – 75.6 per cent of 25- to 34-year-old Irish women are in paid employment.' According to www.ec.europa.eu, 'there were 861,000 women (56 per cent) working in Ireland in 2010'. However, findings suggest that women with young children are less likely to work than those without. 'In 2011, the employment rate in Ireland for women varied from 85.7 per cent for women with a husband/partner and no children to 51.5 per cent for women whose youngest child was aged between 4 and 5 years of age' (www.ec.europa.eu).

- Increases in separation and divorce: 'Major changes in the family can be attributed to factors such as the modernisation of Irish society, a decrease in the adherence to religious regulations, changing attitudes of women etc. 'Ireland, like many other western countries, has seen a major change in the nature and structure of the family unit in recent times' (Tovey and Share 2003:245).

Divorce in Ireland

Divorce was introduced to Ireland by the Family Law (Divorce) Act which came into force on 27 February 1997 (Wood and O'Shea 2003:65). In 1995 Ireland was the only country in the European Union to forbid civil divorce. In November 1996 the electorate in Ireland voted in favour of divorce 818,842 votes to 809,728 after a recount (*Ibid.*: 15). Divorce is seen as the last option by a couple when their marriage breaks down and can have a traumatic effect on all those involved, including the couple, any children and society as a whole. Despite this divorce is a realistic and accepted part of life in twenty-first-century Ireland. The following statistics support this fact:

* The divorced category was the fastest growing marital category in the period since 1996.
* The number of persons recorded as divorced in the 2006 census increased from 9,800 in 1996 to 35,000 in 2002, to 59,500 in 2006.
* The number of divorced people in Ireland increased by more than 150 per cent between 2002 and 2011.
* Since the introduction of divorce legislation in Ireland, the number of divorced people rose from 35,059 to 87,770.
* The number of people identified as "separated" stood at 116,194. This figure was 107,263 in the 2006 census.
* Females accounted for 57.3 per cent of separated persons and 54.3 per cent of divorced persons in 2006. In the 2011 census, there were 65,361 separated women compared with 50,833 separated men, and 49,685 divorced women compared with 38,085 divorced men.
* Limerick City (13.5 per cent) had the highest rate of marital breakdown in the country, followed by Waterford City (12.5 per cent) and Dublin City (12.4 per cent). Cavan (8.2 per cent), Limerick county (7.9 per cent) and Galway county (7.5 per cent) had the lowest rates in 2011 (CSO 2006, 2011).
* The rate of remarriage following divorce increased from 21,400 to 42,960 between the years 2002 and 2011. (www.thejournal.ie 2013)
* 'Male respondents were slightly more predisposed than female respondents to regard divorce favourably' (Rush *et al.* cited in Fanning 2006:152).

Despite increasing numbers and changing attitudes to divorce, it is said that Ireland continues to have the lowest divorce rate in the EU. According to *Eurostat* (2006), in 2003, Ireland had 0.7 divorces per 1,000 inhabitants compared to 3.2 in the Czech Republic and Lithuania' (cited in Lalor *et al.* 2007:63). Figures provided by *Eurostat* in 2012 reflect similar statistics. Along with Malta, 'Ireland (0.7 per cent in 2011) and Italy (0.9 in 2010) were the only other EU member states to record crude divorce rates below one divorce per 1,000 inhabitants. The highest crude divorce rates were recorded in Latvia (4.0 divorces per 1,000 inhabitants in 2011) and Lithuania (3.4). Factors minimising the divorce rates in Ireland could include:

- a dominant religion, Catholicism, which prohibits divorce
- high home ownership rates
- rural populations
- late marriage age
- (relative) cultural homogeneity. (Lalor *et al.* 2007:64)

Divorce is considered to be one of the most stressful events that an individual can experience. 'Men are more likely to be fired from their jobs after a divorce, and the death rate for divorced men and women is higher than that for married people' (Emery *et al.* 1984, cited in Curry *et al.* 2005:312).

FAMILY DISINTEGRATION AND BREAKDOWN: PATTERNS AND REASONS

Violence

'The true numbers of violent episodes that occur in homes up and down the country, as it remains is a largely "hidden problem" taking place behind closed doors, often with no witness present' (Sclater 2000:104). According to Donohoe and Gaynor (2003:245) 'domestic violence refers to violence in the home perpetrated by adults on their partners and/or children'. It was only in the 1970s that violence against women and children was recognised as a social problem. Despite the recognition of this new 'family problem', it is still difficult to estimate the true extent of it, as many feel it difficult to report (Macionis and Plummer 2002:445). Domestic violence occurs across all social classes and includes physical and sexual assault. Men can also be the victims of domestic violence. However the majority of studies document the violence experienced by women. Evidence provided to support this shows that:

- Sixty-five women were murdered in Ireland between 1996 and 2002. One-third of these were murdered by a husband or partner in their own home.
- In 1999, 11,000 calls by women were received by the National Network of Refuges and Support Services (Donohoe and Gaynor 2003:206). 'The most radical remedy available to the court is the barring order. This directs the respondent to leave the place where the applicant or a dependent child resides and prohibits them from re-entering until such time as the court specifies' (Conneely 2005:133). The following table provides some details of the number of applications sought and granted under the Domestic Violence Act of 1996 for a number of different years.

Table 5:5 Applications under the Domestic Violence Act

	1999	2001	2003	2005
Barring orders	4,668	4,470	3,586	3,183
Applications granted	2,219	2,067	1,575	1,265

(Source: Courts Service Annual Report in CSO *Statistical Yearbook* 2006:134)

The Health Service Executive policy on domestic, sexual and gender-based violence acknowledges that 'Domestic violence and/or Sexual violence is a serious health, social and human rights issue' (www.hse.ie). Statistics highlighted in the paper indicate the extent of the problem in Irish society. According to their findings:

- '15 per cent of women and 6 per cent of men have experienced severely abusive behaviour from a partner.
- 11 per cent of the Irish population have experienced a pattern of behaviour with an actual or potential severe impact on their lives.
- 29 per cent of women and only 5 per cent of men report severe abusive behaviour to the Garda Síochána' (McGee *et al.* 2002 cited in www.hse.ie).

According to www.womensaid.ie, 14,792 incidents of domestic violence were disclosed to the Women's Aid National Freephone Helpline in 2012. Of these 'there were 9,912 incidents of emotional abuse, 2,859 incidents of physical abuse and some 1,554 incidents of financial abuse disclosed' (*Ibid.*: 1).

According to the Women's Aid Female Homicide Media Watch 2013, 191 women have been murdered in the Republic of Ireland since 1996. Sixty-one per cent (117) were killed in their own homes (cited in www. womensaid.ie).

Child abuse

In 1999 the Department of Health and Children published the document *Children First: National Guidelines for the Protection and Welfare of Children*. According to Martin (2000:64, cited in Lalor *et al.* 2007:292), 'this was a clear acknowledgment that the profile of child abuse as a social problem had risen considerably in Ireland and was urgently in need of a structured, centralised, socio-legal response'. A child is defined as 'a person under the age of 18 years other than a person who is or has been married' (Childcare Act 1991 cited in Richardson 1999:170). Abuse of children can take different forms. It can be physical, emotional, neglect or sexual. Sexual abuse in Ireland has only been highlighted since around the 1980s, but as with domestic violence, the full extent is not known. According to McGee *et al.* (2002):

- '1 in 5 girls and 1 in 6 boys experience contact sexual abuse in childhood.
- 42 per cent of women and 28 per cent of men experienced some form of sexual abuse or assault in their lifetime' (cited in www.hse.ie: 2013).

The aim of the guidelines were to:

- facilitate professionals in identifying child abuse
- help people identify and report child abuse
- improve current services for children and families in both statutory and voluntary agencies (Lalor *et al.* 2007:292).

The family and social care: legislation and services (voluntary and statutory) protecting families and children

- Child Care (Amendment) Act 2011
- Adoption Act 2010
- Child Care (Amendment) Act 2007
- Criminal Justice Act 2006
- Ombudsman for Children Act 2002
- Children Act 2001
- Youth Work Act 2001
- Family Support Agency Act 2001

- Education Welfare Act 2000
- Protection for Persons Reporting Child Abuse Act 1998
- Child Care Act 1991

The above list mentions some of the legislation that gives the state the right to intervene and to take action to protect children and families. Agencies involved in meeting their needs should problems such as domestic violence arise include:

- The Department of Justice, Equality and Law Reform (Gardaí)
- The Department of the Environment and Local Government
- The Department of Social and Family Affairs
- The Department of Health and Children

Other agencies working in the area of child support and protection are Barnardos Child and Family Services and the ISPCC.

The family is an important social institution which helps hold society together. Sociologists' interest in the area lies in its role as a site of socialisation, a structuring basis of society, and its importance in influencing policy issues (e.g. patterns of work, childcare etc.) (www.pshare.com). The family is a complex and dynamic concept and this is evident in the changes that have taken place in the nature and structure of the family in Irish society. According to Tovey and Share, 'in looking to the future we can begin to discern some important changes' (2003:247). Among these changes we can expect to see:

- increasing numbers of people remaining single
- a rise in the number of one-child families
- more gay and lesbian couples
- more voluntarily child-free people.

6

Social Stratification in Irish Society

CHAPTER OBJECTIVES

After reading this chapter you should be able to:

- define social stratification
- describe the systems of stratification: slavery, caste, estate, class
- explain the concept of social class
- describe class structure in Irish society in relation to health, housing, consumption patterns and education
- describe social mobility in Irish society.

SOCIAL STRATIFICATION DEFINED

'Social stratification: the division of a society into a number of strata, hierarchically arranged groupings' (Mann 1983:366). Stratification is the term used to describe the way in which different groups of people are placed within society.

Social stratification is the term used by sociologists to describe the inequalities that exist between individuals and groups within human societies (Giddens 2001:282). While people may think of stratification in term of assets or property it also refers to all forms of inequality based on class, gender, ethnicity, age, religious affiliation, political status etc. While wealth and income tend to be the most common basis of stratification, people are ranked hierarchically according to their possession of these attributes. 'This sort of ranking leads to groups of people being classified into layers or strata – like geological rock formations – hence the term stratification' (Marsh 2000:268). Societies can be seen as consisting of 'strata' in a hierarchy, with the more favoured at the top and the less privileged near the bottom.

Virtually all societies have some form of stratification or structured inequalities that are organised and that persist over time. The concept of hierarchy (social or otherwise) introduces some notion of inequality that involves making judgments about groups of people, based on social difference. In nearly 'all societies some people are regarded as more important than others, more worthy of respect or more useful than others either within the society as a whole or in certain situations' (O'Donnell 2002:119). According to Babbie (1998:124), large segments of society are stratified, for example men generally do better than women, whites do better than blacks, younger people do better than older people. Different societies value these characteristics differently but it is based on them that individuals and groups enjoy equal (or unequal) access to rewards. Modernisation of society has created new patterns of social inequality that needed to be understood. 'The analysis of social and economic inequality was a central concern of sociology from its inception' (Bilton *et al.* 2002:72). According to sociologists, social stratification is a matter of four basic principles.

Principles of stratification

1. Social stratification is a characteristic of society, not a reflection of individual differences.
2. Social stratification persists over generations.
3. Social stratification is universal but variable.
4. Social stratification involves not just inequality but beliefs. (Macionis and Plummer 2002:178)

SYSTEMS OF STRATIFICATION

Most societies have some form of general stratification placing certain groups of people in superior and inferior positions, a hierarchy of prestige and power. Historically four basic systems of stratification have existed in society. These are slavery, caste, estate and class.

Slavery

This is the oldest and most extreme form of stratification or inequality in which some individuals are literally owned by others as property. 'Between the 15th and 19th centuries the industrial and financial might of modern European powers was directly related to trade in African slaves. This slave labour was crucial to the economic development of the New World and the establishment of black populations in the Americas and the Caribbean'

(Marsh 2000:269). Although the forms that slavery has taken have been highly variable, the majority of slaves were deprived of almost all human rights. As a formal institution, slavery has gradually been eradicated but has not yet completely disappeared. According to Macionis and Plummer (2002:181) although 'the British Empire abolished slavery in 1833 and the American Civil War brought slavery in the US to an end in 1865 . . . it [slavery] still persists in a variety of forms in many parts of the world today'. Brazil was the last to abolish its participation in the transatlantic slave trade in 1888. According to Kelly (2013), about 150 years after most countries banned slavery, millions of men, women and children around the world are forced to be slaves. Although this exploitation is often not called slavery, the conditions are the same. Bales, an English social scientist, suggests that the system of slavery that exists today is different from traditional slavery. He refers to it as modern slavery which is 'not about direct ownership but about control through violence, usually with major elements of economic exploitation' (Bales 2000, cited in Macionis and Plummer 2002:181). He believes that across the world there are about twenty-seven million people in modern slavery, which could include those in

- forced labour
- debt bondage
- prostitution
- servile marriage.

Because of the illegal nature of modern-day slavery data is hard to collate. Child marriage, the marriage of girls under 18, takes place on a massive scale. 'UNICEF recently estimated that globally, almost 400 million women currently aged 20 to 49 were married or entered into a union when they were under 18 years old. This equates to 41 per cent of the total population of women in this age range' (Turner 2013). The UN's International Labour Organisation (ILO) estimates that about 21 million people are in forced labour at any point in time. Other findings presented by the ILO suggest that:

1. 'the above estimate includes trafficking and other forms of modern slavery. The figure does not include trafficking for organ removal, forced marriage or adoption.
2. Asia accounts for more than half of the ILO's 21 million estimate.
3. Women make up the majority of those being exploited, 55 per cent are women and girls, and account for the vast majority of sexually exploited people.

4. Children make up a quarter of all those in slavery.
5. In the year 2005, it was estimated that illegal profits from forced labour amounted to more than 44 billion dollars.
6. People trafficking is the third largest global industry after drugs and arms trafficking'. (Kelly 2013)

Usually modern slaves are found amongst the 'poor, the uneducated, the low-status groups of a society: frequently, of course, these are women and children' (*Ibid.*). Slavery is a closed system of stratification and agencies such as Anti-Slavery International continue to monitor the use of forced labour as well as child prostitution on a global scale (Marsh 2000:269).

Caste

'A caste system consists of a fixed arrangement of strata from the most to the least privileged, with a person's position determined unalterably at birth. The boundaries between castes are discrete – that is, they are distinct and sharply drawn' (Matras 1984, cited in Curry *et al.* 2005:160). Caste systems are closed stratification systems in which people inherit their position and experience little mobility.

This system of stratification is mainly associated with Indian society and the Hindu religion. It is based on a system of religious beliefs that cannot be changed and as a result is a closed system of stratification. The Hindu belief in reincarnation (rebirth) states that individuals who do not abide by the rituals and duties of their caste will be reborn in an inferior position in their next incarnation. The caste position you occupy is determined at birth; you cannot change it throughout your life. 'Caste systems structure the type of contact that can occur between members of different ranks' (Giddens 2001:282). In a caste system, birth determines the shape of people's lives in four crucial ways:

1. Traditional caste groups are linked to occupation, so that generations of a family perform the same type of work.
2. Caste systems ensure that people marry others of the same ranking (endogamy). 'In large part, the boundaries between castes are maintained by regulating who marries whom' (Curry *et al.* 2005:160).
3. Caste systems guide everything in life so that people remain in the company of 'their own kind'.
4. Caste systems are based on strong cultural and religious beliefs (Macionis and Plummer 2002:182).

This system was officially abolished in 1947, but still survives in rural areas, as do the beliefs on which it was based (3,000 years) (Marsh 2000:270). The following outline of the Hindu caste system described by O'Donnell provides an overview of how 'the structure of society is divinely ordained and individuals are obliged to accept it and to carry out their duties within it, without ambition to change (dharma)' (Marsh 2000:270).

THE HINDU CASTE SYSTEM

Brahmans (e.g. priests, teachers)
↓
Kshatriyas (e.g. warriors, landlords)
↓
Vaishyas (e.g. merchants, traders)
↓
Sudras (e.g. peasants, servants)
↓
Haryans (untouchables)
↓
Social Outcastes (e.g. leather-makers, sweepers)

- Each caste is subdivided into thousands of Jatis (sub-castes) with their own restrictions and rituals.
- No mobility between castes is possible.
- Kharma (Hindu belief in reincarnation) results in those who rigidly obey the caste's code (Dharma) being reborn into a higher caste. Those who do not obey the code are reborn into a lower caste.
- Outcastes are segregated – they would pollute higher castes.
- Although higher castes are often richer than lower, this is not necessarily so. The purest 'Brahmans' may reject all possessions, a Haryan leather-maker may become rich (adapted from O'Donnell 2002:123).
- The Brahmans, Kshatriyas, Vaishyas and Sudras are the four main groups Hindus can belong to.

- The 1901 census identified 2,378 main castes and 1,700 sub-castes within just one of these main castes (*Ibid.*: 123).
- According to Leonard (1994) 'The Harijan are considered to be especially polluted. For this reason up until 1973 some untouchables were permitted in the streets only during the morning or evening, while other untouchables could go out only at night' (cited in Curry *et al.* 2005:161).
- Caste systems existed in other societies, such as in the former apartheid system of South Africa where black and white were segregated and stratified. South Africa banned marriage and even sex between the races until 1985 (Macionis and Plummer 2002:192).

'UNICEF estimates that identification and sometimes discrimination based on caste affects 250 million people worldwide'. (www.boundless.com 2013)

Estate

Medieval Europe was a feudal system based on the ideas of estates. The feudal estates consisted of different strata or layers. Three major groups were identified:

1. the nobility or aristocracy
2. the clergy
3. the commoners.

Each of these groups had differing obligations and rights towards each other. This system was closely related to property and political power with land ownership as the key. Although it was not encouraged, movement between the strata was tolerated, especially in towns. It did allow some degree of social mobility.

Class

'A class can be defined as a large-scale grouping of people who share common economic resources, which strongly influence the type of lifestyle they are able to lead' (Giddens 2001:282).

The social class system is a system of stratification that results from the unequal distribution of wealth, power and prestige. It is considered an open system of stratification as unlike the other systems it claims to be based on individual achievement. According to Curry *et al.*, 'In a class system, social standing is determined by factors over which people can exert some control, such as their educational attainment, their income and their work experience' (2005:161). For example, a person who works hard or studies hard can change their social class position. 'Class position is largely determined by an individual's place within the economic system and is to some extent achieved' (Marsh 2000:270).

THE CONCEPT OF SOCIAL CLASS

'Sociologists argue that class position is a major determinant of life conditions and resources, including access to property and income, to education, to housing, to good health and to power' (Drudy 1995:295).

Class systems are considered to be the main form of social stratification in western industrialised societies today and because of this the concept of class is central in social theory and analysis. The economic system of capitalism resulted in the emergence of social classes. Capitalism, according to O'Donnell (2002:124), is an economic system in 'which some people are free to sell what is produced for their own profit, while others are legally free to sell their labour where they like'. The following highlights the main characteristics of class which make it different to the other systems of stratification:

1. According to Giddens (2001:282), 'Classes are not established by legal or religious provisions, membership is not based on inherited position as specified either legally or by custom.'
2. A person's class position is in some part achieved, not ascribed or given at birth as in some other systems of stratification. With this system 'merit' is rewarded and enables a person to rise to a higher social stratum. Movement (or mobility) upwards and downwards in the class structure is possible. A class system is more open so that people who gain schooling and skills may experience some social mobility in relation to their parents and siblings. The fluidity of this system blurs class distinctions making them difficult to define. 'Social boundaries also break down as people immigrate from abroad or move from the countryside to the city, lured by greater opportunity for education and better jobs' (Lipset and Bendix 1967, cited in Macionis and Plummer 2002:184). Class systems put no formal restrictions on inter-marriage between people from different classes.
3. Classes depend on economic differences between groupings of individuals – inequalities in the possession and control of material resources. According to O'Donnell (2002:124), 'As feudalism died out

and social "classes" became established, those families which occupied high-prestige positions under the old order often continued to do so, as they had the wealth or "capital" available to invest in developing their lands, industry or commerce in order to produce a surplus income or "profit".'

4. Class systems operate mainly through large-scale connections of an impersonal kind. For example, inequalities of pay and working conditions are one major base of class differences. Giddens states that 'these affect all the people in specific occupational categories, as a result of economic circumstances prevailing in the economy as a whole' (2001:283). However, it is important to remember that the class we are born into (class of origin) has a huge influence on how we live our lives and on where we end up (class of destination) (Donohoe and Gaynor 2003:71).

CLASS STRUCTURE IN IRISH SOCIETY

'Irish society is often thought of as a classless society' (Tovey and Share 2003:160). Such a statement may suggest that class boundaries are not as severe or defined in Ireland and as a result may seem less constraining, but 'the reality is that they are more rigid and harder to penetrate than in many other societies' (Ibid.: 161). Social class is the main form of social stratification in Ireland and in western industrialised societies today. Researchers studying the area have focused on how race, gender etc., have influenced socio-economic status, but classification by occupation tends to be most common. 'Officially in Ireland a person's social class is measured according to occupation. The social class of children is derived from the occupation of their parent(s)' (Donohoe and Gaynor 2003:71). According to Donohoe and Gaynor there are huge inequalities between the classes in the distribution of wealth and income. It is estimated that 10 per cent of the population own nearly half the wealth in the country, therefore 90 per cent of the population share the other half, but not equally (Ibid.: 71).

Ireland's late and sudden industrialisation brought with it huge changes to the class structure. The pre-industrial class structure was transformed and new lines of class distinction began to emerge. 'However it was not until the 1960s and 1970s that any major transformation in the economy or in the social structure occurred' (IPA 1992:98). Rottman and Hannan (1982) attempted to trace the implications of changes in employment in class terms during the course of industrialisation in Ireland during that period. They distinguished four main class groupings based on the types and levels of resources which families possess:

1. A 'bourgeoisie' made up of substantial property owners (in both the agricultural and non-agricultural sectors) who employ hired labour.
2. A 'petit bourgeoisie' consisting of four categories of farmers and one of non-farmers who are self-employed and do not employ labour.
3. A middle class comprised of non-manual employees, divided by educational qualifications into higher professionals, lower professionals and intermediate non-manual employees.
4. A working class divided into four different categories: skilled manual, service, semi-skilled and unskilled manual workers (cited in IPA 1992:99).

Their findings related to male employment as up until the 1981 census of population, women had their social class ascribed to them according to the occupation of their father or husband. 'Now a woman's social class is derived from her own occupation but some difficulties remain, for example in relation to the classification of the role of mother/housewife/homemaker' (Donohoe and Gaynor 2003:71). According to findings presented by the IPA the class structure of Irish society was characterised by the following:

1920s/1930s

- More than half of the population was engaged in agriculture. Irish society was predominantly 'petit bourgeoisie'.

1940s/1950s

- Decline in numbers of agricultural labourers.
- Decline in number and proportion of farmers who were employers.
- Increase in numbers employed in non-agricultural sectors.
- High levels of emigration as there were not enough jobs in non-agricultural sectors to absorb those leaving agriculture.

1960s

Industrialisation resulted in:

- Growth in number of higher professionals.
- Increase in number of skilled manual workers.
- Decline in number of small shop-keepers.
- Marginalisation of the unskilled manual worker.

1970s

Shape of class structure became apparent.

* Dominant categories of large employers, higher professionals and skilled manual workers.
* Seventy per cent of those at work were salary and wage earners compared to 48 per cent in 1926.
* In 1979 one-fifth of the workforce were professionals, administrators and senior salaried employees.
* Numbers of unskilled and semi-skilled workers declined by nearly half in the period between 1951 and 1979. (IPA 1992:101)

The current Irish social class classification, as outlined by Hyde *et al.* (2004:65), is based on an individual's occupation. It, like the UK classification system, is derived from the Goldthorpe scheme 'which ranks occupations in terms of levels of responsibility and autonomy as well as type of work' (*Ibid.*: 65).

Social class scale in Ireland

Middle class (higher middle class and lower middle class)

1. Higher professional and higher managerial (e.g. doctor, accountant, company director, senior government officer) and farmers owning 200 or more acres.
2. Lower professional and lower managerial (e.g. school teacher, nurse, sales manager) and farmers owning 100–199 acres.
3. Other non-manual (e.g. clerk, secretary, dental nurse) and farmers owning 50–99 acres.

Working class

1. Skilled manual (e.g. building site foreman, supervisor of cleaning workers) and farmers owning 30–49 acres.
2. Semi-skilled manual (e.g. plumber, electrician, fitter, driver, cook, hairdresser) and farmers owning less than 30 acres.
3. Unskilled manual (e.g. machine operator, assembler, waitress, cleaner, labourer, bar-worker, call-centre worker). (Hyde *et al.* 2004:66)

According to Tovey *et al.* (2007:181) 'Class carries a number of broadly accepted separate meanings.' More than just classifying groups of people according to their economic position, 'it is widely understood as an expression of people's lifestyles . . . and it is seen by many as a matter of social esteem, prestige or status . . . (*Ibid.*: 181).

Class and health

'Research on varying aspects of health internationally indicates the powerful effects of socio-economic differentials and data specific to the Irish situation, although not extensive, is convincing and consistent with international findings' (Collins and Shelley 1997 cited in Quin 1999:40).

Hyde *et al.* (2004:69) refer to O'Shea and Kelleher (2001), who claim that when compared to higher socio-economic groupings, those in the lower socio-economic groups are 'more likely to smoke, drink alcohol heavily and have less healthy diets'. According to Daly and Leonard (2002), 'Irish research highlights some of the negative health outcomes of low income for families . . . Poor health was common and one in three households registered health problems in relation to children' (cited in Coakley 2004:122).

The following list details some of the negative health indicators which are often associated with (but not limited to) poorer and less powerful groups in society:

- 'higher levels of chronic physical illness
- higher levels of perinatal mortality
- more financial problems that directly impact on health
- higher levels of smoking and drinking
- lower levels of breastfeeding
- lower levels of consumption of fruit and vegetables
- lower levels of exercise.' (Burke *et al.* 2004:23–9 cited in Tovey *et al.* 2007:295)

Findings show that poorer people, on average, live shorter lives and are subject to more ill health at an earlier age than their rich counterparts, which leads to what Nolan (1989) describes as 'a double injustice – life is short where quality is poor'! (cited in Quin 1999:41). A person's physical health and wellbeing is not the only aspect of their health determined by their social position in society. Fryers *et al.* (2003, cited in Gould 2005:13) refer to a large study carried out in the west and 'found a consistent relationship between rates of mental illness and indicators of social disadvantage, including low income, education, unemployment and low social status'. Apart from maybe adopting some unhealthy coping behaviours such as expressive drinking, it is argued 'that socio-economic differences can create psychological reactions which change people's vision of self-esteem and forms of social cohesion or trust (social networks/social involvement) in society (Wilkinson 1996, cited in Hyde *et al.* 2004:71). Problem drug use (such as heroin) is generally associated with areas of socio-economic disadvantage and poor facilities (Lalor *et al.* 2007:114). When referring to a study carried out in 2002, Health Behaviours in School-Aged Children Survey, they highlighted that 'the significance of socio-economic status (SES) for adolescent health cannot be over-emphasised' (*Ibid.*: 114). Unemployment also is strongly related to poorer than average health. It is seen to have a detrimental effect on both physical and mental health. According to Blane (2003) this is 'not merely because unemployment leads to poverty, but also because of the way in which unemployment removes the person from a web of social relations' (cited in Hyde *et al.* 2004). Although the following table presents statistics dating from 1997, they provide evidence of strong links between health status and socio-economic differentials.

Table 6:1 Socio-economic group related to standardised mortality rates

Socio-economic group	15–24	25–34	35–44	45–54	55–64
		death rate per 1,000			
Farmers	0.9	0.8	1.4	5.6	14.8
Higher professional	0.2	0.3	0.8	3.5	12.8
Salaried employees	1.0	0.6	1.5	3.6	15.2
Skilled manual	0.9	0.7	1.9	6.2	18.7
Unskilled manual	1.9	1.5	3.4	10.7	31.6

(Source: Cleary and Tracy 1997, cited in Tovey and Share 2003:285)

A recent study by the Irish Medical Organisation (IMO) in 2012 presented the following findings in relation to health inequalities:

1. 'Life expectancy at birth is 6.1 years higher for male professionals and 5 years higher for female professionals than their skilled counterparts.
2. Standardised mortality rates (per 100,000 population) are higher among unskilled workers (790) than professionals (456) and higher among those who lived in the most deprived areas (804) compared to those who lived in the least deprived (608).
3. Statistics from the Office of Tobacco Control show that the highest cigarette smoking prevalence rates were in the poorer income groups, and

4. Higher levels of obesity in adults from poorer social groups compared with other groups'. (IMO 2012:3)

Housing

In Ireland housing type and residential patterns clearly relate to social class differences. According to figures presented by the CSO (2006):

- 'The total stock of permanent housing units in April 2006 was 1.77 million of which 1.46 million contained "usual" residents.
- Six out of every ten occupied permanent housing units were built since 1971.
- Owner-occupied dwellings continue to be the most prevalent occupancy status.
- The number of local authority rented dwellings declined at each census between 1961 and 2002 but increased by 17,500 during the most recent intercensal period' (CSO 2006:33).

Quality of accommodation is a central issue in housing policy and is often measured in terms of household facilities such as running water, flush toilet, age of dwelling and overcrowding. 'There is a serious problem with the shortage of social housing for those who cannot afford to buy their own homes – an increasing number, given the rapidly increasing house prices' (Bacik 2004:225). Despite an increase in the number of dwellings 'during the most recent intercensal period their share [owner occupied] of all housing units actually fell from 77.4 per cent in 2002 to 74.7 per cent in 2006 – continuing the downward trend which commenced between 1991 and 2002' (CSO 2006:33). Links have been made between poor housing and poor health. 'International research shows that there is a strong relationship between the neighbourhood environment, housing quality and health . . . poor people, for example, are more likely to live in poor quality built environments and this contributes to poorer health for a variety of reasons' (Lavin et al. 2006 cited in Farrell et al. 2008:42). A survey of the housing stock was undertaken in 1990 (Finn 1992, cited in Quin 1999:51). 'The national survey which involved a survey of over 20,000 housing units, found 5.5 per cent of housing units were unfit for habitation' (Ibid.: 51). A study of cumulative disadvantage carried out in 1999 by Nolan and Whelan 'shows that urban local authority tenants display relatively high levels of psychological distress and comparatively low levels of life satisfaction' (cited in Coakley 2004:122). On the other hand, Cohen (2003, cited in Hyde et al. 2004:72) points out that 'the more affluent areas tend to be better resourced in terms of quality foodstuffs, recreational facilities and public services'.

According to the Community Foundation for Ireland (2013) there are:

1. '1,654,208 private households in Ireland; the average number of people per household is 2.7. The 2011 census recorded almost 475,000 households renting their property, a jump from the 323,000 households renting in 2006.
2. 12.5 per cent of people in Ireland live in a dwelling with a leaking roof or are living with dampness or rot' (2013:1).

The Royal College of Nursing (2012), highlighted that 'poor quality housing can be the cause of numerous physical and mental health problems which can result in unnecessary hospital admissions, force longer than necessary hospital stays (e.g. if homes are not fit to return to) and ultimately cause death'. International research has also identified a link between lack of space and mental ill-health. Impacts on physical and mental health include:

1. 'Excess winter deaths are almost three times higher in the coldest quarter of housing than in the warmest quarter.
2. Children living in cold homes are more than twice as likely to suffer from a variety of respiratory problems than children living in warm homes.
3. One in four adolescents living in cold homes is at risk of multiple health problems compared to one in twenty living in warm homes'. (RCN 2012:7)

Consumption patterns

'Studying consumption patterns in society then can be one way to examine how significant class differences remain for explaining social behaviour' (Tovey *et al.* 2007:479).

There is a relationship between consumption and social class and 'most sociologists would now argue that differences in consumption may be as important as those in occupation or economic position in shaping the stratification system' (*Ibid.*: 479). Ireland has quickly become a consumer society and the following figures from the *CSO Statistical Yearbook* (2006) reflect this:

• Visits abroad by Irish residents increased by 45 per cent: expenditure by these visitors abroad amounted to €4,773 million.
• Domestic trips by Irish residents also increased by 14 per cent with expenditure increasing by 32 per cent (*Ibid.*: 317).

Lalor *et al.* (2007:339) also looked at consumer patterns and found that 'Between 1991 and 2002 the proportion of households with at least one car increased from 59.5 per cent to 78.3 per cent. Households with two or more cars increased from 87,174 to 478,660'.

Research by the Combat Poverty Agency in 1992 (cited in Tovey and Share 2003:490) compared the weekly spending patterns of two household types, one with an income (described as an average family) and one relying on unemployment payments. The surplus money (that left after paying for food, fuel, housing, transport etc.) showed differences in consumption. 'The family on unemployment payments spent a higher proportion of its income (but a lower absolute amount) on drink and tobacco than the "average" family, but the "average" family spent a much higher proportion on clothing, shoes and services of various kinds (mainly related to leisure and recreation such as going to the cinema, or out for a meal, getting clothes dry-cleaned or hair cut, caring for a family pet).'

The 2013 *Survey on Income and Living Conditions* presented the following information on disposable income and consumption patterns in Ireland:

1. 21,440 euro was the average annual equivalised disposable income in 2011. This represented a decline of just over 3 per cent on the 2010 value of 22,138 euro.
2. The at-risk-of-poverty rate increased from 14.7 per cent in 2010 to 16 per cent in 2011.
   (CSO 2013:1)

The study also went on to state that in 2011, the types of deprivation most commonly experienced were in relation to the inability to do the following:

- 'Replace worn out furniture (21.7 per cent)
- Afford a morning/afternoon/evening out (21.1 per cent)
- Have family/friends over for a meal/drink (14.8 per cent)
- Afford heating at some stage in the last year (12.2 per cent).' (*Ibid.*: 5)

Education

Education is a 'crucial mechanism of social exclusion because of the role it plays in the status attainment process and reward structure of Irish society' (Clancy 2003:15, cited in Fanning 2004:55). The term 'educational disadvantage' is defined as 'the impediments to education arising from social or economic disadvantage which prevents students from deriving appropriate benefit from education in schools' (McKeown 2004:1).

Clancy (1999:91) reported that 'in spite of considerable progress in recent years the best estimates for 1995 suggest that about 5,000 students each year leave school without any qualification and that a further 8,000 leave before taking the Leaving Certificate'. This is a huge increase in educational attainment from the figures presented in 1965 by an OECD analysis of education in Ireland. It found the Irish system 'to be grossly neglecting the children of poorer classes in society. It reported that over half (53 per cent) of children left school at or before the age of 13' (Garvin, cited in McVeigh 2006:67). It is estimated that 'approximately 20 per cent of students leave each year without completing the Leaving Certificate' (Lalor *et al.* 2007:158). Figures provided by the Department of Education and Science (2005:22) showed that 'In 2004, 13 per cent of the population aged 18–24 years had achieved at most a lower secondary education (the Junior Certificate) and were not involved in further education or training' (cited in McVeigh 2006:67).

Educational attainment is strongly linked to social class and what seems apparent from statistics gathered is that children from poorer backgrounds do less well academically; for example:

- 'In 2001, 40 per cent of children did not complete the second-level school cycle in certain parts of Dublin's inner city' (Barry 2001:6, cited in McVeigh 2006:67).
- 'In 2004, 69 per cent of a sample of school leavers from a professional background proceeded to further study, compared with just 26 per cent of those with unemployed fathers' (Gorby *et al.* 2006, cited in Lalor *et al.* 2007:171).
- '91 per cent of males from a higher-level professional background complete the Leaving Certificate, compared to only 60 per cent of those from an unemployed background' (*Ibid.*: 173).
- '9.7 per cent of children from "higher-level professional" backgrounds progress to a PLC course, compared to 16.9 per cent of those from skilled/semi-skilled/manual backgrounds and 19.5 per cent of those whose fathers are unemployed' (Gordy *et al.* 2006, cited in Lalor *et al.* 2007:174).
- 'A student whose father is a professional is about 30 per cent more likely to attend university than one whose father is semi or unskilled' (Kenny 2010:10).
- 'While over 90 per cent of young people with parent(s) in professional occupations complete the Leaving Certificate, just two-thirds of their counterparts from unskilled backgrounds do so' (Smith 2009:8).

- '58 per cent of students from higher professional backgrounds achieve 4 or more 'honours' grades in the Leaving Certificate; this is the case for just 16 per cent of those from semi-skilled and unskilled manual backgrounds' (*Ibid.*: 8).

A report by the OECD in 2012 entitled *Equity and Quality in Education* found that in Ireland:

1. 'students from low socio-economic backgrounds are 2.4 times more likely to be low performers than their peers with high socio-economic status, which is slightly above the OECD average of 2.37 times.
2. Students whose parents have low educational attainment have twice the risk of low performance (2.05 times) and, as in most other OECD countries, students with an immigrant background are also at higher risk of low performance by 1.87 times.
3. However, Ireland has a lower than average dropout rate, with only 14 per cent of 25 to 34 year olds not having completed upper secondary education, compared to 19 per cent across OECD countries' (2012:6).

According to Denny (2010:3) 'In Ireland there has been a long standing concern that people from a low socio-economic status (SES) background are heavily under-represented in higher education in general and universities in particular'. It has been estimated that 'persons with a Leaving Certificate tend to earn about 40% more than those without it, while those with a degree tend to earn over 80% more than those without one' (cited in McKeown 2004:4). Clancy argues that 'stratifications in third level reflect those in second level attainment on the basis of parental socio-economic status' (cited in Fanning 2004:67). Among the explanations for levels of educational attainment and social/economic background are those summarised by Drudy and Lynch (1993) and include:

(i)   Attitudes and culture in poorer and working class areas and families, and

(ii)   A lack of interest on behalf of the parents of working class children in their 'child's teachers, school and schooling than their middle-class counterparts' (cited in Lalor *et al.* 2007:160).

There is a strong link between lack of qualifications and unemployment. Educational qualifications are important in securing entry into the labour market. The following statistics provided by Tovey and Share (2003) provide evidence of this.

- 'In 1993 seventy-eight per cent of those without a formal qualification remained unemployed after leaving school.

- In 1997 sixty-three per cent of those unemployed had not finished secondary education.
- A person's earning power and employment opportunities are generally linked to level of education attained. 'The unemployment rate for persons in Ireland aged 18–24 was 25.2 per cent in 2009 while the rate for early school leavers was twice that'. (www.socialjustice.ie 2011:182)

'The class into which we are born influences where we live, how we spend our leisure time, the papers we read, our educational prospects and our earning potential' (Donohoe and Gaynor 2003:71).

SOCIAL MOBILITY IN IRELAND

'Social mobility refers to the movement of people between different levels of the class structure from one occupational group to another' (IPA 1992:107).

Sociologists are interested in social mobility for the following reasons:

1. It can give an indication of the life chances of members of society. It can give an indication of how open a society actually is, for example to what degree a person's background influences their opportunities in later life.
2. The rate of mobility can have important effects on class formation. Giddens (cited in IPA 1992:107) suggests 'that if the rate of social mobility is low, class solidarity and class cohesion will be high'.
3. People's attitudes and aspirations can be affected by social mobility (Ibid.).

Mobility within the class structure is usually considered to be upwards or downwards, but it is also:

Inter-generational: Referring to a person's position in the class system in relation to their parents.

Intra-generational: Referring to a person's position in the structure in relation to other positions they have had at different stages in their life.

Changes in the occupational structure in Ireland brought changes in mobility patterns. 'In the first half of the twentieth century opportunities open to Irish people depended heavily on whether their family owned property such as a farm or small business. Those set to inherit a position in a family enterprise could stay in Ireland. The rest generally had to emigrate or enter the religious life' (Tovey and Share 2003:163).

Movement from an economy based mainly on agriculture meant that many left farming. Industrialisation was not happening at a pace quick enough to absorb those leaving and as a result many were forced to emigrate. 'In 1961 half the gainfully employed men in Ireland worked in farming.

This had decreased to a fifth by 1981 (Whelan 1995:332, cited in Tovey and Share 2003). Research carried out by Breen *et al.* (1990), Whelan (1995), Allen (1998) (all cited in Tovey and Share 2003:163), provides findings that reflect changes in the class structure and mobility patterns in Irish society. The movement from a society dominated by small family business and self-employment to one where individuals are employees in large businesses has resulted in the following:

- By the mid-1980s nearly three-quarters of males were employed in businesses not owned by their family.
- There was an increase in the number of men in the managerial, skilled manual and white-collar occupations.
- There was a decline in unskilled and semi-skilled occupations.
- A study conducted in the late 1980s showed that two-fifths of men aged between 20 and 64 moved into a class position different to that of their parents.
- Ireland had low levels of upward mobility from the working class to the professional and managerial class.
- Women working outside the home still tended to be found in a restricted range of occupations, primarily professional and managerial.
- Women remained largely excluded from the inheritance of productive property such as agricultural land.
- Women changed class through marriage.
- Women were more likely to experience downward mobility. (Tovey and Share 2003:164–5)

Table 6:2 Working males: Changes in class categories 1951–90

	1951	1961	1971	1981	1990
		percentages rounded up			
Employers and self-employed	38	36	28	19	18
Employees					
• Upper middle class	5	8	11	16	18
• Lower middle class	14	16	18	20	20
• Skilled manual	10	12	17	20	18
• Semi/unskilled					
– agricultural	11	8	5	3	3
– non-agricultural	14	13	14	11	9
Total at work	100	100	100	100	100
Total unemployed	4	6	7	10	16

(Source: Breen and Whelan, cited in Tovey and Share 2003:163)

Occupational structure influences and affects mobility patterns but what about those who do not have occupations, who are not in the paid labour force? According to Drudy (1995:306), 'In Ireland this is the condition of a very large proportion of the adult population'. According to the CSO (2012:23), there was significant variation in unemployment rates across social classes in April 2011. Key statistics highlight that:

1. 'Among professionals, only 6 per cent of those in the labour force were out of work.
2. The unemployment rate among managerial and technical workers was also below average at 8 per cent.
3. Almost one third of unskilled workers were unemployed.
4. Over one quarter of skilled manual workers were jobless, this represented 103,277 people or almost one in four of the total number out of work.
5. Farmers and professionals had the lowest unemployment rates among census socio-economic groups in 2011.
6. The largest socio-economic group, with an unemployment rate of 13 per cent was non-manual. This group includes occupations such as clerical workers in financial institutions and government, sales assistants and secretaries'. (CSO 2012:23)

Drudy refers to the 'underclass' and differentiates if from the working class. The underclass is made of 'the poor, the long-term unemployed, substance abusers and marginalised groups such as Travellers' (Tovey and Share 2003:161). A definition of the underclass given by Whelan (cited in Drudy 1995:311) sees it as a social grouping with three features:

(i)   prolonged labour market marginality
(ii)   greater deprivation than is general for the manual working class
(iii) the possession of its own sub-culture.

While opportunities have increased to enable people to move into a better position in society, inequalities do exist. While people are stratified according to attributes such as race, ethnicity, gender etc., Breen and Whelan (cited in Tovey and Share 2003:165) conclude with the statement that 'what most determines one's life chances or eventual position in society is not one's gender but the class or occupational position of the family into which one is born'.

7

Gender Socialisation

CHAPTER OBJECTIVES

After reading this chapter you should be able to:

- define gender
- explain what is meant by gender socialisation
- describe the sexual division of labour – women and the Irish labour market
- describe the relationship between gender and education
- discuss changing gender roles.

GENDER DEFINED

'Gender is the word used to describe social and personality differences between women and men. It refers to that which society defines as masculine and feminine' (Webb and Tossell 1999:47).

Sex refers to the biological differences between male and female; gender, on the other hand, refers to the socially constructed and variable categories of masculine and feminine. Bilton *et al.* describe 'gender as the cultural gloss put on a natural foundation of sex' (2002:131). When we meet someone for the first time we notice whether they are male or female. Such information enables us to interact with them in a socially acceptable manner. Clarke *et al.* (2000:154) argue that children pick up the appropriate sex role by imitating the same-sex parent and being reinforced for behaving in a manner that the particular culture expects of a boy or a girl. 'By reinforcing masculine behaviour in a boy, either parent could ensure that he showed masculine behaviour, similarly for feminine behaviour in a girl' (*Ibid.*: 154). Children learn to behave as 'boy' or 'girl' and also learn that they should not cross the gender roles if possible.

The concept of gender changes over time, and is defined differently between societies and within the same society. We all 'do gender' in our daily social interactions with other people. According to Giddens, 'from tone of voice to gestures and movements to norms of behaviour, all aspects of our existence are gendered. We socially reproduce – make and remake – gender in a thousand minor actions in the course of the day' (2001:106). 'Gender is a social role and like other social roles it is learned through the process of socialisation' (Curry *et al.* 2005:230).

GENDER SOCIALISATION

'As a consequence of early experiences, by the tenth month of life children are already identifying themselves as boys or girls and not long after that their gender identity will be firmly fixed' (Richardson 1981, cited in Curry *et al.* 2005:230).

From the day we are born the process of gender socialisation begins and infants learn what sex they are and what is expected of them as little boys and girls in their society. According to Lieberson *et al.* (2000), 'Naming infants is another way parents gender-mark their child. Most parents use gender-distinct names for their infants' (cited in Curry *et al.* 2005:230). Agents of socialisation such as the family, media, education etc., contribute to the child's understanding of his or her social role. As children grow older they learn the signs and symbols that identify a person's gender. Through constant interactions with people close to them and exposure to the values of their society, 'children gradually internalise the social norms and expectations which are seen to correspond with their sex' (Giddens 2001:108). As we get older gender markers become more prominent and much of our gender socialisation involves learning which markers are appropriate for men and which are appropriate for women. According to Curry *et al.* (2005:230), 'Girls are taught to wear dresses and to behave "properly". When girls grow older they learn to put on make-up and wear high-heeled shoes. Boys are taught to wear pants and to behave "roughly".'

'Socialisation theory offers a straightforward account of the acquisition of gendered identities. Infants are seen as blank slates waiting to be written on by their environment' (Bilton *et al.* 2002:136).

There is a lot of research and theorising on gender development, but three broad traditions can be distinguished. These are as follows:

1. Social learning theories: These theories suggest that differences in gender behaviour are learned in the same way as all behaviours, through a mixture of rewards, reinforcements and punishments (Macionis and Plummer 2002:298). 'Gender processing begins from the moment of birth when baby girls are traditionally covered in pink blankets and boys in pale blue ones' (Webb and Tossell 1999:48). Boys and girls learn 'sex-roles' and 'masculinity or femininity' and are guided to do so by the use of positive and negative sanctions, which reward or restrain behaviour. Boys who receive praise such as 'What a brave boy you are!' or a negative sanction such as 'Boys don't play with dolls' begin to learn and conform to their expected sex role. Children also model or imitate the behaviour of parents and teachers of the same sex and this process also helps children internalise the gender prescriptions of their society. 'If an individual develops gender practices which do not correspond with his or her biological sex – that is, they are deviant – the explanation is seen to reside in inadequate or irregular socialisation' (Giddens 2001:108).

Parents (consciously or unconsciously) tend to treat girls and boys differently in ways that influence their development. For example:

(i)   According to McDonald and Parke (1986, cited in Bilton 2002:136) 'parents are far more likely to engage their infant sons in rough physical play – tossing them up in the air or wrestling with them – than they are their daughters'. They argue that the long-term results of that may be the development of physical confidence or aggressiveness in boys.

(ii)   Webb and Tossell refer to studies that mothers have a tendency to breastfeed boys for longer periods than girls. 'This action, whether it is done unconsciously or not, tends to reflect an inclination to foster independence and responsibility in girls (who are later to be the principal care-givers) whilst tolerating dependency in boys' (1999:48).

2. Cognitive theory: This theory suggests that differences in gender emerge through a categorisation process, for example boys place themselves in a 'masculine' category and then organise their experiences around it (Macionis and Plummer 2002:299).

3. Psychodynamic theories: These are derived from Freud and suggest that 'differences in gender emerge out of emotional struggles between the infant and its caretakers in the earliest years of life' (Macionis and Plummer 2002:299). One of the most influential theories of gender identity is the perspective developed by Nancy Chodorow in her 1978 book The *Reproduction of Mothering*. This theory takes account of the unconscious processes that contribute to a child's learning to feel male or female. For

Chodorow this derives from the infant's attachment to its parents from an early age. Her theory places much importance on the mother rather than the father. For her, 'masculinity and femininity are rooted in strong emotional structures established very early in life and are very hard to transform' (Macionis and Plummer 2002:299). To understand these emotional structures we have to look at the strong attachments between a child and its mother, on whom both the baby boy and baby girl are hugely dependent. In the early years mothers generally care for infants, while fathers tend to remain more emotionally distant. At some point in this time attachment has to be broken in order to achieve a separate sense of self. The child is required to become less dependent on the carer, to test its competence against the outside world. This process of breaking away operates differently for girls and boys. The little girl remains attached while the little boy breaks away. Chodorow believes that as a result:

- Girls remain closer to the mother; the little girl does not outgrow her dependency, she maintains a continuous sense of relationship with the mother.
- Boys' experience is different. Their separation is sharper and involves 'repressing the feminine aspects of themselves and rejecting much of the tenderness that was central to that early relationship' (Bilton *et al.* 2002:137).

As a result of these processes, men are likely to:

(i)   be more dependent and more competitive when dealing with others
(ii)   have difficulty in expressing emotions
(iii)   have a more autonomous sense of self. (Macionis and Plummer 2002:299)

According to Giddens, boys 'learn not to be "sissies" or "mummy's boys". As a result boys are relatively unskilled in relating closely to others, they develop more analytical ways of looking at the world. They take a more active view of their lives, emphasising achievement, but they have repressed their ability to understand their own feelings and those of others' (2001:111).

Girls are more likely to:

(i)   identify with the needs of others more than boys; this asserts itself as a need for mothering in later life
(ii)   have more need and greater ability to sustain relationships with others
(iii)   have greater empathy with others.

'Chodorow's ideas teach us a good deal about the nature of femininity, and they help us to understand the origins of what has been called male inexpressiveness – the difficulty men have in revealing their feelings to others' (Giddens 2001:111). This theory has often been criticised by feminists 'who accuse the theory of blaming mothers for reproduction of male power in their sons' (Macionis and Plummer 2002:299).

There is much in the socialisation of men that discourages them from expressing their feelings. From an early age men are pressurised to hide their true feelings, to always appear strong and in control. 'Big boys don't cry' is a clear message throughout childhood which is reinforced in books and other forms of popular culture' (Webb and Tossell 1999:50).

THE SEXUAL DIVISION OF LABOUR – WOMEN AND THE IRISH LABOUR MARKET

According to the CSO (2006), 'while women are entering the workplace, for instance, there are still significant discrepancies in wages and in the proportions of men and women at senior levels, even in occupations dominated by women' (cited in Lalor *et al.* 2007:337). The following findings from a report entitled *Sexual division of labour –women and the Irish labour market* highlight some of these discrepancies, for example:

• There was a 12.6 per cent pay gap between women and men in Ireland in 2010.
• Women earn on average 17.4 per cent less than men for every hour worked.
• By 2006, women in Ireland were earning 86 per cent of male earnings, although they did work slightly fewer hours than their male counterparts. (www.ec.europa 2013)

'The world of work remains a key site for the expression of gender difference and the positions that men and women hold in the labour market and are a major determinant of wealth, income, power and status' (Tovey and Share 2003:247). Changes in the last decades of the twentieth century had a significant impact on the relationships of Irish women towards the labour market. The following statistics and findings reflect the position of Irish women in the labour market before the economic change occurred in Ireland:

1. Far more women than men spend time on housework and caring.
2. More men than women are employed full-time.

3. Men and women who are employed are segregated into very different kinds of occupations.
4. Employed men earn much more than employed women. (Lynch and Morgan 1995:266)

According to Bacik (2004:92), 'In 1974, the difference between the average hourly earnings of women and men was as high as 40 per cent'. From the 1970s changes in women's position in the labour force began to occur. Expansion in the service industries, from financial to tourism, and investment in Ireland by transnational companies, no doubt influenced these changes. In this period:

• There was a growth of 9 per cent in the number of women employed in the manufacturing industry
• Women's participation rate in the workforce increased from 28 per cent in 1971 to 39 per cent in 1994.
• By 1994 married women made up half the labour force (Smyth 1997, cited in Tovey and Share 2003:250).
• In 1996 married women in the workforce outnumbered single women (Galligan 1998, cited in Tovey and Share 2003:50).

According to the CSO (2011), 'there were 851,300 women and 970,000 men employed in Ireland in 2011'. Although long-term unemployment is now more common among men than women, women are still concentrated in less valued jobs and positions than men. In 2011:

1. '23.7 per cent of women in employment were in professional occupations and 20.9 per cent were in administrative and secretarial occupations.
2. The least gender-balanced occupations were skilled trades, where less than one in ten employees is female, and caring, leisure and other services, where just under one in 6 employees is male.
3. In 2010, the education and health sectors employed the highest proportion of women, accounting for more than 4 out of 5 people at work in the health sector and nearly three quarters of those in education' (CSO 2011:11).

The following table, provided by the Central Statistics Office, shows the employment rate for men and women in Ireland from the period 2001 to 2011.

Table 7:1 Ireland: Employment rate for men and women

Year	Percentage of population aged 15–64	
	Men	*Women*
1994	65.9	40.1
1995	67.1	41.6
1996	67.5	43.2
1997	69.1	45.9
1998	71.1	48.1
1999	73.6	51.2
2000	75.7	53.2
2001	76.2	54.0
2002	75.0	55.2
2003	74.7	55.3
2004	75.2	55.8
2005	76.2	58.0
2006	77.3	58.8

(Source: adapted from CSO Statistical Yearbook 2011)

According to Donohoe and Gaynor, the majority of women employed in Ireland are concentrated into three job types: clerical, service and technical and professional. 'Where women are well represented in a workforce they are not proportionately represented in top positions' (1999:121). 'Women are not well represented at senior level positions: only 36 per cent of medical and dental consultants are women, 53 per cent of primary school managers and 41 per cent of second-level school managers' (CSO 2011:11).

Table 7:2 Ireland: Persons aged fifteen years and over in employment by occupation

Broad occupational group	2000		2005	
	Men	Women	Men	Women
		thousands		
Craft and related	213.0	14.5	260.1	11.7
Plant and machine operatives	134.5	45.8	138.0	29.7
Managers and administrators	222.3	81.3	218.6	98.1
Sales	54.2	81.7	63.0	101.4
Associate professional and technical	62.2	76.4	70.9	100.5
Professional	90.8	75.6	112.5	106.1
Personal and protective service	69.5	96.0	73.4	125.0
Clerical and secretarial	50.0	154.2	58.7	177.7
Other	96.1	53.2	114.9	68.9
Total	992.6	678.8	1,110.1	819.1

(Source: adapted from CSO Statistical Yearbook 2006)

Table 7:3 Persons in employment by occupation 2011

Broad occupational group	Men	Women
Managers, directors and senior officials	93.1	44.9
Professional	145.1	201.6
Associate professional and technical	131.0	77.9
Administrative and secretarial	44.0	178.0
Skilled trades	239.2	23.6
Caring, leisure and other service	22.6	117.0
Sales and customer service	52.9	98.4
Process, plant and machine operatives	127.7	23.2
Elementary	112.5	85.4
Other	2.1	1.0

(Source: CSO 2011:19)

In 2004 men accounted for 58 per cent of persons in employment. The clerical and secretarial group had the highest proportion of women at 75.9 per cent (CSO 2004). 'Almost 50 per cent of women living with a husband/partner in a family unit with children were in employment in June–August 2001 compared with 43.6 per cent three years earlier' (Kennedy 2004:81). There are a number of factors that may have contributed to more mothers entering the workplace in that period, among them smaller families, the economic boom of the nineties and increasing house prices.

'While many women in Ireland have gained greater access to the labour market and by extension to welfare, new inequalities have arisen between groups of women' (Kennedy 2004:78). According to the OECD, in Ireland 'women's labour market participation rates are well below those of the best performing OECD economies, especially for mothers, and high childcare costs and limited supply are major obstacles to participation' (www.nwci.ie 2013:7).

Despite the fact that we now have employment equality legislation, Kennedy states that 'there still remains a gender pay gap with women earning 15 per cent less than men' (2004:81). Bacik (2004:92) points out that this current pay gap is 'a wider gap than exists in most EU states'. Bacik refers to research published by the ERSI in 2002 which shows that other disparities in relation to pay exist, based on marital status. 'While single women tend to earn the least (5 per cent less, on average, than single men), married men tend to be the highest earners, earning 25 per cent more, on average, than single women' (2004:93).

According to the National Women's Council of Ireland (NWCI),

1. 'In 2010, households headed by a male had over 10,000 euro more in disposable income than households headed by a female.
2. In 2011, almost 60 per cent of claimants of the Family Income Supplement (FIS) were women.
3. Poverty rates are highest for households headed by a female, households headed by a lone parent (86.5 per cent of whom are women) and children' (www.nwci.ie 2013:7).

'The *Human Development Report* (1998) states that Irish women are worse off in relation to men and are less likely to be in positions of power than in any other western country' (Donohoe and Gaynor 1999:122). According to Bacik (2004:92), 'The majority of low-paid workers are women, and there are ongoing problems with occupational segregation, often caused by a lack of access to education and training. Three times as many women as men work in "education and health", one-and-a-half times as many in "hotels and restaurants"'. She goes on to provide the following statistics:

* Women still only account for 5 per cent of senior management positions in private and public sectors, and 28 per cent of members on state boards.
* 'Only 21 per cent of judges and 9 per cent of senior counsel among barristers are women – despite the fact that women have been studying law in larger numbers than men for some years, two-thirds of law students nationally are now women' (Bacik 2004:93).
* According to Lalor *et al.* (2007:337), 'Women account for only 14 per cent of TDs in the Dáil and for less than 20 per cent of local authority members.
* Women account for half the Irish population, yet the percentage of women TDs had never exceeded 14 per cent, until the 2011 general election'. (Bacik 2013)

Apart from the obvious benefits of work, that is, to earn money to provide for themselves and their families, work outside the home offers women a source of independence. It also offers them a 'sense of satisfaction, intellectual fulfilment, career progression or a chance to develop personal and social skills' (Webb and Tossell 1999:59). Despite this, the rate of Irish women's participation in the workforce remains low by EU standards. According to Galligan, the main barriers to women's equal participation in the labour force include:

* 'the absence of flexible working hours
* the virtual non-existence of childcare facilities
* lack of appropriate training due largely to the negative attitudes of employers'. (cited in Tovey and Share 2003:251)

Childcare has been identified as a major issue for women in the workplace. According to NWCI (2013) 'Ireland also has one of the lowest levels of investment in childcare and as a result, childcare costs in Ireland are amongst the most expensive anywhere'. Rush *et al.* (2006:157) refer to figures from the *Quarterly National Household Survey* (2004) 'which shows 557,800 people with a principal economic status of home duties, of which 553,400 or 99.21 per cent were women'. Women still have primary responsibility for the care of children even when they are in full-time employment. The work a women does when she arrives home from the office/factory has been referred to as a 'second shift' which involves domestic work, cooking, raising children etc. (Macionis and Plummer 2002:362). According to Richardson (2003), 'Women in the home constitute a sizeable number of Irish parents with little attention paid to them by researchers or policy makers and they receive minimal reward and status for their work' (cited in Rush *et al.* 2006:157).

Although the number of women in the workforce is increasing and the range of jobs they do is broadening, 'the demands inherent in the domestic division of labour are continuing to prevent any fundamental change for most women in respect of work. The gendered division of labour still firmly benefits men to the detriment of women' (Bilton *et al.* 2002:313). For Bacik, 'perhaps most importantly, focused education and training are needed to break down gender stereotypes and to help build a society where all are judged on equal terms, according to merit and regardless of gender' (2004:97). Research carried out by Microsoft to mark International Women's Day found that:

- '28 per cent of women said that prioritising of home life was the most significant obstacle to promotion at work,
- while 27 per cent, most of whom were under 35, said it was lack of support for working mothers' (www.thejournal.ie 2013).

GENDER AND EDUCATION

'Gender is central to the experience of education. People's experiences of "being a boy" or "being a girl" are shaped in many ways by the experience of schooling' (Ryan 1997, cited in Tovey and Share 2003:210). Sociologists are interested in examining how the education process is crucial to the social construction of gender. The educational choices girls make at second level and third level have a huge impact on their educational opportunities. 'At second and third level what is referred to as the "hidden curriculum" is operating, reinforcing traditional male and female roles' (IPA 1992:77).

Dr Damien Hannan carried out a survey in 1979 in subject choice in second level schools in Ireland. His results found differences between boys-only and girls-only schools in the framing of subjects. The following list presents some of his main findings:

- 'In girls schools, science subjects and mathematical subjects were less likely to form part of the core curriculum.
- At Inter Cert level, 88 per cent of boys' schools require that everyone does science while only 9 per cent of girls' schools do.
- In girls' schools science was most often offered as a choice against home economics, commerce, art or music.
- Boys' schools tended to "stream" more than girls' schools'. (IPA 1992:81)

Hannan found differences in the 'school ethos of boys' and girls' schools. Boys' schools had in general a stronger ethos with a clearer career orientation and they offered pupils less choice of subjects' (*Ibid.*: 81). Girls schools had a more modest achievement ethos, a liberal curriculum and wider choice of subjects.

More recent research by Lynch (1999) suggests that males and females are now equally represented in many aspects of education 'with females now making up a slight majority (in the range 51–55 per cent) at post-primary level' (cited in Tovey and Share 2003:210). He also presented the following findings:

- There is an increased number of women in third-level study. According to the CSO (2006), 'In 2006, almost 82 per cent of 18-year-old females were students compared to 62 per cent of males'. Corresponding figures provided by the National Youth Policy Committee 1984 were 35 per cent and 27 per cent (cited in Lalor *et al.* 2007:337).
- Girls out-perform boys in the majority of subjects in the Junior and Leaving Certificates.
- Girls suffer from coeducational schooling, as research has shown that girls receive less attention and encouragement from teachers than do boys' (Lynch, cited in Tovey and Share 2003:213).

According to Lynch and Morgan, 'The experiences of women in education in both the Republic and Northern Ireland are fraught with contradictions' (1995:529). They refer to research by Gallagher (1989) and Clancy (1988) which found that in both systems girls:

- get higher aggregate grades than boys in major public examinations
- are more likely to stay in school after the age of sixteen.

'Boys are considered more likely to leave school early than girls. For example, while 2.6 per cent of girls left school with no qualifications in 1998, 4.4 per cent of boys did so. Similarly, while 11.2 per cent of girls in 1998 left after the Junior Certificate, 19.3 per cent of boys did so' (Lalor *et al.* 2007:166).

However,

- boys outnumber girls in most physical science and technology courses (Lynch and Morgan 1995:529).
- According to O'Connell *et al.* (2006) 'Women now make up the majority of entrants in all fields of study except for "engineering, manufacturing and construction studies"' (cited in Tovey *et al.* 2007:199).

- More girls than boys enrolled in a PLC course (21 per cent of female and 10 per cent of male school leavers). 'This gender disequilibrium may be partly a product of the programmes on offer, many of which are in areas that traditionally provide employment overwhelmingly to women, such as hairdressing, childcare, interior design, secretarial studies and beauty therapy' (Lalor *et al.* 2007:173).

Table 7:4 Persons aged 15–64 classified by highest level of education attained

Highest educational level attained	1999	2001	2003	2005
Males	thousands			
Primary or below	280.8	282.7	253.3	242.4
Lower secondary	311.9	286.7	307.0	310.3
Higher secondary	310.4	315.5	335.2	371.6
Post Leaving Cert	109.7	141.7	133.4	132.0
Third level non-degree	73.4	91.8	104.9	111.0
Third level degree or above	140.3	155.1	195.8	214.7
Other	23.8	28.5	27.3	36.5
Total	**1,250.3**	**1302,1**	**1,357.0**	**1,418.5**
Females	thousands			
Primary or below	250.8	250.8	218.3	203.4
Lower secondary	277.8	252.7	267.6	263.4
Higher secondary	346.1	348.9	375.3	394.9
Post Leaving Cert	123.6	142.6	140.5	134.3
Third level non-degree	89.8	119.5	132.8	150.6
Third level degree or above	126.8	148.7	187.3	222.6
Other	24.0	24.5	23.5	29.2
Total	**1,238.9**	**1,287.7**	**1,345.3**	**1,398.3**

(Source: adapted from CSO Statistical Yearbook 2006:109)

Table 7:5 Persons receiving full-time education and estimated participation rates for ages 15–24, 2010/11

Age	Male	Female	Total
15	29,085	28,005	57,090
16	27,778	27,170	54,948
17	26,203	26,075	52,278
18	21,183	22,771	43,954
19	16,978	19,521	36,499
20	15,109	18,059	33,168
21	13,081	15,503	28,584
22	9,003	10,163	19,166
23	5,807	6,003	11,810
24	4,401	4,325	8,726

(Source: Dept. of Education and Science, cited in CSO Statistical Yearbook 2012:101)

A study entitled *Women and men in Ireland* presented the following recent statistics:

- Women are more likely to have a third-level qualification over men.
- Boys are more likely to leave school early, and girls do better than boys at school.
- 'over half of women aged between 25 and 35 have a third level qualification compared to less than 4 out of 10 men and,
- Men accounted for nearly five-sixths of third-level graduates in engineering, manufacturing and construction and 57 per cent of graduates in science, while women accounted for 82 per cent of graduates in health and welfare, 74 per cent in education and 63 per cent in arts and humanities'. (CSO 2011)

CHANGING GENDER ROLES

'Gender role is a set of socially generated expectations about how men and women should behave' (Clarke *et al.* 2000:127).

Traditionally the mother stayed at home cooking and looking after the children, while the father went to work. The man would not expect to do domestic tasks such as cleaning, shopping and childcare. His role was an instrumental one, that of economic provider or breadwinner, whilst the woman's role was an expressive one, as nurturer and emotional provider. The Eurobarometer study (1993) 'showed that in Ireland as many as 84 per cent of men said they did not have the primary responsibility for even one of a selection of household tasks' (cited in Rush *et al.* 2006:158).

A European Values study (1990 and 1999/2000) provides findings that reflect attitudes towards women's and men's roles in the workplace. What appears obvious is that traditional gender role attributes are 'a continuing source of fundamental cultural division' (O'Connor 1998, cited in Fahey *et al.* 2005:152). See tables below:

Table 7:6 Support for traditional gender role attributes (Republic of Ireland) 1990–99

	1990	1999
	per cent	
A working mother has as secure a relationship with her children as one who does not work outside the home (% disagree)	37	22
A pre-school child suffers if mother works outside the home (% agree)	53	35
A job is all right, but what women really want is a home and children (% agree)	59	37
Being a housewife is just as fulfilling as working for pay (% agree)	72	60
A job is the best way for a woman to be an independent person (% agree)	39	28
Husband and wife should contribute to household income (% disagree)	30	19

(Source: European Values Study 1990 and 1999–2000, cited in Fahey *et al.* 2005:153)

Fahey *et al.* (2005:152) highlight that the 'differences in the attitudes of women and men are of particular interest in this area'.

Table 7:7 Support for traditional gender role attitudes by gender (Republic of Ireland)

	Women	Men
	per cent	
A working mother has as secure a relationship with her children as one who does not work outside the home (% disagree)	19	24
A pre-school child suffers if mother works outside the home (% agree)	32	39
A job is all right, but what women really want is a home and children (% agree)	35	39
Being a housewife is just as fulfilling as working for pay (% agree)	62	57
A job is the best way for a woman to be an independent person (% disagree)	28	25
Husband and wife should contribute to household income (% disagree)	17	21
Fathers are as well suited to look after their children as mothers (% disagree)	18	27
Men are less able to handle emotions in relationships than women (% disagree)	57	47

(Source: European Values Study 1999–2000, cited in Fahey *et al.* 2005:154)

According to Macionis and Plummer, 'the traditional view that working for an income is a man's role no longer holds true' (2002:293). Fathers are generally taking a much more active role in homemaking and family care than before. Families are spending more time together, more mothers are working (part-time or full-time) to contribute to the household budget. 'Maternal and paternal roles are starting to "converge"' (O'Donnell 2002:201). Despite this 'converging', Rush *et al.* state that:

- 'Apart from household repairs, mothers carried out most responsibility for household tasks and childcare duties.
- Mothers emerged as the managers of the internal affairs of the family and this was in spite of over 80 per cent of the mothers expressing the view that husbands should share housework equally.

- The percentage of respondents who agreed that men and women shared the care of sick family members equally declined between 1994 and 2002' (2006:159).

Tovey and Share (2003:228) examine three viewpoints about how relationships between men and women have changed in Ireland over the last three decades.

1. The first view is that 'there has been a huge amount of positive change and progress'. This view pays attention to factors that are indicators that Ireland is becoming a 'modern European state'. These factors include:

   - the appointment and prominence of women in politics and high-profile occupations, for example President Mary McAleese
   - the exposure of abuse against women and children
   - the increasing involvement of men in housework and childcare
   - the increase in numbers of women in the paid labour force.

2. The second view stresses how little has changed in Ireland. This view refers to the extent of gender inequality that still exists in our society. It refers to discrimination against women in the workplace and to their inferior position in relation to wealth and income. In 1992, 'unpaid work in the household sector was still the principal occupation for over 60 per cent of women' (Fahey 1995:222). According to statistics provided by the CSO (2004), 'There was an increasing relative proportion of men in the higher income bands with 10 per cent of men earning €50,000 and over compared to only 2.6 per cent of women.' Failure to address key issues such as childcare, abortion, care of the elderly and other social issues also highlights the widespread inequality that exists between men and women. 'Women's concentration in the so called 5 C's: caring, cashiering, catering, cleaning and clerical has lead to women dominating in the lower paid occupations and contributes in a major way to the gender pay gap' (Barry and Potter 2013:5).

3. The last view sees the nature of gender inequality changing. This developing view sees men as increasingly disadvantaged within Irish society. 'There are concerns over the inability of men to adjust to changes in society, education and the workplace and to develop new models of masculinity . . . "boys are the new girls"' (Tovey and Share 2003:229). This viewpoint expresses concern for:

   - men's poorer health status and shorter life expectancy
   - the academic weakness of boys

- high exposure to violence/higher tendency to suicide
- legal decisions in relation to custody of and access to children.

The essential biological differences between women and men have tended to divide society unequally in terms of women's and men's labour power roles and expectations. In the past, husband and wife had established roles to play. With the converging of maternal and paternal roles, a new problem may emerge – that of role conflict. For example, both members of a partnership are less certain of what is expected of them; a woman may want a man who is strong and authoritarian to associate with masculinity but at the same time want someone to make the dinner or change the baby. A man may want a feminine woman who nurtures and cares for the family while at the same time expecting her to work to supplement the family income. Both partners may have conflicting wishes. 'Working mothers often experience role-conflict and feel guilty that they are neglecting their children . . . Role conflict may be a major source of family conflict' (O'Donnell 2002:52).

Table 7:8 Summary: agree and disagree responses on male role ambiguity

Male role ambiguity	Agree	Disagree
	per cent	
1. With all the changes in gender roles, it's hard to know who's to do what	42	47
2. It's more difficult for a man to find a partner now because women are putting careers ahead of relationships	48	43
3. Women's gains in the workplace have sometimes been at the expense of men	44	44
4. Women can be so independent sometimes that it makes men feel like they are not needed any more	52	42
5. A lot of men are confused about their roles because they are less defined than they used to be	44	47

(Source: Fine-Davis 2011:45)

Gender roles in Ireland in the first half of the twentieth century were much more distinct than they are today. The existence of different views on the relationships between men and women in Ireland, the new focus on masculinity and the experiences of men, the changing structure of the family and occupational structure in Irish society all show to some extent the complexities of the gender issue.

'It seems we have moved on from a time when women were seen to be naturally weak, emotionally unstable and believed to have smaller brains than men, but belief in a direct biological basis for gender difference and inequality persists' (Tovey and Share 2003:233).

8

Deviance and Social Control

CHAPTER OBJECTIVES

After reading this chapter you should be able to:

- define deviance and social control
- outline the social foundations of deviance
- explain the theories of crime and deviance
  - positivist theories of individual crime
  - labelling theory (Lemert)
  - theory of differential association (Sutherland)
  - Merton's strain theory
- discuss crime rates in Ireland.

DEVIANCE AND SOCIAL CONTROL DEFINED

'Deviance may be defined as non-conformity to a given set of norms that are accepted by a significant number of people in a community or society' (Giddens 2001:203).

Deviance means any behaviour that differs from the normal. Most simply put, deviance is the breaking of rules – any rules. For Babbie (1988:131), 'it is the violation of established norms' in a society. Deviance is not a simple concept to define and is a much broader concept than crime; 'virtually any act can be defined as deviant'. According to Curry *et al.* (2005:94), all people are deviant 'because people are not machines'. Terry Simmons argues that most people (you and I included) could be labelled deviant by some existing persons or groups' (cited in Holdaway 1988:11). Generally, 'deviance refers to behaviour that is disapproved of and subject to some form of punishment, behaviour that is outside the rules of society and leads to a hostile and critical response from "conventional society"' (Marsh 2000:656).

A person can be considered deviant if:

1. they reject some or all of the norms and values of society, e.g. a hermit
2. they are part of a group whose members accept different beliefs or practise different behaviour from that common in the general society, e.g. a hippy. (O'Donnell 2002:266)

You can be considered deviant if you speak with your mouth full, stick your tongue out at someone when you meet them for the first time or walk around dressed as a woman when you are in fact a man. What the above examples show is that you do not have to break the law to be deviant. You can even be called deviant when you try to follow all the rules. Consider the example given by Babbie to illustrate this: 'spend the day telling everyone the absolute, unvarnished truth and count your remaining friends at the end of the day' (1988:132).

Some acts are deviant in one society and not another. For example, monogamy is the norm in Irish society, polygamy is not accepted. Homosexuality has been 'decriminalised in many countries but it still carries the death penalty in Iran' (Marsh 2000:657).

'Deviance depends not upon a given action but upon the acceptability of a certain action in a certain circumstance' (O'Donnell 2002:6). Examples of this include:

1. The injection of a drug by a doctor in a hospital may be socially approved; the injection of the same drug by a person 'for kicks' may be condemned and punished.
2. In modern society killing is usually seen as the most serious of offences but when looked at in the context of war, killing can be seen as heroic and people may even be punished for not wanting to take part in killing. (Marsh 2000:657)

Not all crimes are deviant acts and not all deviant acts are crimes. Deviant behaviour can be uncommonly good or brave behaviour as well as unacceptable behaviour, such as theft or vandalism. Murder and incest are both deviant, and breaking norms like these attracts the attention of the authorities. An act that has been declared illegal by some authority is called a crime. But deviance isn't necessarily bad; it can lead to social change. Curry et al. (2005:97) point out that 'like judgement about culture, judgements about deviance and crime are relative. What was deviant at one time might be non-deviant now, and what is a crime in one place might be legal somewhere else.' To illustrate this they use the example of wearing animal fur: this was common for men and women during the 1950s but something that may be frowned upon today. 'In fact, many animal rights activists feel strongly about the issue and have attacked people who are wearing furs. Similarly, many animal species that were once abundant sources of furs have become nearly extinct, and hunting these animals for their pelts is now a crime' (*Ibid.*: 97).

Deviance can be disruptive to social life and as a result, all societies develop some means of controlling it. Why do most people conform to the rules? According to Marsh this can be answered by referring to two basic types of social control or restraint. 'Mechanisms that monitor behaviour and penalise the violation of norms are social controls' (Curry *et al.* 2005:97).

1. **Informal mechanisms of social control** centre around the socialisation process. Children learn from institutions such as the family, education and religion that stealing, cheating etc., are wrong. These informed networks of control range from family and friends through to 'the monitoring done by social workers and psychiatrists, and on to the closed circuit surveillance in shops and shopping centres, the development of electronic tagging and the rise of private policing' (Macionis and Plummer 2002:413).

2. **Formal mechanisms of control** involve legal and formally established sanctions, such as the law, the police and punishment system. The criminal justice system is society's formal response to crime (Marsh 2000:659). 'A sanction is a method of enforcing obedience' (O'Donnell 2002:262). These can also be referred to as rewards or punishments to ensure people accept the approved behaviour of their society. Rewards and punishments can be formal or informal.

Formal rewards can be in the form of a bonus or promotion at work for employees who have worked hard in the socially approved ways to achieve their benefits or success. An informal way of rewarding a person could include a child's 'being given sweets for helping out his/her mam'. A formal negative sanction or punishment would include a prison sentence for a child abuser while an informal sanction would include ignoring someone who has offended us. 'Positive sanctions tend to be more effective than negative ones in ensuring social control' (O'Donnell 2002:264).

Social control aims to ensure that people abide by the general rules and expectations of the society in which they live. 'Sociologists studying deviant behaviour seek to understand why certain behaviours are widely regarded as deviant and how these notions of deviance are applied differentially to people within society' (Giddens 2001:204).

THE SOCIAL FOUNDATIONS OF DEVIANCE

Deviance as well as conformity is shaped by society. According to Macionis and Plummer (2002:418) there are three social foundations of deviance:

1. Deviance varies according to cultural norms – behaviour is only considered deviant when examined in relation to cultural norms. The norms that govern Irish life differ to those that govern the life of someone living in India. Laws also differ from place to place. In some Arab countries a man is permitted to have up to four wives. A man in Irish society who tried to do the same would face prison. In Amsterdam the use of soft drugs is permitted and 'there are even shops for their sale. In the rest of Europe, marijuana is outlawed' (Macionis and Plummer 2002:418).

2. People become deviant as others define them that way – 'Deviance is not a simple quality, present in some kinds of behaviour and absent in others. Rather, it is the product of a process which involves responses of other people to the behaviour' (Keating, cited in Marsh 2002:209). For example, if you help yourself to stationery in a shop you are stealing and deviant, but if you do so at work by 'borrowing' their supplies, you may not be seen as deviant. Whether such activity is seen as criminal or not depends on how others perceive, define and respond to the situation. 'Deviance is the result of interaction between rule-breaker and witness and not merely the result of what the rule-breaker does' (Tovey and Share 2000:271).

3. Both rule-making and rule-breaking involve social power – norms and their application are linked to social power. 'The law, Karl Marx asserted, amounts to little more than a strategy by which powerful people protect their interests' (Macionis and Plummer 2002:418).

THEORIES OF CRIME AND DEVIANCE

Positivist theories of individual crime

'Positivist theories focus on the characteristics and causes of a criminal type' (Macionis and Plummer 2002:419).

Much of the early work on crime attempted to explain it as something done by criminals that was essentially biological in character. Sociologists at that time studied groups of convicted criminals and focused on innate qualities within individuals as the source of crime and deviance. They believed that criminal types could be identified by certain anatomical features. An Italian physician, Caesare Lombroso, worked in prisons and in 1876 declared that criminals have a distinctive physique. 'He investigated the appearance and physical characteristics of criminals, such as the shape of the skull and forehead, jaw size and arm length and concluded that they displayed traits held over from earlier stages of human evolution' (Giddens 2001:205). He declared that features common to criminals included low foreheads, prominent jaws and cheekbones, protruding ears, excessive hairiness and unusually long arms.

His work was flawed; 'had he looked beyond prison walls, he would have realised that the physical features attributed exclusively to prisoners actually were found throughout the entire population' (Macionis and Plummer 2002:419). Although Lombroso's work was discredited, similar theories emerged. Sheldon in 1949 distinguished three main types of human physique and claimed that one type was directly associated with delinquency. The mesomorph (the muscular, active type) according to the theory, is 'more aggressive and physical and therefore more likely to become delinquent than those of thin physique (ectomorphs) or more fleshy people (endomorphs)' (Giddens 2001:205).

Other researchers looked for psychological explanations of crime. They focused on personality types and looked more for psychological defects: 'people who took illegal drugs were (and indeed still commonly are) thought to suffer from personality defects of various sorts, such as a poorly developed super-ego, or excessive narcissism, or were people with "addictive personalities"' (Tovey and Share 2003:310).

The positivist theories (biological or psychological explanations) have three major characteristics. According to David Matza (1964):

1. They focus on the criminal as a specific type of person.
2. The look for ways in which criminals differ from others.
3. They seek out explanations for criminal conduct as in some way of control of the criminal who perpetrates criminal acts. (cited in Macionis and Plummer 2002:420)

The main weakness of this approach is that it offers no insight into how some kinds of behaviour come to be defined as deviant in the first place. 'Both biological and psychological approaches to criminality presume that deviance is a sign of something wrong with the individual, rather than with society' (Giddens 2001:207).

Labelling theory

'This theory focuses on the processes by which some people label other members of society as deviant. According to labelling theorists, people's labels rather than actions are important' (Clarke *et al.* 2000:134).

Labelling theory is the name for the sociological view that people often take on the statuses assigned to them by the opinions of those around them. For example, someone widely and unjustly regarded as a thief may begin stealing, 'A woman labelled unfairly as sexually loose may eventually loosen up her sexuality to match this image' (Babbie 1988:39). Labelling is a process by which:

1. People are identified in a particular way.
2. They then receive special attention as a result of the label being attached to them.
3. They come to be regarded by others and to see themselves in the way they are described by the label. (O'Donnell 2002:266).

Labelling not only affects how others see an individual but also influences the individual's sense of self. Edwin Lemert (1972) made a distinction between primary and secondary deviance. Primary deviance refers to what Lemert called the 'initial act of transgression'; the deviant act remains 'marginal' to the person's self identity – 'a process occurs by which the deviant act is normalised' (Giddens 2001:210).

In some cases, however, normalisation does not occur and the person is labelled as a criminal or delinquent. 'Lemert used the term secondary deviance to describe cases where individuals come to accept the label and see themselves as deviant' (Giddens 2001:210). If this happens, the label can become central to a person's identity and lead to a continuation or intensification of the deviant behaviour. 'The development of secondary deviance is one application of the Thomas theorem which states situations defined as real become real in their consequences' (Macionis and Plummer 1997:213).

Who labels? Labelling theorists stress the importance of power in both the enforcement and the construction of laws. Those with power benefit from it, and those without power are disadvantaged when laws are constructed and enforced. 'Law enforcement by the police and courts is a selective process in which certain social groups are more vulnerable to arrest, prosecution and punishment' (Bilton *et al.* 2002:390). The actions of those doing the labelling are of as much concern as those of the labelled. 'The focus on the process of labelling raises the issue of who has the power to define and impose their definitions of right and wrong on others' (Marsh 2000:663).

According to Giddens, 'By and large the rules in terms of which deviance is defined are framed by the wealthy for the poor, by men for women, by older people for younger people, and by ethnic majorities for minority groups' (2001:209).

Labelling theory is considered an important approach to studying criminality. It is important because it sees no act as being intrinsically criminal. Acts are seen as being defined as criminal by the powerful, through the formation of laws and their interpretation and enforcement by the guards, courts etc.

It is along these lines that the theory has also been criticised. For example:

1. There are certain acts such as murder, theft etc., that are prohibited across nearly all cultures.
2. Labelling theorists neglect the processes that lead to acts defined as deviant.
3. It is not clear whether labelling actually does have the effect of increasing deviant conduct. (Giddens 2001:211)

Theory of differential association: Sutherland

This theory was first described by Sutherland in 1934. Edwin Sutherland advanced that deviance is learned through interaction with others. 'Any person's tendency towards conformity or deviance depends on the relative frequency of association with others who encourage conventional behaviour or norm violation' (Macionis and Plummer 2002:422). He believed that criminal behaviour is learned in interaction with other persons, especially within intimate personal groups, in a process of communication. According to Mann (1983:93) learning includes:

- techniques of committing the crime, and
- the specific direction of motives, drives, attitudes and definitions of legal codes.

Sutherland linked crime with differential association. Most simply put, his idea was that 'in a society that contains a variety of subcultures, some social environments tend to encourage illegal activities whereas others do not. Individuals become delinquent through associating with people who are the carriers of criminal norms' (Giddens 2001:209). For him, criminal activities are learned in much the same way as law-abiding ones. This theory sees criminal behaviour as an expression of general needs and values just as non-criminal behaviour is an expression of the same needs and values. This theory rejects the idea that psychological differences separate criminals from non-criminals.

According to Curry *et al.* (2005:107), 'differential association is nothing more than a fancy restatement of the saying "birds of a feather flock together".' This theory of differential association has often been used to explain urban youth gangs. The attractions of youths to gangs, according to these theories, may include:

* social support, group identity, recreational opportunities and physical protection
* economic opportunities not available in legitimate community. 'In exchange, gang members must conform to the gang's culture, which includes petty deviance, violence and crime'. (*Ibid.*: 107)

However, while this might explain some instances or situations, Curry *et al.* believe it fails to address two major issues:

(i)   'most youths who encounter crime do not become deviant
(ii)   most people living in high crime areas are not criminals'. (2005:108)

Merton's strain theory

Robert Merton argues that deviance is generated by the structure and culture of the environment in which the individual lives. For him all societies establish goals of success and provide a means for achieving them. However, there are situations in which people cannot achieve the goals by normal means. Merton uses the term 'anomie' when he refers to these situations (IPA 1992:161). He carried out his study in the US in the 1930s and from its findings found that people in society are oriented to the goals associated with monetary success. For him society placed demands on individuals to accumulate wealth and achieve success, but largely denied them the opportunities to do so effectively. Society wanted people to achieve these goals by approved means. This was the path to conformity. When the institutional means of attaining these goals is denied to an individual they may respond to the situation by deviating in one of four different ways:

* innovation
* ritualism
* retreatism
* rebellion.

1. **Conforming:** People who conform are those who accept the goals of their society and set about achieving these goals in a generally acceptable way. The majority of the population falls into this category, for example someone who gains wealth and status by hard work and talent.

2. **Innovation:** The innovators are people who accept the goals of the society but not the accepted means of achieving them, for example a person who seeks wealth but does so by means of robbery, gambling etc. For some innovators, opportunities to achieve wealth by any other means are not available to them. 'Members of organised crime are considered innovators because they accept society's goal of materialistic success, but instead of following the legitimate means to acquire wealth, they substitute deviant means such as drug dealing (Curry *et al.* 2005:106).

3. **Ritualism:** Ritualists are people who do not believe in the goals, but go through the socially approved motions for fear of disapproval. 'For example, a young couple may reject the values of our society in relation to marriage, but still do marry, even though they do not regard it as sinful to live together without marriage' (O'Donnell 2002:259).

4. **Retreatism:** Retreatists avoid decisions on, or reject, society's goals or methods of achieving them and withdraw from society as much as possible. This group could include some alcoholics, drug addicts, hermits etc.

5. **Rebellion:** Rebels openly reject the values of the society, both the goals and means of achieving them. They usually advocate radical alternatives to the existing social order.

Table 8:1 Merton's Theory of anomie and its adaptations

		Cultural goals, e.g. wealth, success	Institutional means, e.g. college, hard work etc.
1.	Conformity	+	+
2.	Innovation	+	–
3.	Ritualism	–	+
4.	Retreatism	–	–
5.	Rebellion	+ –	+ –

(+) signifies acceptance

(–) signifies rejection)

(+ –) signifies rejection and substitution of new goals and standards

(Source: adapted from Holdaway 1988:72)

'According to Merton, the "strain" between a culture's emphasis on wealth and the limited opportunity to get rich gives rise, especially among the poor, to theft, the selling of illegal drugs etc.' (Macionis and Plummer 2002:420). According to Tovey and Share this theory 'assumes that people are not naturally aggressive and selfish but that these qualities are fostered to them by an anomic society – one which encourages people to believe that only wealth and consumption can give their lives meaning and worth but which nonetheless denies many of them the chance to achieve these goals' (2003:305).

This approach explains crime in terms of the structure and culture of society rather than in terms of the individual. However, it has been criticised for offering explanations of crime that are too generalised. For example, not all people who have restricted opportunities turn to crime (Marsh 2000:63).

CRIME RATES IN IRELAND

'Crime may be defined as an act that breaks the criminal law, it can be followed by criminal proceedings and formal punishment' (Marsh 2000:656).

Crime is an issue of major public interest. According to McCullagh (1999:410) 'one of the major changes in Irish society over the past thirty years has been the growth in the level of recorded crime and in the accompanying perception that there is now a significant crime problem in that society'. The rise has been attributed to increasing levels of violent crime, such as murder and assault, and of property crimes such as burglary and car theft, many of which are felt to be drug related (Ibid.). 'While there has been concern in relation to the rise in the homicide rate, the official statistics suggest that violent crime is at a very low level in Ireland' (O'Connell 2002, cited in Tovey et al. 2007:313). The statistics provided by the 2003 Annual Report on crime reported that 'there were 45 murders recorded in 2003 which was a decrease of seven over that recorded in 2002. When murders and manslaughters are combined, the total of 52 recorded in 2003 represents a decrease of 12 per cent of the 59 recorded in the previous year'. According to O'Mahony, 'the statistics indicate that the level of violent crime is about half the US rate, a third of the EU average and a quarter of that for Denmark or England and Wales' (2002, cited in Tovey and Share 2003:300). 'The highest percentage decreases in recorded offences between 2010 and 2011 included homicide offences which decreased by 27%'. (CSO 2011:7)

Sexual assaults against adults and children are now recognised as a major social and criminal problem in Ireland. In 1997 there were 279 sex offenders in our prisons, a number comprising 12 per cent of all adult male prisoners in Irish prisons (Murphy, cited in Cotter 1999:298). 'Over 400 rapes of females were recorded by An Garda Síochána in 2002 compared with fewer than 40 in 1975' (Kilcommins *et al.* 2004:121). During the same period the total number of sex crimes jumped from 161 to 3,171. 'Expressed as a rate this is a sixteen-fold increase, most of which occurred between the years 2000 and 2002' (*Ibid.*: 121). According to O'Donnell (2002) there are a number of possible explanations for this:

Table 8:2 Indictable/headline offences and murders recorded

Year	Indictable/headline offences recorded	No. of murders
1950	12,231	9
1960	15,375	3
1970	30,756	11
1980	72,782	21
1990	87,658	17
2000	73,276	39
2001	86,633	52
2002	106,415	52
2003	103,360	45
2004	98,964	37
2005	101,659	54

(Source: adapted from An Garda Síochána Annual Report in CSO Statistical Yearbook 2006)

1. 'The first is the increased likelihood that victims will come forward.
2. There is evidence that "historic" offences are now being reported, particularly where the victims were male' (Leon 2000) and
3. 'This has resulted from a growing awareness of the prevalence of child sexual abuse, and the erosion of the stigma and fear that caused victims to suffer in silence' (cited in Kilcommins *et al.* 2004:121).

Table 8:3 Victims of assault and sexual offences by sex, 2005

Offence	Male	Female	Total
Assault causing harm	2,861	809	3,670
Sexual offences	353	1,381	1,734

(Source: An Garda Síochána Annual Report in CSO Statistical Yearbook 2006:133)

Table 8:4 Detection rates (Irish Crime Classification System) 2007–11

Offence group	2007	2008	2009	2010	2011
Homicide offences	90	86	80	83	86
Sexual offences	60	65	62	59	57
Attempts/threats to murder, assaults, harassments and related offences	59	59	60	62	62
Dangerous or negligent acts	99	99	100	100	100
Kidnapping and related offences	58	62	50	62	68
Robbery, extortion and hijacking offences	49	50	52	54	49
Burglary and related offences	24	26	24	25	23
Theft and other offences	36	38	37	38	36
Fraud, deception and related offences	44	53	56	51	45
Controlled drug offences	98	99	99	99	99
Weapons and explosives offences	87	91	89	90	90
Damage to property and to the environment	23	22	22	23	23
Public order and other social code offences	91	93	94	94	94
Road and traffic offences	99	99	99	99	99
Offences against government, justice procedures and organisation of crime	98	98	98	98	98
Offences not elsewhere classified	65	68	67	62	51

(Source: CSO 2013:7)

'The characteristics of young offenders in Ireland have been described in numerous studies. Overwhelmingly they are the children of the poor, they are early school leavers, they have experienced broken homes and many have lived in residential child care' (Lalor *et al.* 2007:249). In 1996 there were 14,285 offences committed involving juveniles (An Garda Síochána, 1996). This figure increased to 19,915 in 2003. Despite increasing numbers Lalor *et al.* (2007:250) highlight that 'the numbers of young people who come to the attention of the Gardaí and the justice system are small relative to the numbers of young people in the general population'. They provide the following figures:

- The highest number of young people cautioned in 2005 was in Dublin (at 16.43 per 1,000 of the population)
- The lowest number of young people cautioned in 2005 was in the Northern region (at 9.56 per 1,000 of the population).

Despite the dearth of indigenous Irish studies on the social profile of prisoners at regular intervals, 'it is widely known that most prisoners have a history of social exclusion, including high levels of family, educational and health disadvantage, and poor prospects in the labour market' (IPRT 2012:6). While the incidence of some offences decreased, such as burglary and vehicle offences, there was a steady increase in the number of detections relating to drink offences. For example drink-related offences accounted for 17 per cent of referrals in 2001 and for 20.7 per cent in 2003 (An Garda Síochána 2003). The breakdown of offences by juveniles detailed in the 2005 An Garda Síochána Annual Report shows that '4,164 offences (19.4 per cent of the total) were "intoxicated in a public place" or "purchase/ possession/consumption of alcohol"' (cited in Lalor *et al.* 2007:253).

'In recent years around about 600,000 offences per annum, have been known to the Gardaí. Over 80 per cent of these (half a million) are non-indictable offences – misdemeanours not thought serious enough to warrant trial by jury, but which can be summarily dealt with by a district court' (Tovey *et al.* 2007:313). 'While these crimes are generally not seen as serious they can include offences that have a major impact, such as drink-driving, joy-riding and some assaults' (O'Mahony 2002, cited in Tovey and Share 2003:300). They also present the following statistics:

- The majority of offences are traffic offences such as speeding, driving with no tax or insurance.
- Of approximately 100,000 'indictable offences' recorded annually since the early 1980s over 95 per cent have been property crimes.

Table 8:5 Arrests and convictions for drink-driving offences

Year	No. of arrests	No. of convictions
1997	7,541	4,379
1999	9,570	5,853
2001	12,841	6,790
2003	11,344	3,060
2004	11,646	4,140

(An Garda Síochána Annual Report in CSO Statistical Yearbook 2006:134)

In 2002 burglary accounted for almost one quarter of all headline crime. According to An Garda Síochána (2003), 'The rate of recorded burglary escalated in the early 1980s. In four out of five burglaries property is stolen and in most cases the value is less than €500. Most burgled goods are not recorded' (cited in Kilcommins *et al.* 2004:125). According to the CSO (2013:6), burglary and related offences increased by 8 per cent between 2010 and 2011. It also found that in 2011, 'almost 40 per cent of burglary offences were recorded in the Dublin Metropolitan region' (*Ibid.*: 37).

Table 8:6 Robberies and aggravated burglaries

Offence	1997	1999	2001	2003	2005
Involving firearms	252	290	232	313	353
Involving use of syringe	893	384	371	287	165

(Source: An Garda Síochána Annual Report in CSO Statistical Yearbook 2006:133)

According to O'Mahony (2000:3), Ireland has seen an emergence of:
- violent and intimidatory crimes like gangland assassination, torture and murder of isolated old people for their money
- a growth in more vicious crime
- an exposure of previously hidden crime such as child sex abuse, rape and 'white collar crime' at all levels in society
- a growth in serious levels of drug abuse which has impacted on the nature of crime – from individual addicts to organised criminal gangs.

Table 8:7 Crime recorded in 2006 and 2011

Headline	2006	2011
Homicide	138	63
Dangerous or negligent acts	19,280	9,940
Sexual offences	1,415	2,052
Controlled drug offences	14,232	17,709
Kidnapping and related offences	81	104
Burglary and related offences	24,788	27,439
Thefts and related offences	74,500	76,924
Frauds, deception and related offences	4,167	5,311

(Source: www.cso.ie 2012)

Infanticide (baby killing) was a serious problem in the nineteenth century; the last recorded case of it was in 1983. 'Its disappearance reflects a changing social and moral environment. Since the 1970s the stigma associated with lone motherhood has largely evaporated and the use of institutional confinement for unmarried mothers and their children has ended' (Kilcommins *et al.* 2004:117).

Although official statistics rarely provide full information on the background offenders, such information that is available tends to suggest that the majority of crimes are committed by young adult working-class males (IPA 1992:170). According to research carried out by Paul O'Mahony on prisoners in Mountjoy prison, the 'typical prisoner was male, had left school before the legal minimum age, had limited experience of the world and work and was likely to have serious emotional and personal problems, such as a history of drug abuse or psychiatric difficulties' (cited in McCullagh 1999:410). Research by Rottman (1984) provides an analysis of people 'apprehended' for indictable offences in the Dublin Metropolitan Area. He found that:

• most of these people were male (84 per cent)
• most were very young (one-quarter were under sixteen and a further half between seventeen and twenty)
• 80 per cent of the seventeen- to twenty-year olds were unemployed
• they came from specific locations in Dublin that at the time were socially or physically deprived. (cited in Tovey and Share 2003:305)

According to the IPA (1992:170), women commit far fewer crimes than men, for example the annual reports on crime 'show that around 10 to 15 per cent of those convicted of offences in any year are women' (Bacik 2002, cited in Tovey and Share 2003:135).

Table 8:8 Sentenced prisoners in custody by age and sex, 31st August 2011

Age	Male	Female	Total
16–17	24	0	24
18–20	256	5	261
21–24	622	28	650
25–29	810	31	841
30–39	1,052	28	1,080
40–49	472	14	486
50 and over	261	7	268
Total	3,497	113	3,610

(Source: Irish Prison Service Annual Report in CSO Statistical Yearbook 2012:119)

Who are the victims of crime? A survey carried out by Breen and Rottman in 1985 provided the following findings of the most likely victims:

- those in higher social classes
- young middle-aged
- living in middle-class housing estates. (cited in Tovey and Share 2003:305)

The 1998 CSO survey also provided useful information about the risk of victimisation and fear of crime. It reported that:

- 'Men aged 18–24 were most vulnerable to theft or assault, with risk declining by age.
- Elderly were a low-risk group but reported feeling unsafe.
- The proportion feeling that crime was 'a very serious problem in Ireland today' was higher for women in every age group and increased with age for both men and women'. (Kilcommins 2004:105)

According to a report published by the Department of Justice, Equality and Law Reform:

1. 'More females than males were "very worried" about rape, physical attacks by a stranger, burglary and being mugged/robbed, and
2. Older groups were found to be more concerned about property crime while younger age groups tended to be more worried about violent crime'. (2009:vii)

'In one year in the 1980s the increase in serious crime was greater than the total amount of such crime in the one year of 1947' (O'Manony 1999:120). He referred to Rottman, who he considered was the first person to address the effects of modernisation on crime in Ireland. Rottman's 1980 study suggested that crime rates in Ireland prior to the mid-1960s 'were such as to be almost imperceptible and no signs of pending increases could be found'. His explanation for these low levels of crime included:

- Ireland's stagnant economy
- the very high level of emigration
- a highly conservative political and social culture.

He associated increasing crime rates from the late 1960s on with:

- intense and rapid modernisation
- a shift from an agricultural to an industrial economy
- growth in affluence and Ireland's becoming a more stratified society
- greater availability of desirable and stealable goods such as cars.

'The new patterns of criminal activity typically associated with industrialisation and urbanisation are an increase in the incidence of property crime, high levels of juvenile delinquency and female crime, and patterns of crime that are more sophisticated' (IPA 1992:173). Although our crime figures remain low by international standards, the last twenty to thirty years 'have seen a dramatic decline in the average person's sense of personal security and interpersonal trust' (O'Mahony 1999:3).

According to Casey (2002) 'Evidence of very high levels of alcohol and drug abuse (by international standards), of high rates of suicide among young males, of significant increases in violent assault and sexual offences, and of a sharp rise in the homicide rate, has led one leading professor of psychiatry to conclude that there are worrying trends to suggest that the civic order is in disarray' (cited in Kirby 2004:36).

As sociologists we need to become aware of the existence and extent of crime in our society. We need to try to identify the possible causes of crime if we hope to reduce it or eradicate it.

9

Ageing and Older People

GROWING OLD – BIOLOGY AND CULTURE (A DEMOGRAPHIC PROFILE)

With falling birth rates and improvements in healthcare, the number of older people in the population is increasing. An increasing proportion of the population is made up of elderly members in our society. According to the Central Statistics Office (2011) there are over 500,000 persons over the age of sixty-five in Ireland. People are living longer and longer. The European Commission provides the following statistics that reflect this marked increase in life expectancy:

- 'The population of the EU will be slightly higher in 2060 (517 million, up from 502 million in 2010). Nearly one-third of the citizens will then be aged 65 or over.

- Life expectancy at birth is projected to increase from 76.7 years in 2010 to 84.6 in 2060 for males and from 82.5 to 89.1 for females' (2012).
- 'Among individual countries, the most aged are Greece and Italy, where 24% of the population was aged over 60 or older in 2000' (Mirkin and Weinberger 2013:41).

Table 9:1 Proportions of over-65s in selected European countries, 1993 and projections for 2025

Country	1993	2025
	per cent	per cent
Sweden	18.6	21.2
Italy	15.9	25.1
Britain	15.8	19.0
Germany	15.1	22.9
Greece	14.8	23.0
Poland	10.7	16.4
Turkey	4.4	9.2

(Source: adapted from Giarchi and Abbot 1997, cited in Cole 1999:70)

Table 9:2 Countries with the highest shares of 60+ in 2011 and 2050 (among countries with 2011 population of 1 million or more)

	2011		2050
	per cent		per cent
Japan	31	Japan	42
Italy	27	Portugal	40
Germany	26	Bosnia and Herzegovina	40
Finland	25	Cuba	39
Sweden	25	Republic of Korea	39
Bulgaria	25	Italy	38
Greece	25	Spain	38
Portugal	24	Singapore	38
Belgium	24	Germany	38
Croatia	24	Switzerland	37

(Source: Bloom *et al.* 2011:2)

This ageing of the population is general throughout Europe and may create an economic advantage for those countries with younger populations. 'In Europe Italy has the greatest proportion of older people (22.7 per cent estimated for 2020), while the Irish Republic has the youngest population, with older people comprising 15.9 per cent of the population by 2020' (O'Donnell 2002:228).

The following information provides the principal demographic results from the 2012 census in Ireland.

Table 9:3 The elderly population in Ireland, 2012

	Aged 65–69	70–74	75–79	80–84	85 and over
			thousands		
Persons	181.5	132.7	103.6	71.0	60.5
Males	90.6	64.4	47.6	29.4	19.4
Females	90.9	68.3	55.9	41.6	41.1

(Source: CSO 2012:13)

'In France the age of 121 has already been achieved. At the moment women are seven times as likely as men to become centenarians' (Denscombe 1998, cited in Marsh 2000:545).

The following highlights population projections for the elderly population in Ireland:

1. The proportion of people in Ireland aged sixty-five years or older is due to increase from 11.1 per cent of the overall population in 2002 to 23.9 per cent by 2050.
2. By 2050 one in four of the population will be over sixty-five.
3. Life expectancy is also set to rise. In 2000 life expectancy was 74 for men and 79.4 for women. By 2050 it is expected to be 79 for men and 84 for women.
4. The number of the very old (those aged eighty and above) will increase from 23 per cent of the total elderly population to approximately 27 per cent by 2050 (Stratton 2004:10).

Because the elderly now represent a growing group in society, distinctions have been made, and we now refer to the elderly as:

1. the 'younger elderly' (sixty-five to seventy-five years)
2. the 'older elderly' (seventy-five to eighty-five years)

3. the very old (eighty-six years and over). (Macionis and Plummer 2002:329)

On average people live to much older ages than they did over a century ago. Underlying this gain in lifespan are medical advances and improvements in nutrition, hygiene and healthcare. Some sociologists refer to the changing demographics of the elderly as the 'greying of the population'. 'Nearly all developed countries will witness the ageing of their populations in the next decades' (Giddens 2001:163). Peter Peterson 'has described this shift as a "gray down"' (1999, cited in Giddens 2001:163). According to his findings:

1. One in every seven people in the developed world is aged over sixty-five.
2. In thirty years' time this will have risen to one in four.
3. By 2030 the proportion of people over sixty-five will range from 33 per cent in Australia to almost 50 per cent in Germany.
4. The number of the 'old old' (those aged over eighty-five) is expanding more quickly than the 'young old'. Over the next half century the number of people over eighty-five will grow six-fold. This process is sometimes referred to as the 'ageing of the aged' (Giddens 2001:613).

Table 9:4 Expected rise in numbers of older people

1996	2002	2010	2030	2050
413,900	436,001	484,481	817,767	1,136,623
11.4%	11.1%	11.7%	17.7%	23.9%

(Source: Stratton 2004:10)

There are three reasons why sociologists need to consider old age more fully than they do at present:

1. Demographic factors: 'The role of demographic factors could be very significant on the size of the population pool in need of social care services such as personal care, home help and surveillance' (O'Loughlin 1999:235).
2. Ageing as an important social process in its own right.
3. Ageing as a key feature in class, gender or ethnic experience (Webb and Tossell 1999:199).

'Across the world the expectation that people will live longer, and that an increasing proportion of the population will be older is having repercussions on demographic, economic, medical and social frameworks'

(Marsh 2000:545). As the elderly population continues to grow, the demands on social services and health systems will increase as well. As the old-age-dependency ratio groups grow, increasing strain will be placed on available resources. Pensions will need to be paid for more years than they are at present. 'In the light of demographic projections, governments, interest groups and policy makers are being forced to look ahead and to develop proposals for meeting the needs of a changing population' (Giddens 2001:163). Gerontology, the study of ageing and the elderly, concerns itself not only with the physical process of growing old, but also with social and cultural factors connected to ageing.

1. **Physical processes of ageing:** 'The ageing process starts at birth and slowly begins to accelerate when we are in our late twenties when the first physical signs such as greying hair or facial lines begin to show, and early aches and pains start to establish' (Webb and Tossell 1999:198). However, by the time we reach old age most of us are psychologically adjusted to cope and have become accustomed to having to 'live with a gradual diminishing physical capacity' (*Ibid.*: 198). For Cole (1999:71), 'growing old is a chronological and biological fact. The body changes with age and death is an eventuality that none of us escapes, but these simple truths tell us little of the social experience of old age'.

2. **Social processes of ageing:** Sociologists say that old age, like ageing in general, is socially constructed. In contemporary industrial societies, old age is defined by reference to retirement. For Cole, 'This experience of old age is a social one because it is society that defines what it is to be old and what meaning, expectations and status are attached to it' (1999:71). Some elderly people have commented that their advancing years have no effect on how they see themselves, but it has changed the way in which other people have related to them (Bilton *et al.* 2002:86). An experiment conducted in New York over a three-year period highlights 'the fact that elders within a society are handicapped not so much by their physical disabilities as by the attitudes and psychological barriers that are set up by other people' (Webb and Tossell 1999:199).

Ageing is not a uniformly experienced phenomenon. While there are examples of older people living well into their eighties and nineties and living full and active lives, ageing is also accompanied by a set of unfamiliar challenges. The elderly in our society remain 'largely on the periphery, unable in many cases to enjoy the benefits of a developed society to which they have all made contributions' (Webb and Tossell 1999:198).

THEORIES OF AGEING

A number of sociological theories have been used to understand the ageing process. Two theories we will look at are (a) disengagement theory and (b) role and activity theory.

Disengagement theory

'Disengagement promotes the orderly functioning of society by removing ageing people from productive roles while they are still able to perform them. It is functional for they as ageing individuals with diminishing capacities can presumably look forward to relinquishing some of the pressures of their jobs in favour of new pursuits of their own choosing' (Macionis and Plummer 2005:355).

This theory was first presented by Elaine Cumming and William Henry (1961). They commenced a study, beginning in the 1950s, that 'followed' a group of healthy older people over a number of years to observe the changes that occurred as they got older. The study followed a sample of 275 older adults in Kansas City. 'Even though the sample was small and did not represent the entire United States, many sociologists found the theory intriguing and it quickly gained a wide following' (Curry *et al.* 2005:70).

According to Hyde *et al.* (2004:173), 'The central premise of the theory is that the older person disengages from social activities in preparation for death. . . . The underlying belief is that because the timing of death is unpredictable, it would be socially disruptive if people died while strongly engaged in social and work activities'. Jones (1994) refers to it as 'the quiet closing of the doors' (cited in Hyde *et al.* 2004:173).

Disengagement, which involves older people disengaging from their roles in society, creates opportunities for young people to enter them, to develop and society could continue (Scambler 2000:155). According to Fennell *et al.* (1988) 'Disengagement is seen to begin for men and for women at widowhood' (cited in Hyde *et al.* 2004:173). Victor (1994) also cited in Hyde *et al.* (2004:173), 'Because retirement is more abrupt than the loss of the domestic role, ageing is considered to be more problematic for men'. Scambler (2000:151) raises an important point: 'questions about whether older people wanted to "disengage" or were forced to do so by society were not asked'.

Bond *et al.* highlight a number of problems with this particular perspective on ageing. They argue:

1. This theory condones the social isolation and marginalisation of older people. It can also lead to poverty, as most workers cannot so readily disengage from paid work because they may not have the financial security to rely on.
2. The theory is seen as ageist in the sense that it assumes identical experiences for older people (cited in Barry and Yuill 2002:114).

Macionis and Plummer highlight another problem of the disengagement theory: that 'it makes the elderly appear too passive and too much like victims' (2005:356).

Activity theory

'Activity theory proposes that, to the extent that people do disengage, they substitute "new lives" for the ones they leave behind. Activity theory thus shifts the focus of analysis from the needs of society (as stated in disengagement theory) to the needs of the elderly themselves' (Macionis and Plummer 2005:356).

This theory, developed by Havighurst (1963), believes 'that elders should exercise, participate in community affairs, engage in volunteer work, go to school and otherwise live actively. Such activity seems to be correlated with a sense of well-being and health' (Curry et al. 2005:71). According to Hyde et al. (2004:174), 'Successful ageing according to this theory is about extending middle age pursuits into old age'.

While the concept is good, this theory also has its problems. For example:

- Financial restrictions can limit the choices available to older people.
- Many people who have been disengaged may have little to do and as a result experience isolation and loneliness.
- How does this theory apply to older people who suffer from poor health?

Overall, the problem of both these theories 'concerns the assumption that people change dramatically when they enter old age' (Curry et al. 2005:72).

TRANSITIONS AND PROBLEMS OF AGEING

A lot of problems and challenges experienced by the elderly are very much compounded by society's attitudes towards them. Webb and Tossell believe that the use of terms such as 'pensioner', 'geriatric' etc., words commonly used in association with elders, 'helps to perpetuate the stereotyped image of their dependency and perceived uselessness, and so deny their human validity' (1999:199). Among the problems of the elderly are loss of role (resulting largely from retirement), loss of relatives and friends, separation from children who live elsewhere, poverty as a result of unemployment etc.

'Older people in modern societies tend to have lower status and less power than they used to have in pre-modern cultures. In these cultures, as in non-western societies today (such as India or China) old age was believed to bring wisdom, and the oldest people in any given community were commonly its main decision-makers. Today, increasing old age normally brings with it something of the reverse . . . the accumulated knowledge of older people often seems to the young no longer a valuable store of wisdom, but simply behind the times' (Giddens 2001:162). According to Hamel (1990) 'Because our culture places such a premium on youth, ageing may spark frustration, fear and self-doubt' (cited in Macionis and Plummer 2002:329). The next section will look at some of the challenges and issues faced by the elderly in Irish society. For Stratton (2004), 'if the resource implications of the changing reality of Irish society are not met, then the likelihood is that the level of vulnerability among older people will increase.' The following table provides an overview of the issues and implications of the greying of the world.

Table 9:5 Issues and implications of the greying of the world: A summary

Issue	Implication
Disability	• Growing need for health services and finance for support
Retirement	• Changing shape of life course • New patterns of both 'work' and leisure in later life • Changing incomes of the elderly
Poverty	• Greater strain on finances for some groups in old age – living longer
Family	• New roles: the young old look after the old old • Assisted conception means older people may have children
Psycho-social	• Problems of isolation through bereavement etc. • Needs for new meanings of later life and communities of support • New identities for the ageing?
Politics	• The rise of the grey vote, a new politics of ageing
Culture	• Shifting images of ageing as more and more people fit the category, and hence more facilities become available
Community	• New retirement colonies for different groups, e.g. lesbian and gay communities in Palm Springs

(Source: Macionis and Plummer 2005:348)

Retirement

'Retirement itself is a product of a wage-labour society, and more specifically of one where there is provision for income when employment has ceased, i.e. pensions' (Cole 1999:71).

According to Stratton (2004), 'In 2000, 13.6% of men over 65 and 2.4% of women over 65 participated in the labour market. By 2050, these rates will fall to 11.7% for men and 2% for women.'

Although the idea of retirement is familiar to us and seen as a socially acceptable period in which state and/or private pension provision is made, it is usually a recent creation, becoming commonplace in industrial societies during the nineteenth century. Retirement pensions were first introduced in 1899 by the German Chancellor Otto Von Bismarck. At the time the age set was seventy but was lowered to sixty-five in 1916 (Macionis and Plummer 2002:331). Retirement 'offered those who left the labour market a legitimate role as an ex-worker' (Bilton *et al.* 2002:87).

Table 9:6 Recipients by type of old age pension

Year	Old Age Contributory Pension	Retirement Pension	Old Age Non-Contributory Pension	Pre-Retirement Allowance	Total
1995	69,179	65,761	102,984	15,023	252,947
1996	67,988	69,740	101,624	14,151	253,503
1997	70,022	71,793	98,835	13,647	254,297
1998	71,706	75,316	95,890	13,897	256,809
1999	76,241	78,868	93,023	13,149	261,281
2000	86,217	78,370	90,652	12,521	267,760
2001	94,871	80,326	89,061	11,807	276,065
2002	105,295	83,055	87,828	11,222	287,395
2003	113,970	86,509	86,733	10,957	298,169
2004	118,383	88,870	85,172	11,228	303,653
2005	124,611	91,047	84,445	11,058	311,170

(Source: Dept. of Social and Family Affairs, in CSO Statistical Yearbook 2006:90)

In Ireland the Old Age Pension Act was introduced in 1908, but this was a strictly means-tested pension for people over seventy years old. The

1960s saw the introduction of the Contributory Old Age pension (1961) (Mills 1999:6–7). The pension age was reduced from seventy to sixty-six by 1977. In 1970 a retirement pension for those aged sixty-five began (O'Loughlin 1999:225). While pensions have saved many people from the fear of becoming destitute, Edmondson sees pensions 'in the context of a work-oriented, youth-orientated society, they also create an image of older people as debarred from the mainstream of life' (1997:165).

Kennedy in *Ireland in the Coming Times* suggests 'that the National Pensions Board (NPB) estimates did not take sufficient account of the improvement in mortality over the past decade' (1997:148). She states 'The National Pension Board made projections of the cost of social welfare pensions between 1990 and 2035 in 1990 prices. The cost projections were based on lower population estimates of those aged 65 years and over than the 1995 CSO projections used in this paper' (1997:148).

Private and public pensions provide an economic foundation for retirement. In some poor societies where no pension scheme exists, 'most people work until they become incapacitated' (Macionis and Plummer 2002:331).

'As the pattern of work changes in industrial societies, so there is a pronounced tendency for people to retire at earlier and earlier ages – sometimes by choice, sometimes through compulsory redundancies' (Macionis and Plummer 2002:331). Reasons for early retirement could include the following:

- It allows more 'younger workers', who may have more up-to-date skills, access the labour force.
- Sophisticated technology may reduce the need for everyone to work, but requires that those who do have the relevant skills and training.
- Lowering of retirement age could be linked to growth in unemployment.

While retirement is welcomed by many, a recent study in Ireland by Fahey and Russell (2001) 'suggested that approximately 70 per cent of 55–69 year olds currently in employment favoured a more gradual system of withdrawal from the workforce' (cited in Hyde *et al.* 2004:170). The move from working life to retirement is not an easy one and it can pose some problems for many older people. 'Retirement is likely to be particularly hard for those for whom work was an important source of social status, identity and most importantly, independence' (Turner 1993, cited in Bilton *et al.* 2002:87). Work is important in our personal identity; it gives us a purpose in life. Exiting the labour market through retirement can lead to many feeling socially excluded, socially isolated as well as experiencing a significant drop in their living standards. 'Overall, the elderly tend to be more materially disadvantaged than other segments of the population. Retirement results in a loss of income that may cause a significant drop in elderly people's standard of living' (Giddens 2001:165).

Bilton *et al.* state that 'the differing experience of the impact of retirement tends to reflect differences between the incomes that older people take with them to retirement' (2002:87). For Blaikie (1999) 'working-class retirement may often lack "an active concept of retirement" whereas middle-class retirement – with better resources – has led to an expanding consumer market and culture' (cited in Macionis and Plummer 2002:331).

In our society, fewer women than men have faced the transition of retirement but this trend continues to change as the proportion of women in the labour force continues to rise.

'The pensions upon which the retired depend have become more unequal than in the past, in that many new pensioners enjoy higher levels of support via private or employment-related pensions' (Bilton *et al.* 2002:87). A result of this is an increase in income inequalities among pensioners which 'points to the need for us to differentiate among older people themselves as much as between them and younger generations' (*Ibid.*). A study entitled *Fifty plus in Ireland 2011* presented the following key findings:

- 'Among those aged 50–64, 62% of men and 46% of women are at work compared to 16% of men and 8% of women aged 65 to 74
- Of men aged 65–74, 82% describe themselves as retired, compared to 52% of women. However, 36% of women aged 65–74 report that they are "looking after home or family".' (TILDA 2011:220)

A recent Eurobarometer report found that 'almost three quarters of Irish people believe that they should be allowed to continue working past their official retirement age compared to 60 per cent of their European counterpart' (Department of Health and children 2013:25).

Social isolation

'For many people growing old can be a time of social withdrawal and loss – loss of job, income, health, independence, role, status, friends and relatives. It is unsurprising that this can be a period of loneliness and social isolation' (Marsh 2000:545). In 2011, it was reported that 'loneliness was the biggest problem for older people living alone' (Walsh and Harvey 2011, cited in CARDI 2013).

Potential isolation and loneliness can be a result of:

1. retirement cutting the older person off from friends and workmates
2. loss of status as a result of retirement, loneliness and disorientation; having to restructure the daily routine
3. death of spouse or partner may leave an older person on their own
4. limited physical mobility preventing the older person from meeting others
5. the decline of the extended family resulting in many old people living isolated lives, either independently or surrounded only by peers in old people's homes. (O'Donnell 2002:229)

The following figures from the 2006 census provide details on the number of elderly living alone in Ireland.

Table 9:7 The elderly population living in private households and living alone

Age group and sex	Persons in private households	Persons living alone: Total	Persons living alone: As a percentage of persons in the age group in private households
Aged 65 years and over			
Persons	422,242	121,157	28.7
Males	191,372	41,939	21.9
Females	230,870	79,218	34.3
Aged 70 years and over			
Persons	286,194	94,137	32.9
Males	123,922	29,951	24.2
Females	162,272	64,186	39.6
Aged 75 years and over			
Persons	174,467	65,119	37.3
Males	70,586	19,074	27.0
Females	103,881	46,045	44.3

(Source: CSO Statistical Yearbook 2006:63)

The problem of social isolation falls heavily on women, who typically outlive their husbands. Life expectancy rates at birth for Ireland were 75.1 years for men and 80.3 years for women in 2001–3 (Census 2000:14). The census of 2006 provides us with statistics that show for the age group seventy-five and over, 47,045 women lived alone compared to 19,074 men (CSO 2006:63). 'As with everything to do with old age, it is strongly structured by gender.' (Arber and Ginn 1995, cited in Macionis and Plummer 2002:333)

Macionis and Plummer (2002:332) point out that living alone is not the equivalent of feeling lonely. They use a survey from Walker and Maltby (1997) to illustrate this point: Fear of crime is another factor that tends to strand large numbers of old people in their homes. The Health Promotion Strategy (1998) 'Adding years to life, life to years' highlighted security as a growing problem for older people. 'In 1994 19 per cent of older people in urban areas and 8 per cent in rural areas were burgled, while 4 per cent of males and 5 per cent of females were assaulted or mugged. The state of fear among older people generally has been heightened by the publicity surrounding these incidents' (Stratton 2004:17/18). The Centre for Ageing Research and Development in Ireland makes the following recommendations to address the problem of loneliness among older people:

1. 'Ensuring older people have an adequate income to support their lifestyle,
2. Encouraging life-long learning to improve educational levels,
3. Providing access to health and social services, and
4. Encouraging greater flexibility in employment policies to allow those who wish to work longer to remain in the labour force'. (2013:5)

Table 9:8 Old and lonely: proportion of older people who often feel lonely by country (%)

% feeling lonely often	Country
<5	Denmark
5–9	Germany, The Netherlands, UK
10–14	Belgium, France, Ireland, Luxembourg, Spain
15–19	Italy
20 or more	Portugal, Greece (36%)

(Source: adapted from Walker and Maltby 1997, cited in Macionis and Plummer 2003:332)

Poverty and inequalities

Our society values people who work because the [...] wealth of a nation. Despite the fact that many of th[...] work in the past, they lack the purpose attributec [...] to do so. 'In this way elders share a common stat [...] unemployed' (Webb and Tossell 1999:200). Lacl [...] problem faced by many older people. Retirement re [...] that may cause a significant drop in elderly people's standard of living.

According to Tovey and Share (2000:130), 'Poverty in Ireland is found decreasingly among the retired or elderly and increasingly among the unemployed (and consequently families with children). This contrasts with the situation in some other EU countries where they make up a much larger proportion of those in poverty, as do those in work – the "working poor".'

The true extent of poverty among the elderly may be difficult to detect. A report in 2000 by the ESRI, *Monitoring Poverty Trends in Ireland*, presented data that 'shows that between 1997 and 2000 those aged 65 years and over living below the relative income poverty line almost doubled' (cited in Stratton 2004:12). Stratton goes on to highlight that:

- 'Based on the 2000 Living in Ireland Survey, 6.6% of all older people in Ireland are living in consistent poverty.
- In terms of living standards, almost half of the older population live below the poverty line. . . . and older women living alone in rural areas in particular are most at risk of poverty' (2004:13).
- In 2011, elderly people living alone had the lowest average weekly income when compared with those living in other household compositions.
- 'An analysis of the elderly group by age showed that those who were 80 or over had the highest at-risk-of-poverty rates (13.3% in 2009 and 12.5% in 2011), followed by the youngest group of elderly people, those aged between 65 to 69 years'. (CSO 2013:9)

Despite these figures, poverty among the elderly can remain hidden from view. According to Macionis and Plummer, there are a number of reasons for this:

1. Personal pride – many elderly people may conceal their financial problems even from their own families in the desire to maintain the dignity of independent living.
2. Admitting to having financial difficulties may be admitting that they can no longer provide for themselves (2002:334).

the elderly

buse or 'granny battering' has recently been identified as a problem researchers, although the extent of the problem is difficult to estimate because, like violence against women and children, many victims are reluctant to talk about it. But it is an area that requires considerable attention because 'as the proportion of elderly people rises so does the incidence of abuse' (Holmstrom 1994 cited in Macionis and Plummer 2002:333). According to a report on the National Study of Elder Abuse and Neglect, incidents of elder abuse have increased since 2009. 'In 2011, there were 2,302 cases of elder abuse reported to the HSE, a rise of 9 per cent on the previous year' (Barry 2013). Abuse of older people takes many forms from passive neglect to active torment – which includes verbal, emotional, financial and physical harm (Macionis and Plummer 2002:333).

Recent evidence highlighted in the media over the last years has brought the public's attention to the need to protect our old. While abuse of the elderly may seem unreal, we have to look at how certain arrangements in society can contribute to it. Often the cause lies in the stress of caring – financially and emotionally – for ageing parents. 'Today's middle-aged adults represent a "sandwich generation" who may well spend as much time caring for their ageing parents as for their own children' (Macionis and Plummer 2002:333). Naughton *et al.* (2010) have identified a number of risk factors for elder abuse – being female, of advanced age and lower socio-economic status may be factors, and 'physical impairment and dependence on others for assistance with activities of daily living are the most consistently identified factors, followed by older people co-habiting with family and being socially isolated' (2010:1).

Ageism and discrimination

'Ageism is a set of beliefs originating in the biological variation between people and relating to the ageing process' (Bytheway 1995 cited in O'Loughlin 1999:222).

Ageism is prejudice and discrimination against the elderly. Whether we admit it or not, there is a tendency in society to regard 'older people as out of step with the youth-orientated consumer society' (Bilton *et al.* 2002:88).

Ageism distances older people from mainstream culture and generates a fear of the ageing process. It does so by providing stereotypes regarding the competence and need for protection of the elderly. Just like racism or sexism it can be blatant or subtle. It can be manifest in many ways, for example:

1. An older person may be refused a job because of their age. It is often believed that older workers are less competent than younger ones.
2. Elder abuse (highlighted above). Biggs (1999) argues that 'professional staff have the same negative stereotypes of the elderly as those found in the wider culture. They may also give priority to the organisational demands of the institution in which they work rather than to the individual needs of its residents, resulting in ill treatment or neglect' (cited in Bilton *et al.* 2002:88).

'Ageist behaviour includes talking down to older people, according less weight to their opinions, needs and beliefs and taking their health and welfare needs less seriously' (Third Age 2013). Eamon Timmins, spokesperson for Age Action, said, 'the facts that complaints on grounds of age were the second largest category of cases under the Equal Status Act and the third largest when it comes to employment equality, shows the challenges we face if Ireland is to become a truly age-friendly society' (2012).

Activist groups have started to fight against ageism and are seeking to encourage a positive view of old age and older people. 'There is a certain lack of understanding about the status of older people in Irish society. Challenging the power of ageism will require facing the reality that it is a shared experience and seeing ourselves in terms of the broader context of the whole of our lives' (O'Loughlin 1999:235).

Death and dying

'Ireland's death statistics (mortality) now mirror those of other relatively affluent countries . . . In regard to lowering premature mortality (death before 65 years) Ireland trails behind other EU member states' (Quin 1999:28).

Despite the fact that we all die, modern societies try to foster 'eternal youth' by separating life from death. 'Death is physically removed from everyday activities' (Macionis and Plummer 2002:536). In the past people died at home in the presence of family and friends. Today most deaths occur in hospitals, nursing homes or hospices. According to Aries, (1974) 'Even hospitals commonly relegate dying patients to a special part of the building, and hospital morgues are located well out of sight of patients and visitors alike' (cited in Macionis and Plummer 2002:536).

Bereavement

'A most devastating form of stress experienced by individuals is bereavement – a state characterised by loss' (Clarke *et al.* 2000:145). The intensity and experience of grief is unique for everyone, but studies suggest that most people experience a number of stages. According to some researchers bereavement parallels the stages of dying described by Elisabeth Kubler-Ross (1969). The five stages she identified are:

1. anger
2. denial
3. negotiation
4. resignation
5. acceptance
   (cited in Macionis and Plummer 2002:537)

'All experts agree that how family and friends view a death influences the attitudes of the person who is dying. Specifically, acceptance by others of the approaching death helps the dying person do the same. Denial of the impending death may isolate the dying person, who is then unable to share feelings and experiences with others' (Macionis and Plummer 2002:537).

Other areas of concern for the elderly

These include:

- Moving from one's home to residential accommodation. While this can cause feelings of dependence for some older people, Norman (1998) 'suggests that the loss of a home is experienced as a bereavement in terms of its level of disruption to an older person' (cited in Barry and Yuill 2002:114).
- The move of an older person to 'institutional' care can undermine their sense of self and autonomy. Bromley believes that it could do so to 'such an extent that he or she increasingly conforms to societal expectations of senility' (*Ibid.*: 114).
- Increasing mental health problems among the elderly – according to Drury (2005:121) 'Approximately 5 per cent of people over 65 have a dementia and the figure increases to 20 per cent of those aged over 80'. Suicide rates also increase with age. Keogh and Roche (1996) state that in 'almost all countries the highest [suicide] rate is found amongst males aged 75 years and over' (cited in Drury 2005:122).

Care of the elderly

The increase in the population of older people is going to have a significant influence on many aspects of Irish life. Statistics on the elderly show that there is both a need and a demand for health and social care services over the coming decades, in both non-residential and residential institutions for the dependent elderly. 'Traditionally many day services for older people were provided by voluntary organisations, with nuns from religious orders providing much of the expertise. With the decline in the number of religious, these services are increasingly coming under the remit of the Health Service' (Gallagher 2005:289). According to Vincent (2003), population ageing is a highly emotive subject and can lead to an inflated sense of crisis about the growing social "burden" of older people' (cited in Pierce 2006:202). However, organisations such as Age Action and Age and Opportunity work to challenge negative attitudes to ageing while encouraging the participation of older people in all areas of society. Age Action Ireland, in their Positive Ageing Cross-Border Project (2007), presented findings that highlighted the major problems older people face across the Border region. Forums were held in a number of locations and the organisers 'engaged with 150 older people and representatives from older people focused organisations residing and operating in the Border region' (Age Action 2007). One of the key questions they asked was 'What issues do you face as an older person living in the Border region?' The following table presents the responses to that question:

Table 9:9 What issues do you face as an older person living in the border region?

Issue	Explanation
Access to services	• Closure of central services such as banks and post offices • Lack of personal service in larger towns • The distance to travel to access services, even more problematic if you don't drive etc.
Ageism	• Barrier of old age • Perceptions and definition
Carers	• Carers are penalised • Need to be better funded
Equitable benefits	• Free units of electricity in Republic of Ireland • Free telephone line rental costs in Republic of Ireland • Living Alone Allowance in Republic of Ireland • Fuel allowance in Northern Ireland

Health services	• Border areas need an Accident & Emergency Department and a doctor on call • There are no choices with regard to health services when you live in the border region • The downgrading of the local hospital (Monaghan)
Isolation	• Due to living on your own • Rural and urban • Men and women • Relatives living in other countries and further apart
Personal and home security	• In the home and personally when 'out and about' • The closure of Garda stations in rural areas • The increasing rate of burglaries aimed at older people • Media scare-mongering • The need for more Neighbourhood Watch Schemes • The cost of fitting alarm systems • Getting work done by 'cowboy builders'
Premises for community groups	• Premises are needed for activities but this can attract large costs and a need for volunteers
Roaming charges	• Roaming charges are very costly, and people are being penalised for living in the border region • Phone companies not very helpful when contacted and asked about charges
Transport	• The lack of transport • Hard to get funding for transport • Routes are too specific • The difficulties in getting a driver • Insurance can be very costly for smaller groups
Volunteers and new members	• Enticing new (sometimes younger) members to groups • Attracting volunteers – people don't seem to have the time, it's always the same people doing all the work.

(Source: *Ibid.* 2007)

The problems and challenges older people face today – ageism, abuse, poverty – should give us a sense of real concern. Failure to identify and confront these problems means they will become ours one day.

10

Race and Ethnicity

CHAPTER OBJECTIVES

After reading this chapter you should be able to:

- define race and ethnicity
- define prejudice
- define discrimination
- discuss immigration and social change in Ireland
- discuss racism and ethnic relations in Ireland – a case in point: Travellers.

RACE AND ETHNICITY DEFINED

Race

'The idea of "race" as type is based upon a belief that all humans do not share a common origin and that humanity is divided into distinctive groups. It is therefore a polygenetic theory, that is a theory that humanity has several origins rather than one' (Haralambos and Holborn 2004:154). According to Macionis and Plummer, 'race usually refers to a category of people sharing biologically transmitted traits'.

The word 'race' came into the English language at the beginning of the sixteenth century. When it was used at that time it was simply to refer to groups of people connected by common origin. It was used loosely to refer to likeness or similarities of people of shared descent (Mann 1983). The concept of race took on a whole new meaning in the eighteenth and nineteenth centuries. During this period the scientific theories of 'race' arose and it took on a different, more dangerous meaning. 'Peoples of the world – within and beyond Europe – were being classified and ranked into superior and inferior races with allegedly inherent capacities and characteristics'

(Bilton *et al.* 2002:162). This new approach to race and the beliefs about the different capacities of distinct races offered an explanation and justification for the ruling powers such as England and other European countries to exercise control over colonies and their people.

Samuel James Morton, a Philadelphian doctor, based his arguments on the measurement of skulls. In 1839 Morton distinguished five races:

1. 'Caucasian (from Europe, India and parts of North Africa and the middle East)
2. Mongolian (Chinese and Eskimos)
3. Malay (from Malaysia and the Polynesian Islands)
4. American (native Americans from North and South America)
5. Ethiopian (from sub-Saharan Africa)'. (Haralambos and Holborn 2004:155)

Morton equated cranial capacity with the size of the brain, and the size of the brain with intellectual development. 'From his measurements Morton claimed that "Caucasians" had the largest cranial capacity and Ethiopians the smallest. He believed therefore that Europeans were more advanced than sub-Saharan Africans' (*Ibid.*: 155).

Joseph Arthur de Gobineau (1816–82), who is sometimes called the father of modern racism, proposed the existence of three races:

1. White (Caucasian)
2. Black (Negroid)
3. Yellow (Mongoloid)

According to Giddens (2001:245), Gobineau believed that 'the white race possesses superior intelligence, morality and will-power; it is these inherited qualities that underlie the spread of Western influence across the world. The blacks, by contrast, are least capable, marked by an animal nature, a lack of morality and emotional instability'.

Scientific ideas about racial difference continued to have a significant impact in the twentieth century. They influenced Hitler and the Nazi party, the Ku Klux Klan in the US and the architects of Apartheid in South Africa, and have cost the lives of millions of people.

Superficial differences between people do exist. We do have different skin colour, facial features, hair texture etc. These superficial differences 'are nothing more than indicators of how the human race has adapted to its various climatic surroundings during the evolutionary process' (Webb and Tossell 1999:82). Since the end of World War II 'race science' has been thoroughly discredited. Scientists today are continuing to challenge the links between biology and behaviour that had underpinned earlier beliefs. According to Donohoe and Gaynor (1999:100), 'in the biological/ physiological sense it is not possible to divide human groups according to race'. The results of an international study, the Human Genome Project, were published in 2001. They indicated 'that every person on earth shares 99.99 per cent of their genetic code with all other people. There is no separate Jewish race or Irish race. There is no evidence of racial differences in intelligence that could not equally be accounted for by environmental factors' (O'Donnell 2002:249). We are all members of a single biological species; we are all members of the human race.

Migration and inter-marriage over the course of human history means that people the world over display a bewildering array of racial traits. 'No society lacks genetic mixture, and increasing contact among the world's people will ensure that racial blending will accelerate in the future' (Macionis and Plummer 2002:259).

However, the term 'race' remains a powerful social concept which is widely understood and used. For Bilton *et al.* (2002:164) 'Race remains a potent basis for identity – our sense of sameness and difference'. In social life, nineteenth-century ideas about racial characters are still used by members of powerful groups to set at a distance members of weaker groups. According to Bilton *et al.* some social scientists wish to focus on ethnic differences as opposed to racial differences. To forget or ignore the concept of race would be in a way like ignoring the millions who have suffered or died because of it (and who continue to do so). To avoid this, some scholars therefore 'choose to us the word "race" in inverted commas to reflect its misleading, but commonplace usage' (Giddens 2001:246).

Ethnicity

'Ethnic group is used to describe groups of people who share common cultural characteristics, for example language, dress, food, religion, customs, beliefs and traditions' (Donohoe and Gaynor 1999:101).

'Ethnicity is used in ethnic relations literature to refer to a sense of cultural awareness and identity within groups that share a common history or heritage' (Marsh 2000:391).

According to Mann (1983:114), the first recorded use of the word 'ethnicity' dates from 1953. The word itself derives from the Greek word 'ethnos', meaning 'a people'. Ethnicity is sometimes confused with race, but while the two can sometimes go hand in hand, it is important to make a distinction between them. Race has a firm sense of biological difference while ethnicity relies on cultural heritage (Macionis and Plummer 2002).

To qualify as an ethnic group, a group must fulfil the following objective scientific criteria:

1. they must be biologically self-perpetuating
2. they must be racially different
3. they must share fundamental cultural values and cultural difference
4. they must be socially separated from other groups
5. language barriers must be present
6. they must be self-ascribed and externally ascribed
7. they must show signs of organised and spontaneous enmity (Ní Shuinear 1996:55–9).

'Members of ethnic groups see themselves as culturally distinct from other groups in a society, and are seen by those other groups to be so in return' (Giddens 2001:246). People in ethnic groups see themselves and are seen by others as having a distinct identity. Their ethnicity is central to the individual and group identity. In Ireland, the Travellers are an ethnic group, as are the different groups of refugees from various countries (Donohoe and Gaynor 1999:101).

PREJUDICE

'Prejudice is defined as hostile or negative attitudes based on ignorance and faulty or incomplete knowledge. It is characterised by a tendency to stereotype, that is a tendency to assign identical characteristics to whole groups regardless of individual variations' (Twitchin *et al.* cited in Rattansi 1992:25).

Prejudice is difficult to define and can take many forms. Weber (cited in MacGréil 1996:18) states that 'Prejudice is acquired through learning, as part of normal socialisation and in developing social identity through group membership.'

The following list highlights some of the key characteristics of prejudice:

1. It is an attitude – a prejudgment.
2. Prejudices can be positive or negative.
3. Prejudices are irrational. They are not based on reasonable, factual evidence. They are usually based on hearsay.
4. Prejudice is based on fear.
5. Prejudices are based on a lack of knowledge.

Gordon Allport, a leading authority on social prejudice, identified the following five progressively severe stages of behaviour that could result if social prejudice was acted out and not corrected:

Stage 1: Antilocution or ridicule

Stage 2: Avoidance or shunning

Stage 3: Discrimination

Stage 4: Physical attack

Stage 5: Extermination or expulsion. (Allport 1954, cited in MacGréil 1996:21)

Whether we acknowledge it or admit it, we all have prejudices. In almost all societies, if not in all, each new generation of people is taught 'appropriate' beliefs regarding other groups. People commonly hold prejudices (negative or positive) about individuals of a particular race, ethnicity, class, sexual orientation and so on. 'Our positive prejudices tend to exaggerate the virtues of people like ourselves, while our negative prejudices condemn those who differ from us' (Macionis and Plummer 2000:261). Prejudice is most often applied by the more powerful in society, by those with authority and influence, to the less powerful. 'Whatever its cause, an ignorance of those to whom it is directed is nearly always present' (Webb and Tossell 1999:16).

DISCRIMINATION

'Discrimination means policies, practices or behaviour which lead to the unfair treatment of individuals or groups because of their identity or their perceived identity' (Donohoe and Gaynor 2003:64).

Discrimination is the expression of prejudice; it is a matter of behaviour, for example denying Travellers access to bars and restaurants etc. When we speak of discrimination we are referring to any action that involves treating categories of people unequally. Common types of discrimination include:

1. age
2. class
3. culture
4. gender
5. health status
6. HIV status
7. marital status
8. cognitive ability
9. mental health

10. offending background
11. physical ability
12. place of origin
13. political beliefs
14. race
15. religion
16. responsibility for dependants
17. sensory ability
18. sexuality. (Clarke *et al.* 2000:19–21)

Discrimination can be subtle or blatant but either way the effect of it on an individual can be serious. Those who experience discrimination can feel rejected and powerless and it could result in a loss of their self-esteem and confidence.

Unfortunately, the problem of discrimination is extensive and results in inequality in access to services and the disqualification of members of one group from opportunities open to others. The most damaging form of discrimination is institutional discrimination 'which refers to bias in attitudes or action inherent in the operation of society's institutions, including schools, hospitals, the police and the workplace' (Macionis and Plummer 2002:267).

An analysis of a society's health and social problems would show a truer picture of the extent of institutional discrimination in operation in our society. As a society we must learn to tackle intolerance, the problem that links all forms of discrimination. 'It is not unusual to be suspicious of those not like us in appearance, beliefs, background and much more. The real challenge in developing anti-discriminatory practice in the caring services is to develop a more tolerant attitude to differences between people' (Clarke *et al.* 2000:19). Fighting intolerance means fighting fear.

IMMIGRATION AND SOCIAL CHANGE IN IRELAND

'Immigration is the primary reason for the increase in the population from 3.9 million in 2002 to 4.2 million as recorded in the 2006 census. The level of inward migration is such that 10 per cent of the population – 400,000 people – are foreign nationals (Lalor *et al.* 2007:310). According to Bacik (2004:183), 'for the first time in our history, Ireland is experiencing more inward than outward migration'. However, since 2008, the patterns of international migration have changed once again, and Ireland is once more a country of net emigration.

An indication of long-term migration is provided by analysing the usually resident population by place of birth. The following table provides such an analysis for 2002 and 2006.

Table 10:1 Population by nationality 2006 and 2011

Nationality	2006	2011
	thousands	
Poland	63,276	122,585
UK	112,548	112,259
Lithuania	24,628	36,683
Nigeria	16,300	17,642
Romania	7,696	17,304
India	8,460	16,986
Philippines	9,548	12,791
Germany	10,289	11,305
USA	12,475	11,305
Czech Republic	5,159	5,451
Brazil	4,388	8,704
Total non-Irish	**419,733**	**544,357**

(Source: CSO 2012)

Ireland had relatively little immigration in the twentieth century. However, this pattern changed dramatically with the Celtic Tiger years of the 1990s. 'Ireland has rapidly become a multi-ethnic society, transforming within the past two decades from a country historically seen as one of emigration to one of notable in-migration' (Feldman 2006:93). Many of the new migrant workers in Ireland were from the more recently acceded EU member states. According to Lalor *et al.* (2007:310), 'In the two years 2004–6, almost 230,000 people from these countries received PPS (Personal Public Service) numbers in Ireland, with more than half of these being received by Polish people.' People from Asia account for 55,628 of our population, while people from Africa account for 42,764 of our population (CSO 2006:69). Recent statistics show that migration from Ireland has certainly increased, for example:

- 'the figure for 2012 represents over 240% increase from the low of 2002, when less than 26,000 migrated.
- The level of migration to Ireland has decreased significantly: in 2010, this figure was at its lowest level since 1994, when around 30,100 people moved to Ireland.
- In the period of 2002–2012, over 860,000 people moved to Ireland, while over 550,000 left Ireland.
- Over 87,000 people migrated from Ireland in 2012'. (Gilmartin 2012:2)

Bacik states that for non-EU citizens 'there are basically only two ways to live and work legally in this country: by taking up a job here in respect of which an Irish employer has obtained a work permit for them, or by claiming asylum' (2004:183). According to Moran (2005, cited in Feldman 2006:94), 'Between the years 1996 and 2004, almost 63,000 applications for asylum were made, the annual numbers of which peaked in 2004 at over 11,000 compared to only 31 in 1991.' An asylum seeker is looking to be recognised as a refugee by the Department of Justice. The process of granting refugee status can take up to two years. 'Once such status is granted, the holder has the same rights and privileges as Irish citizens' (Lalor *et al.* 2007:310). 'Since 1999, more than 8,000 asylum seekers have had their applications for refugee status in Ireland turned down and have been subsequently served with deportation orders' (Bacik 2004:188). Asylum seekers make up a very small proportion of migrant flow. According to Gilmartin, ' while asylum applicants live in Ireland as their application is being processed, a very small percentage – around 10 per cent – are granted asylum or leave to remain in Ireland in the longer term' (2012:9).

Because they are not allowed to work while they are waiting for the outcome of their application for refugee status, asylum seekers encounter a number of problems. Among these include dependence on social welfare benefits and few opportunities to integrate with the local community. As a result they can be seen as 'scroungers', are often attacked or abused and blamed by some for problems they may be experiencing. 'They offer an explanation for the housing crisis, the lack of available jobs, and the continuance of poverty – experiences which many marginalised groups face. Racism helps people to make sense of economic and social changes by making a simple and erroneous casual connection between asylum seekers and social problems' (Loyal and Staunton 2001:42). According to Moran, 'Asylum seekers and refugees, by the nature of forced exile, are more likely to be confronted with greater experiences of personal and social upheaval than economic migrants' (2005:183). As a result, they are more likely than the rest of the population to face mental health difficulties and problems. Fanning *et al.* (2002:5) 'indicate that asylum-seeking families in Ireland under direct provision experience extreme levels of income poverty and extreme deprivation including inadequate diet and inability to purchase sufficient and adequate food' (cited in Kennedy 2004:90).

'Arriving in Ireland as a migrant worker can present many challenges; linguistically and culturally and whatever their reason for being in Ireland, people from different national and ethnic backgrounds are vulnerable to racist abuse' (European Monitoring Centre on Racism and Xenophobia 2006, cited in Lalor *et al.* 2007:310). The National Consultative Committee on Racism and Interculturalism (NCCRI) issue of *Spectrum* in March 2003 noted an increase of 60 per cent in the number of racist attacks reported to them. 'Racist abuse, assaults, harassment and other forms of cultural disrespect were the most common forms of incident, and the NCCRI commented that some of these were of a particularly serious nature' (Bacik 2004:200). A study undertaken by Gallup on behalf of the FRA found that '73% of black African respondents in Ireland believed that discrimination based on ethnicity and immigration status was widespread in the country' (cited in ICI 2011). A 2010 study by the Teachers' Union of Ireland involving 332 second and third level colleges found that '28% were aware of racist incidents that had occurred in their school or college during the previous month' (*Ibid.*:9). Racism in Ireland affects a range of groups who are not black, such as Travellers, asylum seekers, migrant workers and Muslims.

'These changes have posed challenges, given the absence of a well-established policy infrastructure or expertise in Ireland in relation to immigration, race equality and multiculturalism, and the government's slow – and often negative – response' (Feldman 2006:94). The Irish government in May 2004 decided to remove many benefit entitlements from new immigrants and their families for an initial two-year period. However, this changed because 'In February 2006, the government clarified that EU law imposed reciprocal obligations on EU states to recognise the entitlements of citizens from other EU countries resident in their own countries. This meant that the removal of entitlement set out under the 2004 Act could not apply to immigrants from EU countries' (Fanning 2006:91). However, Fanning points out that the criterion of two-year residency eligibility continues to apply to immigrants from non-EU countries (*Ibid.*: 91). The decision of the government to make restrictive changes to the work permit system in June 2009 also had the potential to exacerbate racism towards migrants. 'These changes were intended to make it difficult for migrant workers who had been made redundant to remain and work in Ireland' (MCRI 2010:4). According to CSO, 'there were a total of 544,357 non-Irish nationals living in Ireland in 2011, representing 199 different nations' (2012). Ireland is and will continue to be a racially and culturally diverse society. We need to tackle racism up front, and for Bacik (2004:202), 'Most importantly, there is a need for a coherent immigration policy that facilitates economic migration to Ireland and that emphasises the positive contribution of immigration to Irish economy, society and culture.'

RACISM AND ETHNIC RELATIONS IN IRELAND: A CASE IN POINT – TRAVELLERS

'Racism equals prejudice plus power. In other words, racism is a combination of individual racial prejudice and society's support' (Webb and Tossell 1999:82). The roots of racism are to be found in the past, at a time when it was used to justify the African slave trade and the system of imperialism. Its underlying belief was that one racial category was innately superior or inferior to another and thereby the superior group had right to dominance. 'Although the term race has a long history, the term racism only entered common usage after the Second World War as a way of describing the horrors of the Holocaust' (Bilton *et al.* 2002:178).

Racism remains a widespread and serious social problem. Despite attempts to dispel the notion that inferiority or superiority can be justified by skin colour or physiognomy, racism is still extensive. Scientists now refer to 'new racism' (or cultural racism) which uses the idea of cultural differences to exclude certain groups' (Barker 1981, cited in Giddens 2001:252). New racism implies that discrimination is now experienced by individuals or groups not because of their biological differences but because of their cultural arrangements. Those groups in a society that stand apart from the majority can 'become marginalised or vilified for their refusal to assimilate' (Giddens 2001:252).

'The fact that racism is increasingly exercised on cultural rather than biological grounds has led some scholars to suggest that we live in an age of 'multiple racisms' where discrimination is experienced differently across segments of the population' (Modood and Bethoud 1997).

Racism is more than simply the ideas of a few racist individuals; it is much more deep seated than that. It is embedded in the very structure of our society. Institutional racism is rife, 'the practices and procedures of so many of our organisations are consciously or unconsciously racist in that they operate unfavourably towards and therefore discriminate against people from ethnic minorities' (Webb and Tossell 1999:82). The following example will show how institutions such as the health service, the educational system etc., all promote policies that favour certain groups while discriminating against others.

Travellers and racism in Ireland

'Travellers are widely acknowledged as one of the most marginalised and disadvantaged groups in Irish society. Travellers fare poorly on every indicator used to measure disadvantage: unemployment, poverty, social exclusion, health status, infant mortality, life expectancy, illiteracy, education and training levels, access to credit, accommodation and living conditions. The circumstances of the Irish Travelling people are intolerable. No humane and decent society, once made aware of such circumstances, could permit them to persist' (ESRI 1986, cited in Irish National Co-ordinating Committee for European Year Against Racism 1997).

Travellers are an ethnic minority group who make up approximately 0.6 per cent of the population of Ireland. According to the census (2012:27) 'there are 29,573 Irish Travellers nationally'. Travellers as a group have a long history (dating back to the twelfth century) and an identity marked by a number of common characteristics – an oral tradition, their own language etc. Travellers can be considered an 'ethnic group because they regard themselves and are regarded by others as a distinct community by virtue of the following characteristics:' (Kenny, cited in Centre for Gypsy research 1992:171)

1. They have a long shared history.
2. They have their own values, customs, lifestyles and traditions associated with nomadism.
3. They came from a small number of ancestors . . . one becomes a Traveller not just by choice but by birth.
4. They have their own language called Cant, Gammon or Shelta and are also recognisable by their accents and use of language.
5. They have an oral tradition rich in folklore and also have a distinctive style of singing.
6. The majority adhere to a form of popular religiosity in the Roman Catholic tradition (Centre for Gypsy Research 1992:17). '21,549 Travellers identified themselves as Roman Catholic' (Census 2002, cited in www.nccri.com).

The Traveller Community in Ireland experiences prejudice and social discrimination at all levels of society. Because they are a distinct and unique group, recognised by themselves and others, they face an ongoing struggle for survival. They face much opposition and pressure to conform to sedentary society; resistance to doing so means they experience low social status and exclusion, 'which prevents them from participating as equals in society' (DTEDG 1992:4). The discrimination experienced by the Travelling Community is a result of the widespread hostility and prejudice of the settled people/community towards them and it affects all aspects of their lives.

The following section provides some statistics on the Travelling Community in Ireland and examines the effects of discrimination on Travellers in relation to the following:

1. general lifestyle
2. health
3. accommodation
4. education
5. economy.

Statistics on the Irish Travelling Community

According to the 2011 census, 29,573 Travellers were enumerated. This figure represents a 32 per cent increase on 2006. 'Galway (2,476 persons) was the county with the highest proportion of Travellers in 2011, followed by South Dublin with 2,216 Travellers. In contrast, there were only 152 Travellers enumerated in Waterford city' (CSO 2011:28).

Other statistics provided by the census show that:

- The average age of Irish Travellers was 22.4 compared with 36.1 for the general population.
- Over half of all Travellers (52.2 per cent) were aged under 20.
- 29.1 per cent of Irish Travellers were aged 9 or under in 2011.
- Irish Traveller males of retirement age and above (65+) numbered only 337, accounting for 2.3 per cent of the total male population.

General discrimination

'Research into the living circumstances of Irish Travellers shows that they are: a uniquely disadvantaged group, impoverished, under-educated, often despised and ostracised, they live on the margins of Irish society' (ESRI 1986, cited in MacLaughlin 1995:27). Although Travellers experience prejudice and discrimination in Irish society, there is an unwillingness among the Irish public to acknowledge this behaviour as racist. Two key reasons have been identified for this:

1. People still equate racism with skin colour. It is frequently said 'that Travellers cannot experience racism because they are white, are not a different "race" nor a different nationality' (National Co-ordinating Committee for European Year Against Racism 1997:6).
2. There is also a tendency for Irish people to deny that racism exists in our country and in themselves.

According to the Committee (1997:6) Ireland is not unique in this context; it goes on to say that 'the forms of prejudice and discrimination experienced by the Travelling Community equate with racism in the international context'. The ethnic status of the Travelling Community has been contested by the majority settled community. Travellers and their way of life are seen as the problem. According to Noonan, 'Those who do not accept Travellers as an ethnic group have usually inverted this relationship and have viewed Travellers from a pathological perspective which blames them as "deviants", "drop-outs", "failed settled people" or a culture of poverty' (1996:170). Crowley (1999:244) believes that such definitions of Travellers deny them as a people with their own history, culture etc., and instead see them as a people in need of rehabilitation and assimilation. Such beliefs need to be examined and analysed against a tradition which:

1. 'prioritised sedentarism over nomadism, and
2. legitimised the social and cultural values of settled communities and property-owners while undermining the position of the propertyless' (MacLaughlin 1995:27).

Travellers are often viewed as scroungers and thieves, while the use of terms like 'knackers' and 'itinerants' debase Travellers to the level of a racial minority. The level of racism (individual and institutional) and the degree of anti-Traveller exclusion is very high. A survey carried out by the Irish Traveller Movement in 1994 provided the following results:

1. Eight out of ten Travellers were refused in a pub.
2. Five out of ten Travellers were asked to leave a shop.
3. Three out of ten Travellers were asked to leave a hairdressers.
4. Two out of ten Travellers were asked to leave a laundry.
   (McDonagh, cited in The Parish of the Travelling Community 2000:115).

MacGréil (1996:341) in his study *Prejudice in Ireland Revisited* refers to the Travelling peoples as 'Ireland's Apartheid'. In this study (1988–9) he tried to gauge how close settled people were willing to get with the Travelling Community. He then compared the results of this study with the results of a similar one carried out in 1972–3. 'The findings were surprisingly negative and show a substantial deterioration in the Dublin sample since 1972–3':

- Only one in seven of the national sample would welcome a Traveller into the family through marriage.
- Fifty-nine per cent (three out of five) would not welcome Travellers as next-door neighbours.
- One in ten would deny citizenship to Irish Travellers. (MacGréil 1996:327)

The following remarks made by a Fianna Fáil councillor at a Waterford County Council meeting (cited in National Co-ordinating Committee for European Year against Racism 1997:9) highlight the extent of the last finding – 'The sooner the shotguns are at the ready and these 'Travelling people are put out of our country the better. They are not our people, they aren't natives.'

On further examination of research findings, MacGréil found that 'way of life' was the dominant reason for not welcoming Travellers into the family (77 per cent). One-fifth of the respondents gave 'not socially acceptable' as their main reason. MacGréil concluded that 'the Irish people's prejudice against the Travellers is one of caste-like apartheid' (1996:341). A more recent report carried out by the ESRI between November 2007 and March 2008 monitored the changes in public attitudes to the Traveller community over a period of 35 years. Findings presented showed that:

- '73 per cent of respondents agree that Travellers "should be facilitated to live their own way of life decently".
- 39.6 per cent would welcome a member of the Traveller community into the family through kinship.
- 18.2 per cent would deny Travellers citizenship (8.9 per cent have as "visitors only" and 9.3 would "debar or deport" Travellers).
- 79.4 per cent would be reluctant to buy a house next door to a Traveller'. (MacGréil 2010)

Anti-Traveller racism in Ireland is rooted in a belief that the way of life of settled people is the norm. This ideology is at the root of the social, economic and geographical exclusion of Travellers from Irish society. According to Donohoe and Gaynor (2003:79) most of the difficulties and problems experienced by Travellers 'are caused not by ignorance and lack of education on the part of the Traveller, but by ignorance, prejudice, discrimination and lack of education on the part of the settled community'. The following statistics on Traveller health, education and accommodation provide very graphic evidence of the extent of institutional racism towards them in our society.

Traveller health

'Travellers are only now reaching the life expectancy that settled Irish people achieved in the 1940s' (Barry *et al.* 1987, cited in Task Force on the Travelling Community 1995:135).

Statistics on the health status of the Travelling Community in Ireland provide evidence of the harsh reality of the intolerable living conditions of the majority of the Traveller population. The last comprehensive statistical analysis of Traveller health took place in 1987. This study, the Travellers' Health Status Study (Barry *et al.* 1989), found that 'the infant mortality rate for Travellers in 1987 was 18.1 per 1,000 live births compared to the national figure of 7.4' (cited in Crowley 1999:244). An All-Ireland Traveller Health Study, 'Our Geels', was carried out in 2010. This study compared Travellers' health status with that of the settled community. Its findings showed that:

- The gap in the life expectancy of Traveller men, as compared with men generally in the population, has increased from 10 years to 15 years since 1987.
- The suicide rate for Traveller men was seven times that of the rate for men generally.
- Traveller men have four times the mortality rate of the general population.
- Traveller women have three times the mortality rate of the general population.
- The infant mortality rate for Travellers is 3.6 times the rate of the general population.
- In both males and females, deaths due to respiratory conditions and heart disease are higher than expected.
- Traveller children also have higher reported prevalence of hearing, eyesight and speech problems than children in the general population. (Quirke 2012:11–14)

According to the 2008 census, only eight of the Traveller population were aged over eighty-five years. Poor living conditions, social exclusion and racism are the main cause of Travellers' inferior health status. Another contributing factor to the inferior health status of Travellers is the failure of health services to meet and adapt to their specific needs. For Fanning (2002, cited in Tovey and Share 2003:285), 'in particular they [health services] have not adequately responded to Traveller culture and how it may shape perceptions of and responses to ill health and services'.

Traveller accommodation

In 1960 four per cent of Travellers were housed. By 1980 this figure was just under 40 per cent. MacLaughlin's statistics and figures illustrate how dramatically Traveller accommodation changed in the twenty-year period between 1960 to 1980. His figures also show that in 1980:

- a further 15 per cent of Travellers were living on serviced sites.
- almost half of all Traveller families were still living on the roadside and that there were almost 300 Traveller families on the roadside in the Dublin area alone. (1995:27)

'The most recent count of Traveller families provides further evidence of institutional racism. It identified 1,127 families as living on the side of the road without basic facilities and subject to the constant threat of eviction. This figure is out of a total of 4,521 families identified in the count, which took place in 1997' (Crowley 1999:244).

Travellers live in the following types of accommodation:

1. standard housing (in mixed housing schemes)
2. group housing schemes (all Travellers)
3. official halting sites – permanent sites have full services, temporary ones often do not
4. unofficial halting sites (on the roadside). This accounts for about 35 per cent of Traveller accommodation. (Donohoe and Gaynor 2003:78)

Donohoe and Gaynor refer to a survey by the Dublin Accommodation Coalition for Travellers which highlights the appalling living conditions of some of these Travellers:

- Sixteen per cent of Travellers had no water supply.
- Fifty-three per cent of Travellers had no electricity supply.
- Thirty-six per cent of Travellers had no toilet.
- Fifty-three per cent of Travellers had no bath or shower facilities.
- Ten per cent of Travellers had no rubbish collection. (2003:78)

Local authorities were required by the Housing (Traveller Accommodation) Act 1998 to draw up a five-year plan in relation to Traveller accommodation. Failure to address the needs of the Travelling Community, to ignore their ethnicity by enforcing assimilationist policies, encourages anti-Traveller racism and heightens tensions between the Traveller and settled communities. As MacLaughlin (1995:80) states, 'Local authorities often "hide" halting sites away from towns and cities and locate them in isolated areas away from shops, schools and community services. They particularly ignore Traveller preferences for small extended family sites and pay more attention to placating the majority population than addressing the needs of Travellers.'

According to the 2011 census there are now more Travellers in permanent accommodation. A breakdown of the findings shows that:

- 'Of the total 7,765 Irish Traveller households, 4.5% had only one room compared with 1.5% for all private households in the state in 2011.
- Almost 1 in 3 Irish Traveller households living in mobile or temporary accommodation had no sewage facilities in 2011. These dwellings housed over 800 people.
- One in five Irish Travellers in mobile or temporary accommodation had no piped water source in 2011.
- In 2011, more than one in four Irish Traveller households in permanent accommodation were without access to a car'. (2012:37/38)

Table 10.2 Accommodation type of households containing Travellers 2006–11

Accommodation type	2006	2011
Detached house	1,133	1,837
Semi-detached house	1,322	2,448
Terraced house	1,329	1,714
Flat/apartment/bedsit	342	580
Caravan or other mobile accommodation	1,355	920
Not stated	349	266
Total number of households containing Irish Travellers	**5,830**	**7,765**

(Source: CSO 2012:36)

Traveller education

'The formal education system (especially second level) is seen as negative by many Travellers for a number of reasons: feelings of "difference" and discrimination, lack of flexibility towards nomadic lifestyles, the higher levels of family responsibility of Traveller girls and the potential role of the education system in undermining Traveller culture' (Lodge and Lynch 2004:96, cited in Tovey *et al.* 2007:238). The educational status of Travellers provides further evidence of racism. According to the Report of the Special Education Review Committee 1993 (cited in Crowley 1999:245), it was estimated that 'of the 5,000 Traveller children of primary school age, 4,200 were attending'. Donohoe and Gaynor provide the following information in relation to Traveller education:

1. About 90 per cent attend primary school.
2. More than half of these are segregated into special classes or schools.
3. Only 12 per cent continue into secondary school and a mere handful proceed to do the Leaving Cert. (2003:79)
4. Eighty per cent of adult Travellers are unable to read (Dept. of Health and Children 2002:5).

Table 10:3 Distribution of Traveller students in mainstream post-primary schools

School year	First year	Second year	Third year	Trans. year	Fifth year	Sixth year	PLC	Total
2000–01	531	319	183	27	67	38	13	1,178
2001–02	582	397	220	31	86	49	16	1,381
2002–03	650	482	272	26	102	62	14	1,608
2003–04	626	527	341	44	113	63	15	1,729

(Source: Lodge and Lynch 2004:95, cited in Share *et al.* 2007:239)

Recent figures provided by the CSO in relation to Travellers and education show that:

• 'Of the 12,442 Irish Travellers who had completed their full time education, 7,319 provided information on the age at which their education ceased.

- The results show that 4,041 of the~ the age of 15.
- Only 3.1 per cent continued their
- In 2011, 17.7 per cent of Irish T~
- In 2011, the number of Travel~ (2012:32)

Two key reasons identified~ Community in education are:

1. Failure to address their dis~ and
2. Segregation in early childhood services and ~

According to Kenny, 'improvement of the educat~ for Travellers depends on proactive change within schools: if e~ provision from the central policy-makers through to the local classrooms were informed by principles of anti-racism and inter-culturalism, the need for special support for Travellers would be pared back to its true extent, because at least an alien school programme would not be confounding the difficulties confronting Traveller children' (1997, cited in Tovey and Share 2003:223).

Traveller economy

Many Travellers live in poverty and depend on social welfare for survival. Up until the twentieth century Travellers had an economy based on a range of activities such as tin-smithing, seasonal farming and recycling. However, with the increased use of materials such as plastic and machinery for repairs, their skills and occupations became obsolete, and forced many of the population to move to urban areas. Many Travellers today try to remain self-employed by dealing in scrap and recycling but 'because this economy is marginalised, the majority of Travellers live in poverty' (Donohoe and Gaynor 2003:77). According to Irwin (2006), 'Travellers are eight times more likely to be unemployed than settled people' (cited in Lalor et al. 2007:304). 'Furthermore, unemployment among male Travellers is 73 per cent compared with 9.4 per cent for the male population overall' (Bacik 2004:203). 'Unemployment in the Irish Traveller community was 84.3% in 2011, up from 74.9% five years earlier'(CSO 2012:32).

Over the years, the government has made clear and explicit attempts to respond to Travellers' needs. Some of these attempts can be seen in:

Commission on Itinerancy, 1963
e Travelling People Review Body, 1983
the Task Force on the Travelling Community, 1995.

e progress made by these reports, much of the work done to
e plight of the Travelling Community has been carried out by
ch as the Irish Travellers Movement, National Traveller Women's
Pavee Point Travellers Centre etc. MacLaughlin views 'the upsurge
veller awareness groups under a leadership drawn from the Traveller
mmunity itself as [having] done much to redress the devaluation of
raveller culture, both by the settled community and more damagingly, by
Travellers themselves' (1995:82).

The Traveller Community suffers significant disadvantages in comparison to the general population. Travellers in Ireland experience the effects of ethnocentrism – 'the belief that one group of people's way of life is the best way to live and is the way every group should live, even if this way of life has to be forced on another group' (McDonagh, cited in *The Parish of the Travelling Community* 2000:116). A nationwide survey carried out in 2002 examined attitudes to Travellers and minority groups. 'It indicated that 42 per cent of the population held negative attitudes towards Travellers' (BAI 2000, cited in Jackson 2005:263). Jackson also cites another public-attitudes survey published by the government's Know Racism campaign in February 2004. The findings showed that:

- '72 per cent of respondents agreed that the settled community did not want members of the Traveller Community living amongst them.
- 48 per cent disagree that Travellers make a positive contribution to Irish society'. (Brown 2004, cited in Jackson 2005:263)

The situation of the Travelling Community reflects our ethnocentric and racist nature. 'Despite widespread and profound ignorance of Traveller culture, most government and local authority departments have presumed to know what is best for Travellers' (Noonan 1996:173). We need to confront this ignorance and begin to acknowledge and appreciate the many varied and wonderful cultures around us. Easier said than done, but maybe the following challenge offered to us by Crowley will make us sit up and think: 'I would like to pose racism as a challenge to white people and settled people – both groups of which I am a member. White people and settled people benefit from a racist society – we are affirmed, we are resourced. As such we cannot be neutral – we can only be racist or anti-racist' (Crowley 1999:87).

11

Sociology of Health

CHAPTER OBJECTIVES

After reading this chapter you should be able to:

- define health
- discuss the contribution of sociology to health studies
- outline the social causes of illness
- provide a sociological analysis of health and illness
- understand what is meant by sociology of the body
- discuss the relationship between health and gender
- explain the social aspects of health – social class, ethnicity
- describe the incidence of suicide in Ireland.

HEALTH DEFINED

In its 1946 Constitution, the World Health Organisation defined health as a 'state of complete physical, mental and social well-being' (Tovey and Share 2000:234). This definition of health sees it in a holistic way, and because of this problems arise. Tovey and Share suggest that few of us, if asked, could claim such an ideal and cite research by MacFarlane (1997) that reveals that up to '95 per cent of the population experiences some sort of ill health in any two-week period.'

'Health status' is the term used to describe the present state of illness or wellness in a community. Doorley (1998:17) describes health status in terms of 'rates of death and illness in a community, the prevalence of good and poor health practices, rates of death and disease (chronic and infectious) and the prevalence of symptoms/conditions of well-being' (cited in Tovey and Share 2003:276).

Tovey and Share in their chapter 'The Body, Health and Illness' highlight that the most common indicators of health status are:

1. life expectancy
2. death rates
3. morbidity rates (rates of certain diseases)
4. patterns of lifestyle
5. self-perceived health. (2003:276)

They believe that a lack of available information on these indicators at a local level has made it difficult to analyse health patterns in Ireland and as a result these have not informed policy-making in a critical way.

THE CONTRIBUTION OF SOCIOLOGY TO HEALTH STUDIES

Sociology examines the social dimensions of health, illness and healthcare; 'it seeks an understanding of individuals and their health by reference to the society in which they live' (Hyde *et al.* 2004:6). According to Daykin, the sociology of health and illness is concerned with the following key questions:

- 'What accounts for socio-economic inequalities in health and illness?
- How do social structures, institutions and processes affect the health of individuals?
- What are the characteristics of health care work?
- What is the nature of the doctor-patient relationship?
- How do lay people make sense of health and illness?
- What impact do health care services have on individuals and society?' (2001:102–3)

'Sociology allows us to investigate patterns of health and illness. This embraces the branch of social research known as epidemiology' (Tovey *et al.* 2007:282). Hyde *et al.* argue that sociology can increase health professionals' understanding of:

- 'the nature of health and illness (the social causes and social distribution of mortality and morbidity)
- experiences of health and illness
- the social context of healthcare' (2004:7).

According to Tovey *et al.* (2007:282), 'The sociology of health and illness has also contributed a great deal to our understanding of the medical industries and the medical professionals and other workers that operate within them.'

SOCIAL CAUSES OF ILLNESS

According to Bilton *et al.* (2002:358), 'the sociology of health and illness is concerned with the social origins and influences on disease rather than with exploring its organic manifestation in individual bodies'. Macionis and Plummer (2002:514) regard 'Health as much a social as a biological issue' and believe that it can tell us a lot about how a society works. Sociologists believe that you cannot ignore the important role of social and environmental influences on patterns of health and illness. 'The improvements in overall public health over the past century cannot conceal the fact that health and illness are not distributed evenly throughout the population' (Giddens 2001:144). Societies that tend to show large variations in levels of sickness and early deaths are likely to be organised very differently from those where people live longer and experience less illness (Macionis and Plummer 2002:514). Macionis and Plummer (2002) believe that the characteristics of the surrounding society shape the health of its population. For them, the key aspects of health include the following:

1. **People judge their health relative to others:** 'As standards of health vary from society to society, health is sometimes a matter of having the same diseases as one's neighbours' (2003:514).
2. **People often equate 'health' with morality:** Conformity to cultural norms is often encouraged by ideas about good health. According to Morgan *et al.* (1983, cited in Bilton 2002:438), homosexuality was classified as a disease until 1973 when the American Psychiatric Association voted that it no longer be seen as an illness. 'Those who contract a sexually linked disease may be looked upon as morally suspect. Indeed, some countries require potential immigrants to take HIV and Syphilis tests before they are given visas' (Macionis and Plummer 2002:514).
3. **Cultural standards of health change over time:** 'People's perception of health and illness is culturally variable, highly context-specific, dynamic and subject to change' (Bilton *et al.* 2002:358). They give the example of suntan, which many associate with health and good looks, rather than leading to 'wrinkled skin or skin cancer'. The smoking ban in this country since 2004 shows how attitudes to smoking and its dangers have changed over the years.
4. **Health and living standards are interrelated:** High levels of infectious disease are found in poor societies that contend with malnutrition and poor sanitation. In Irish society, Traveller accommodation provision

was criticised for 'Inadequate provision with one-quarter of families living on the side of the road without access to basic facilities' (Crowley 1999:250).

5. **Health relates to social inequality:** Certain groups of people tend to enjoy much better health than others. According to Giddens, 'health inequalities appear to be tied to larger socio-economic patterns' (2001:145).

Balanda and Wilde (2001) reported that 'those in the "lowest" class are fifteen times more likely to die from homicide, six times more likely to die from respiratory disease, and seventeen times more likely to die of alcoholism' (cited in Tovey and Share 2003:284). Activities such as smoking, poor diet and higher consumption of alcohol, which are detrimental to good health, tend to be higher among the lower social classes. This argument sees individuals as bearing primary responsibility for poor health, as many lifestyles are freely made (Giddens 2001:147).

SOCIOLOGICAL ANALYSIS OF HEALTH AND ILLNESS

Structural functionalism perspective

From the functionalist viewpoint, 'a basic function of medicine is to keep people healthy so that they can serve the society. Another function of medicine, of course, is to treat and cure sickness' (Curry *et al.* 2005:416). One of the dominant functionalist theorists of the mid-twentieth century was Talcott Parsons (1902:79). He saw medicine as a social system's way of keeping its members healthy. 'From this point of view, illness is dysfunctional, undermining the performance of social roles and thus impeding the operation of society' (Macionis and Plummer 2005:555).

Parsons used the concept of the 'sick role' in relation to the study of health and illness. 'The concept is used to analyse sickness as a social role, not merely as a biological entity and physical experience' (Barry and Yuill 2002:11). The sick-role mechanism is one way in which society regulates sickness in order to minimise its disruptive effect. According to Scambler (1997:171), 'Parsons defined illness as a form of deviance on the grounds that it disrupts the social system by inhibiting people's performance of their customary or normal social roles.' To minimise this disruption the sick role 'provides an exemption from normal role obligations but is conditional on the sick person seeking appropriate, that is medical, help. The sick role therefore legitimised social deviance – behaviour that violates social norms, but is linked to a medical solution or cure' (Cleary and Treacy 1997:3).

The sick role, which people ideally enter when they become ill, confers on them both rights and obligations. The rights are:

- 'An exemption from responsibilities such as work and social obligations, which needs to be legitimised by a physician in order to be valid, and
- that the sick individuals avoid any blame or responsibility for their condition' (Daykin 2001:115).

Sick people are at the same time obligated

- to want to get well as soon as possible and
- to consult and co-operate with medical experts whenever the severity of their condition warrants it.

'Failure to meet either or both of these obligations may lead to the charge that people are responsible for the continuation of their illness, and ultimately to sanctions, including the withdrawal of the rights of the sick role' (Scambler 1997:172).

Parsons' work has not gone without criticism, for example:

- According to Myers and Grasmick (1989) 'Parsons' notion of the sick role illuminates how society accommodates illness, as well as some non-illness solutions, such as pregnancy' (cited in Macionis and Plummer 2005:555).
- In this scheme the doctor operates as the 'gatekeeper', regulating access to the sick role. Hyde *et al.* (2004:23) see 'Parsons' benign view of the health professions as altruistic and impartial service-providers has of course been contested.' Parsons, in his work, overlooked the conflict that could occur between the patient and the practitioner and 'he misguidedly assumed that the practitioner would always act in the best interests of the patient' (Barry and Yuill 2002:11).

Marxist and political economy perspective

The ideas of this approach are based on the thinking of Karl Marx (1818–83). 'Marx advanced a theory that held that whilst individuals have choices, these choices are limited by the society in which they live – or more correctly by the economy in which they live' (Hyde *et al.* 2004:23).

Political economy writers such as Doyal saw that society was structured around the needs of capitalism as an economic system and drew broadly on this theory and applied it to health in a number of ways:

- Occupational disease, industrial accidents, and the manufacturing and marketing of harmful consumer products are all causes of ill health that can be linked directly back to the processes of industrial capitalism.
- 'This burden of disease is disproportionately felt by those in lower socio-economic groups.
- Society does not do enough to prevent these problems or promote health because society's resources are channelled towards the maintenance of production over and above the social goal of securing and improving public health'. (Daykin 2001:119)

'The central argument of the political economy approach to health is that capitalist economies based on profit-making create ill-health in society' (Hyde *et al.* 2004:24).

The symbolic interactionist perspective

'Symbolic interactionists have become increasingly interested in the patient's subjective experience of illness on a day-to-day basis, and the impact that illness has on the lives of the patients and their caregivers' (Lawton 2003 cited in Curry *et al.* 2005:421).

Interactionists are interested in the social context in which healing takes place and in how it can affect the speed and course of recovery. They also look at the family and friends of patients and find that generally patients who belong to such a network do better than patients who do not.

Social networks provide:

- emotional and material support
- information about treatments, doctors and hospitals.

According to Bloom *et al.* (1991), 'Isolated patients, in contrast, receive little or no help from other people, lack information and may not have the emotional strength to face the disease alone' (cited in Curry *et al.* 2005:421). Interactionist perspectives 'have had a strong influence on research in medical sociology, much of which is focused on interactions between professionals and patients, and the experiences of people with particular conditions' (Daykin 2001:121).

SOCIOLOGY OF THE BODY

'The importance attributed to the body in contemporary culture marks an unprecedented trend in the individualisation of the body, where concern with health and body image is an expression of individual identity, and yet the body has never been so central to political life' (Hyde *et al.* 2004:127). The field known as 'sociology of the body' is relatively new. Sociologists in this area investigate the ways in which our bodies are affected by social influences. 'Our bodies are deeply affected by our social experiences, as well as by the norms and values of the groups to which we belong. It is only recently that sociologists have begun to recognise the profound nature of the interconnections between social life and the body' (Giddens 2001:144).

Interest in the social importance of the body has been 'stimulated by a number of factors' (Nettleson and Watson 1998, cited in Tovey and Share 2003:270). These include:

1. a politicisation of the body
2. demographic change
3. rise in the consumer culture
4. the development of new technologies
5. the development of communications technologies.

Feminists and disabled groups have played a big part in the politicisation of the body. Feminists focus on how women's bodies have been controlled and abused in a range of cultures, for example, analysis of childbirth and eating disorders has highlighted the role of advertising and the medical industry in this control and abuse. 'While the growth in consumerism is associated with new diseases such as anorexia, obesity, heart disease and diabetes, and advertising images are associated with growing bodily angst even amongst children, the cultural significance of the cultivation of a well-toned, fit and muscular body is that it conveys a modern value system of consumer choice, personal autonomy and self-mastery' (Hyde *et al.* 2004:126). Disabled groups on the other hand focus on how society discriminates against those who do not fit in with the dominant view of the 'normal' body.

People are now living longer and this has led to new issues, such as quality of life in later years. A rise in consumer culture, which is saturated with images of the ideal body, means that people are now spending more on cosmetics, fashion, surgery etc. Adele Clarke (1995:147) estimates that plastic surgery is a '$1.75 billion a year industry in the US, with about 1.5 million people undergoing plastic surgery of some kind!' (cited in Macionis and Plummer 2002:170). The development of new technologies is also having a huge effect on our bodies. Boundaries between humans and new technology are questioned with the development of new surgical techniques such as organ transplants and cosmetic surgery. Finally, digital cameras, the internet etc., have made it difficult to distinguish between the 'virtual' and the 'real'. In an age where a person can continuously retouch their own family photograph album, the physical body may become a touchstone of 'reality and authenticity' (Tovey and Share 2003:271). Overall, people today are increasingly preoccupied with getting their bodies under control. Examples of this can be seen in people's preoccupation with diets, fitness regimes etc. For teenagers, being popular is related to appearance and image. According to Lalor et al. (2007:138), 'Young males evaluate their growing body more in terms of body efficiency and physical ability'. Young women evaluate themselves in terms of physical attractiveness and the reactions of others. 'In comparison to young men, they are more dissatisfied with their bodies, wanting to be thinner (even more so than healthier) and more influenced by the media' (Trew et al. 2006, cited in Lalor et al. 2007:138). Sociologists studying 'the body' attempt to analyse 'how people view, use and feel about their bodies within a range of social settings and structural situations' (Tovey and Share 2003:271).

HEALTH AND GENDER

What is the relationship between health and gender? How does gender impact on health experience? Men and women do have specific conditions related to their genes and biological make-up, for example women experience childbirth and menstruation; testicular cancer is a condition specific to men. According to Marsh, 'the main differences in health experience are related to the social construction of gender: that is, the ideas we, as a society, have about what is expected of men and women' (2000:477).

In Ireland, as in most other countries, health status is clearly patterned by gender. Statistics provided by the Department of Health in 1997 showed that 'while there had been much improvement since the middle of the century, women in Ireland have a lower life expectancy and a higher premature mortality rate than average' (cited in Quin 1999:39). These figures surrounding Irish women's health were looked at in the EU context and also highlighted a plight experienced by Traveller women 'who have a life expectancy of 12 years less than average, reflecting a lifestyle and service that grossly neglects their needs' (Ibid.). According to Hyde et al., 'In developed countries women presently live longer than men. For example, in Ireland the average life expectancy for women born between 1995 and 1997 is 6.5 years longer than that of men (79.5 years and 73 years respectively)' (2004:73). Although women report more illness than men, they live longer; 'women are more likely to visit doctors than men, and more likely to be admitted to hospitals' (Macionis and Plummer 2005:551). Naidoo and Wills (2000:3) argue that women are socialised to be passive, dependent and sick: 'women readily adopt the sick role because it fits with preconceived notions of feminine behaviour. Men by contrast, are encouraged to be aggressive and risk-taking both at work and in their leisure time' (*Ibid.*: 37). Similar to this idea is that suggested by Hyde *et al.*, 'that gender processes operate at the level of data collection, with women more likely to report illness to research interviewers, whilst male stoicism may prevent men from doing likewise' (2004:74).

Research by Balanda and Wilde (2001, cited in Tovey and Share 2003:286) found that the following causes of death are more likely to apply to women in Ireland:

1. meningitis
2. congenital malformation of the nervous system
3. disease of the skin and of the musculo-skeletal system, such as rheumatoid arthritis and osteoarthrosis.

Mahon (1997), also cited in Tovey and Share (2003:286), has found that 'Irish women have rates of certain cancers (colon, breast, larynx and oesophagus) and ischaemic heart disease that are among the highest in the EU'.

According to Balanda and Wilde (2001:12):

- 'Men were more likely to die prematurely than women for most major causes of death.
- Men were more likely to die of homicide/assault (over twice as likely).
- Men were three times as likely to die as a result of transport accidents'. (cited in Hyde *et al.* 2004:73)

Hyde *et al.* (2004:73) go on to cite Busfield (2002) who states 'that men are more likely to suffer behaviour disorders such as violence, drug or alcohol abuse and are more likely to commit suicide'.

Researchers are interested in attempting to answer questions on why women live longer than men. The following factors are considered:

1. Biology: Nathanson (1984) states that 'some researchers have suggested that the extra chromosome carried by women confers some protection, in part making them more resistant to disease in childhood' (cited in Marsh 2000:478). Women generally fare better than men across the life course. 'At each age, the age-specific mortality rate for boys is higher than for girls, although recently death rates have decreased by 29 per cent for males and by 25 per cent for females, narrowing the differential in death rates slightly' (Macionis and Plummer 2005:551).

2. Behaviour: Do men take more risks than women? Are they more likely to take part in dangerous sports or violent activities? Eurostat (1995, cited in Macionis and Plummer 2002:523) reported that violent deaths as a result of suicides and accidents are the single most important cause of death amongst young men between 15 and 24 in the EU (as elsewhere). The suicide rate for males has also increased sharply in Ireland and other western societies. Statistics presented by Balanda and Wilde state that 'Irish males are now nearly four times more likely to end their own lives than females' (2001, cited in Tovey and Share 2003:286). Alcohol-related activities are also higher among men. Marsh suggests that this could be related to the fact that drinking alcohol is a 'more socially acceptable response to stress for men than it is for women' (2000:479). Hyde *et al.* raise concerns about the hidden health risk behaviour of women. Such behaviour, they believe, 'has been a pre-occupation with ideals of thinness, which can manifest in constant and excessive dieting, including eating disorders and cigarette smoking as a means of weight reduction' (2004:76).

When it comes to mental health, gender differences also emerge. According to Rhodes and Goering (1998), 'Women experience certain disorders more commonly than men, especially depression and anxiety-related disorders. Alcoholism, substance misuse and anti-social personality are more common in men' (cited in Kennedy and Hickey 2005:105). Kennedy and Hickey's work presents the following findings:

- More men than women are admitted to psychiatric hospitals.
- 'The gender difference in depression is not seen until after adolescence and decreases again at the menopause'. (Stoppard 2000 cited in Kennedy and Hickey 2005:105)

Across adolescence, a rise occurs in depressive feelings and depressive disorder, especially in young women. Across the 11- to 14-year-old age range, young females showed an increasingly higher rate of depression than males' (Lalor *et al.* 2007:141).

Table 11:1 Irish psychiatric admissions for selected diagnosis, 1997–2000

	Depressive disorders		Personality disorders		Neuroses	
Year	Male	Female	Male	Female	Male	Female
1997	2,772	4,133	670	701	643	875
1998	2,973	4,341	598	727	681	975
1999	3,096	4,221	611	722	623	868
2000	3,148	4,382	549	624	539	851

(Source: Dept. of Health and Children 2003, cited in Kennedy and Hickey 2005:106)

Recent studies on the health differences between men and women continue to show key differences. For example, a report entitled *Equal but Different – A framework for integrating gender equality in Health Service Executive policy, planning and delivery* highlighted that:

- Women are less likely to be diagnosed with coronary heart disease than men.
- Women may be more aware of their health than men and may have better access to their GP than men because of their children.
- Women are more likely to have a medical card and less likely than men to receive treatment in a private hospital or to have health insurance.
- Death rates resulting from suicide, drug-related poisonings, accidents at work, lung cancer and heart disease are higher among men than women.
- The death rate for males in the 15- to 24-year age group was more than three times that of the female rate in 2010.
- Men are also less likely than women to seek health advice, discuss their health problems and to access medical services. (NWCI 2012:17/18)

According to Kennedy and Hickey, 'women's economic power, access to childcare, training, education and employment as well as security and safety are prerequisites for good mental health' (2005:114).

SOCIAL ASPECTS OF HEALTH

Social class

'The association between social class and health status shows that death and disease are socially structured, as opposed to randomly distributed throughout the population, and that they vary in line with the difference in living standards' (Blane 2000:114). Class position has a huge impact on one's health status. One of the important studies to look at health inequalities was the Black Report (1980, updated in 1992 as the *Health Divide*). This study was carried out in the UK and one of its most shocking findings was 'that the child of an unskilled manual worker will die around seven years earlier than a counterpart born to professional parents' (Macionis and Plummer 2002:251). The Black Report suggested four types of explanation of social class differences in health. These are:

1. **Artefact:** The association between social class and health is an artefact of the way these concepts are measured.
2. **Social selection:** Health determines social class through a process of health-related social mobility.
3. **Behavioural/cultural:** Social class determines health through social class differences in health-damaging or health-promoting behaviours.
4. **Materialist:** Social class determines health through social class differences in the material circumstances of life (Blane 2000:115). 'Research has consistently indicated (for example Balanda and Wilde 2001) that in advanced industrial economies like Ireland, the UK, Australia and the US, poor health status is associated with variation in social class' (Tovey and Share 2003:284).

Tovey and Share list health factors (negative factors) associated with poorer and less powerful groups. These include higher levels of:

1. perinatal mortality
2. admission to psychiatric hospitals
3. standardised mortality rates
4. incidences of diseases such as pneumonia, cancer and heart disease
5. deaths from accidents, suicide and homicide. (2003:284)

Doorley (1998:37) provides some examples of how health status in Ireland varies according to socio-economic group:

- 'Perinatal mortality is highest among children of unemployed men, and
- the percentage of children breast-fed (the desirable method from a health perspective) varied in 1991 from 65 per cent among higher professional groups to 10 per cent in the unskilled manual groups'.

SOCIO-ECONOMIC GROUPING AND HEALTH STATUS IN IRELAND

- Unskilled manual men were twice as likely to die prematurely than higher professional men.
- Unskilled manual men were eight times more likely to die from an accidental cause than higher professional men.
- Persons in the unskilled manual category were almost four times as likely to be admitted to hospital for the first time for schizophrenia than those in the higher professional category.
- In the early 1990s women who were unemployed (and in the lowest socio-economic group) were over twice as likely to give birth to low-birth-weight babies as women in the higher professional group.
- Persons within the socio-economic group 'unskilled manual' had worse health than professional groups in all years and for all the conditions which were analysed in this report.

(Source: Barry *et al.* 2001:7, cited in Hyde *et al.* 2004:67)

In a paper on health inequalities presented by the Irish Medical Organisation, statistics showed that:

1. 'Life expectancy at birth is 6.1 years higher for male professionals and 5 years higher for female professionals than their unskilled counterparts.
2. There are higher levels of obesity in adults from poorer social groups.
3. Standardised mortality rates (per 100,000 population) are higher among unskilled workers than professionals and higher among those who live in the most deprived areas compared to those who live in the least deprived'. (IMO 2012:3)

Although there is a trend towards better health the links between health status and socio-economic inequalities have not disappeared; according to Giddens 'some scholars believe that the relative health inequality between the richest and poorest members of society is widening' (2001:145). Research available for the Irish situation is consistent with international findings. 'The findings that poorer people, on average, live shorter lives and are subject to more ill health at an earlier age than their rich counterparts leads to what Nolan (1989:2) describes as a 'double injustice – life is short where quality is poor' (cited in Quin 1999:28).

Ethnicity and health

'There has been little sociological research into the health needs and possible health inequalities that impact on new ethnic groups' (Hyde *et al*. 2004:82, cited in Tovey *et al*. 2007:297).

Hyde *et al*. refer in their work to two studies, one by the Refugee Resettlement Project in 1998 and one by Kennedy and Murphy-Lawless (2003) researching refugees' needs in relation to living standards since arrival in Ireland and in relation to maternity services here (2004:85). The Refugee Resettlement Project surveyed Vietnamese and Bosnian refugees and the findings showed 'that only 17 per cent of Bosnian respondents reported an improvement in living standards since arriving in Ireland, while 40 per cent reported a noticeable fall' (*Ibid*.: 85). Kennedy and Murphy-Lawless' research on the needs of refugees and asylum seekers in relation to maternity services in Ireland found that:

- 'some respondents did not have basic toiletries . . .
- Many did not have cots for their babies, nor access to a bath, and
- Following the baby's birth, these mothers often shared single beds with other children in hostels' (Hyde *et al*. 2004:85).

Some of these inequalities or differences in health status are a result of discrimination and racism. The Travelling Community has been identified as having a particularly poor health status. 'The main cause of Travellers' inferior health status is to be found in poor living conditions, social exclusions and racism' (Tovey and Share 2003:285). Health services in Ireland have failed to address the specific needs of Travellers and this may have shaped their perception of, and responses to, ill health and health services' (Fanning 2002, cited in Tovey and Share 2003:285). Among some of the challenges encountered by ethnic minorities in relation to their health status are:

1. a lack of knowledge of the services available to them
2. lack of entitlement or restricted entitlement to services due to immigration status
3. financial cost of health services
4. poor 'out of hours services' for those in employment
5. late presentation to health services. (CAIRDE 2006:21)

SUICIDE RATES IN IRELAND

'Over 500 people die by suicide in Ireland each year. Fifty per cent of these deaths are under the age of 30 and suicide is now the number one killer of young men in Ireland' (www.irlfunds.org 2004). 'There were 507 suicides registered in Ireland in 2012, or 11 per 100,000 of the population. This compares with 525 suicides registered in 2011, a decrease of 3.5%' (CSO 2013:1).

These suicide trends reflect similar trends in international suicide statistics. According to Deleo *et al.* (2002:185), 'Suicide was the thirteenth leading cause of death worldwide in 2002, when an estimated 815,000 people took their own lives. This represents an annual global mortality rate of about 14.5 per 100,000 population – equivalent to one death every 40 seconds' (cited in Allen 2005:88).

More recent statistics provided by Paul Corcoran of the National Suicide Research Foundation Ireland show that:

1. 'An estimated one million people die by suicide annually worldwide.
2. Annually, 10–20 million people attempt suicide worldwide.
3. It is the 10th leading cause of death worldwide.
4. Suicide is the second leading cause of death in 15- to 34-year-old Europeans' (cited in NSRF 2013).

Table 11:2 Suicide mortality by sex 1970–2011 (Ireland)

Year	Total	Males	Females
1970	52	44	8
1975	148	104	44
1980	216	143	73
1985	276	216	60
1990	334	251	83
2001	519	429	90
2008	506	386	120
2011	525	439	86

(Source: CSO Dept. of Vital Statistics (2004), cited in Allen 2005:90) (NSRF 2013)

Among the reasons proposed to explain these trends are:

1. social changes
2. loss of religious faith
3. loss of community solidarity
4. rise in individualism
5. family breakdown
6. substance abuse
7. the Celtic Tiger affluence
8. unemployment
9. lack of services.
   (www.irlfunds.org 2004)

'Ireland has the 6th lowest rate of death by suicide in the EU' and 'Ireland ranks fourth highest in the EU for deaths by suicide for 5–24 year olds, at 13.9 per 100,000' (NOSP 2012).

According to Rutter and Behrendt (2004) there are risk factors for suicide in young people. They include:

• poor self-concept
• a history of victimisation (bullying and rejection)
• attachment insecurity
• poor coping style, feelings of hopelessness and hostility
• poor social support
• a lack of sense of belonging to a community or group
• loss (of role status, relationships, physical capabilities).
  (cited in Lalor *et al.* 2007:149)

'Suicide in modern Ireland is not someone else's problem, it is everyone's problem. Turning the tide of suicide in Ireland will require leadership, dedication and commitment over time to avoid this tragic legacy being passed on to the next generation' (www.irlfunds.org 2004:5).

An understanding of the sociology of health and continued research on the health inequalities that exist (as a result of social factors such as gender and class) will hopefully reduce differentials between socio-economic groups. The end result may be a health service that benefits all members of its society.

12

Demography and Urbanisation

CHAPTER OBJECTIVES

After reading this chapter you should be able to:

- define demography
- discuss the historical perspectives in relation to population
- describe the population structure in Ireland in terms of:
  - birth and death rates
  - life expectancy
  - infant mortality
  - migration: emigration and immigration
  - demographic changes and their relationships to individuals and society
- define what is meant by urbanisation
- describe the human impact on the environment.

DEMOGRAPHY DEFINED

'Demography is the study of human populations, particularly their size, structure and development' (O'Donnell 2002:215).

Demographers – those who study trends in population – are concerned with measuring the size of populations and explaining their rise and decline. According to Clarke *et al.*, demography, the study of population, consists of two primary aspects: structures and processes:

1. Structures examine how the population is made up, for example how many single-parent families or people over eighty live in an area.
2. Processes examine the rate of change of variables such as births, deaths and migration. (2000:117)

'Demography is customarily treated as a branch of sociology, because the factors influencing the level of births and deaths in a given group or society, as well as migrations of population, are largely social and cultural' (Giddens 2001:603). Population patterns are governed by three factors: births, deaths and migrations. In 1950, the population of the world was 2.5 billion; this increased to 3.76 billion in 1970, to 5.2 billion in 1990. In 1950, the population of Europe was 15.6 per cent of the world's total. This had decreased to 9.5 per cent in 1990 (Courtney 1995:39). In 1950 the annual growth in world population was 28 million per year; this increased to 72 million by 1960. Statistics provided by the United Nations show that there were 5.3 billion people in the world in 1991 and estimate that by the year 2050 this figure will have increased to 10 billion people (Marsh 2000:517). According to Marsh, the biggest increase in population is expected to take place in Africa and Asia; areas of the developing world. 'The developed world commands the majority of the world's income, but its population at 1.2 billion is only 29 per cent of that of the developing world' (2000:517). 'The current world population is 7,181,044,697. It has a daily increase of 215,060' (Geohive 2013).

HISTORICAL PERSPECTIVES: THEORIES OF POPULATION GROWTH

A number of theories have tried to explain the potential impacts of population growth. Two of these are the Malthusian Theory and Demographic Transition Theory.

1. Malthusian Theory: Thomas Malthus (1766–1834), an English clergyman, was the first to carry out a major systematic study of population. In his *Essay on Population* (1798), he claimed a 'law of population' – 'that the human species, when unchecked, goes on doubling itself every 25 years' (O'Donnell 2002:215). His global argument was that population increases in a geometrical progression (1, 2, 4, 8, 16 . . .) while food supply or subsistence increases in an arithmetical progression (1, 2, 3, 4, 5) when conditions are favourable. Malthus believed that positive and preventive checks would slow the tide of population increase. Positive checks such as famine, disease and war slow down population increase due to increasing mortality. Preventive checks bring about decreasing fertility and are achieved by late marriage, sexual abstinence and family planning (Courtney 1995:40). Some used this theory to argue against improving the conditions of the poor, as doing so would only mean that more people would survive and this would speed up the collapse of the population (O'Donnell 2002:215).

2. Demographic Transition Theory: This theory directly opposes the ideas of Malthus. 'Whereas for Malthus increasing prosperity would automatically bring about population increase, the thesis of demographic transition emphasises that economic development, generated by industrialism, actually leads to a new equilibrium of population stability' (Giddens 2001:603). This theory links demographic changes to a society's level of technological development and it attempts to answer questions such as why population increase is higher in poorer countries than in richer countries. It answers these questions 'by analysing birth and death rates at four stages of a society's technological development' (Macionis and Plummer 2002:603). These stages represent societies at different levels of industrialisation and technological development, for example:

Stage 1: Societies at this stage have not yet experienced industrialisation. These societies have high birth rates and high death rates. Birth rates are high because of the absence of effective family planning and because of the economic value of children. Low living standards, lack of medical technology etc. are among the factors that contribute to a high death rate. Population increase at this stage is modest as deaths almost offset births.

Stage 2: This stage sees populations increase. It is characteristic of societies at the start of industrialisation. The advent of technology 'expands food supplies and science combats disease'. Rapid population growth occurs because death rates fall but birth rates remain high. 'Most of the world's least economically developed societies today are still in this high-growth stage' (*Ibid.*: 603).

Stage 3: Societies at this stage are mature industrial economies. Birth rates drop as most children at this stage survive to adulthood and the cost of raising children increases. More and more women are working outside the home and there is widespread availability of contraception making family planning more effective. As birth rates follow death rates downward, population growth slows further.

Stage 4: This stage corresponds to a post-industrial economy. Birth rates continue to fall and population growth is very slow.

This theory has been criticised on the grounds that 'current economic arrangements only ensure continued poverty in much of the world. Unless there is a significant distribution of global resources . . . our planet will become increasingly divided into industrialised "haves", enjoying low population growth, and non-industrialised "have nots", struggling in vain to feed soaring populations' (Macionis and Plummer 2002:603).

Malthus' prediction regarding the collapse of the population has not taken place. He underestimated the advances in industry, technology and communications that have occurred. 'Since 1950, the growth in world trade, the impact of the so-called "green revolution" in agriculture and the use of technology have prevented the type of global catastrophe predicted by Malthus from occurring' (Marsh 2000:518).

THE POPULATION STRUCTURE IN IRELAND

Demography, from the Greek word meaning description of people, provides statistical information on human populations. The components of population consist of birth and death and the natural movements of people – migrations. According to Quin (1999:29), 'Ireland's demographic profile is changing in the same way as in other countries in the EU'. Information on the demographics of a society is very important if we are to try and understand that society. 'The nature of human society cannot be fully understood without a clear comprehension of the integral role played by population processes in the dynamics of social life' (Courtney 1995:39). The Central Statistics Office (CSO) in Ireland collects, compiles and analyses population statistics. The census of population gathers demographic, social, economic and administrative data at a given time relating to all persons and households in a country (*Ibid.*: 43). The following information provides an overview of the population structure in Ireland and the changes in the demographic patterns that have taken place here.

Birth and death rates

'Birth rate refers to the number of live births per 1,000 of the population in a given year while death or mortality rate is the number of deaths per 1,000 of the population in a given year' (O'Donnell 2002:223). According to figures from the Central Statistics Office in 2012, 'the population of Ireland was 4,588,252 persons compared with 4,239,484 in 2006'. An analysis of the age and sex composition of the population indicates the effect of the peak in the number of births which occurred in 1980, the sharp decline which followed over the next fifteen years and the subsequent partial recovery over the past decade. In 2012, 'there were 2,272,699 males and 2,315,553 females in Ireland' (CSO 2012).

In the 1920s Ireland's fertility rates were unusually high when compared to other European countries. 'Even as late as 1987 Ireland's fertility rate was the highest of any developed country with the exception of the former Soviet Union' (Coleman 1992, cited in Tovey and Share 2003:134). According to Tovey and Share,

- Ireland had the lowest proportion of first births and the highest proportion of births that were the fourth or subsequent child of the same mother.
- Ireland was the most youthful country in the industrialised world in the 1980s with nearly one-third of its population under fifteen. (2003:141)

Between 1980 and 1996 Ireland's birth rate fell by about one-third (Fitzgerald 1999:270). An analysis of population trends by NCB Stockbrokers (2006) 'estimates that of EU countries Ireland will have the highest proportion of under-15s in the population by 2010' (cited in Lalor et al. 2007:334). New figures from the ESRI show that:

- 'Ireland has the highest birth rate of any of the 27 European Union countries.
- Over 74,000 babies were born in Ireland last year, a slight fall at 16 births per 1,000 of population.
- Almost 24% of births in 2011 were to mothers born outside of Ireland'. (2012)

According to the *Statistical Yearbook of Ireland* (2006:57) the death rate continues to fall steadily. Among statistics it provides are those that show that:

- 'There were 27,441 deaths registered in 2005; 13,904 males and 13,537 females.
- The number of deaths in 2005 fell below 28,000 for the first time ever.'

According to Hunter (2011), 'while death rates from many diseases are declining, there are significant issues with the level of chronic disease and obesity in younger people'.

Table 12:1 Average annual births, deaths and natural increase for each intercensal period, 1926–2006

Period	Total births	Total deaths	Natural increase
	thousands		
1926–36	58	42	16
1936–46	60	43	17
1946–51	66	40	26
1951–56	63	36	27
1956–61	61	34	26
1961–66	63	33	29
1966–71	63	33	30
1971–79	69	33	35
1979–81	73	33	40
1981–86	67	33	34
1986–91	56	32	24
1991–96	50	31	18
1996–2002	54	31	23
2002–06	61	28	33
2006–11	73	28	45

(Source: adapted from CSO 2012:8)

There have been changes in the behaviour of Irish people in relation to birth, marriage and family formation. The following trends in fertility have emerged: 'smaller families, later motherhood, more voluntary childlessness, more single-parent families, more "only children" and more children born outside legal marriage' (Tovey and Share 2003:149).

Life expectancy

'The expectation of life is the average number of years a person can expect to live at a given age' (O'Donnell 2002:221). According to the United Nations (2003), 'In Ireland the average life expectancy is 76.7 years compared for example to 33.4 years in Zimbabwe' (cited in Hyde *et al.* 2004:91). People are living longer as a result of long-term falls in mortality, and increase in longevity is associated with developments in biomedicine. 'A baby boy or girl born in 1926 could expect, on the basis of the mortality figures at that time, to live on average to about 57 years' (*Statistical Yearbook of Ireland* 2006:58). It goes on to say 'By contrast, the estimated life expectancy for people born in 2002 is 75.1 years for boys and 80.3 years for girls. Assuming that similar trends continue into the future, male life expectancy in Ireland may be approaching 83 years by the year 2037 and female life expectancy should be about 87 years' (*Ibid.*: 59). 'Life expectancy for Irish males is currently 76.8 years while it is 81.6 years for women'. (Hunter 2011) According to the 2012 census, 'The average age of the population of the state as a whole increased by half a year to 36.1 years since 2006'.

Table 12:2 Population by sex and age groups, 2012

Age group	Males	Females
	thousands	
0–4 years	186.0	178.6
5–9 years	166.1	158.7
10–14 years	156.4	149.0
15–19 years	141.3	134.4
20–24 years	138.6	139.2
25–29 years	163.5	177.7
30–59 years	832.6	970.3
60–69 years	200.6	200.8
70–84 years	141.4	165.8
85 years and over	19.4	41.1
Total	2,269.6	2,315.8

(Adapted from CSO 2012:13)

Infant mortality

'Refers to the number of deaths among infants under one year of age for each thousand live births in a given year' (Macionis and Plummer 2002:594). This is regarded as a good guide to the state of health and health services in a country. There is a decline in the perinatal mortality rate. 'This rate is estimated at 6.1 per 1,000 live births and stillbirths in 2011 compared with 6.8 per 1,000 live births and stillbirths in 2010. This represents a reduction of over 10%' (ESRI 2012).

Migration – emigration and immigration

Migration refers to the movement of people into and out of a particular territory. The eighteenth and early nineteenth centuries saw a huge growth in the population in Ireland but did not have an economic system to sustain it. In 1841 the population of Ireland was a little more than half that in England and Wales which had a population of 15.9 million. 'After the famines of the 1840s Malthus' 'ideal' was achieved when the Irish population overall declined dramatically and continuously until 1926 from 8,177,744 to 4,228,553, by 48 per cent' (Courtney 1995:48). According to research by Geary (1951), Drudy (1995) and Ryan (1990) (cited in Tovey and Share 2003:134-5):

- In the first half of the 1900s, Ireland's population was the only one in the world whose population declined, with its excess of emigration over natural increase.
- More women emigrated than men.
- Between 1600 and 1922 seven million people left Ireland for North America. Four million left in the years from 1846 to 1925 (MacLaughlin 1994, cited in Tovey and Share 2003:145).
- Between 1890 and 1990 it is estimated that over two million Irish people emigrated to Britain.

Courtney estimates that up to a quarter of all Irish-born people live outside the country (1997:26).

'In recent years, Ireland has experienced a phenomenon that has been largely absent for most of its recent history: substantial immigration' (Tovey and Share 2003:155). With immigration rising to record levels, Ireland faces a dramatic change in its population composition as the number of foreign nationals living in the state approaches 400,000, accounting for 8 to 9 per cent of the population of 4.13 million (Humphreys 2005). A study by the CSO of population and migration estimates, covering the period April 2004 to April 2005, showed that:

- one-third of immigrants to Ireland in that year came from the new accession states

- seventeen per cent of immigrants were from Poland (11,900)
- ten per cent of immigrants were from the UK (6,900)
- nine per cent of immigrants were from Lithuania (6,300)
- twelve per cent of immigrants were from other accession states (8,200)
- ten per cent of immigrants were from the rest of the EU15 (7,100)
- two per cent of immigrants were from the USA (1,600)
- thirteen per cent of immigrants were from the rest of the world.

According to the 2006 census, these figures have increased and the following statistics indicate this. Of those present and resident in the state on census night:

- 63,276 were from Poland
- 112,548 were from the UK
- 24,628 were from Lithuania
- 12,475 were from the USA
- 35,326 were from Africa
- 46,952 were from Asia.
  (CSO 2006:73)

A report entitled *This is Ireland* by the Central Statistics Office reported the following key findings:

1. Between 2006 and 2011, there was an increase in the number of residents who were born outside Ireland. It stood at 766,770 persons accounting for 17 per cent of the population.
2. The groups showing the largest increase were those already well established in Ireland. 'The fastest growing groups were Romanians (up 110%), Indians (up 91%), Polish (up 83%), Lithuanian (up 40%) and Latvians (up 40%)' (2012).

Historically, population patterns in Ireland have been affected by factors including emigration, low levels of urbanisation, low incomes, the dominance of rural livelihoods and private property relations and the influence of the Roman Catholic Church (Tovey and Share 2003:143). Modernisation of Irish society has resulted in population patterns that resemble the majority of western countries. According to Tovey and Share, 'now the patterns may be affected by trends such as higher educational levels, increasing costs of raising children for longer periods of time and the widespread entry of married women into the workforce' (2003:143).

Table 12:3 Breakdown of distinctive demographic trends, 1926–2006

Years	Demographic trend
1926–51	The population was stable at just under 3 million as a result of the moderate natural increase being counterbalanced by net outward migration.
1951–61	High net outward migration flows were responsible for the population falling to its lowest level of 2.8 million in 1961.
1961–71	The natural increase exceeded declining net outward migration leading to an increase in population during 1961–6 – the first significant intercensal population increase.
1971–79	A reversal in net migration from outward to inward alongside an increase in births led to an average annual population growth rate of 1.5 per cent over the period.
1979–86	Net outward migration resumed, though not on a scale sufficient to offset the natural increase in population.
1986–91	A declining natural increase coupled with high net outward migration led to a small fall in population.
1991–2006	Both natural increase and significant net inward migration have culminated in record population growth for the most recent intercensal period.

(CSO 2006:12)

More recent changes in the Irish demographic profile show two key factors:

1. A reduced but still significant net immigration in the years 2007 to 2009, the fall largely as a result of the decreased flows of people from new EU member states.
2. Increased emigration from Ireland.

Key findings from a 2013 report entitled *Generation Emigration* provided the following statistics:

- 89,000 people left Ireland in the year up to April 2013, this was up 2.2 per cent on the previous 12 months.
- 21,900 moved to the UK last year, making it the most popular destination for people of all nationalities leaving Ireland. This was almost three times the 2008 figure.

- Australia remains the second most popular destination.
- The number of people in the age category 25–44 emigrating increased rapidly. It rose from 31,300 in 2011 to 41,000 last year (cited in *The Irish Times* 2013).

Demographic changes and their relationships to individuals and society

'The decreasing percentage of children in Irish society and the increasing number of older people are reshaping the demographic profile of Irish society' (Rush 2006:61).

'The impact of changing demography is of significance for the provision and development of different areas of Irish Social Policy in the coming decades' (Quin 1999:4). Changes in demography can put pressure on existing services within society. Population structures can affect health and social care priorities, education, welfare and housing. Estimates of current and future population structures form the basis of planning in these areas. Statistical information from census returns, surveys and the registration of births, deaths and marriages allows the demographic scientist to identify trends and make projections (Clarke *et al.* 2000:17). For example:

- If a society is experiencing rapid growth we can generally expect the birth rate to be high and the number of young people in the population to be large. Society will need to accommodate these young people and direct its resources towards schools, teachers and childcare.
- 'The old population has increased at every census since 1961. People are living longer as can be seen in the changes in the population aged over 65 which increased by 14.4 per cent since 2006' (CSO 2012). An increase in the numbers of this age group is very likely to place increasing demands on health and personal social services. Society will have to devote more resources to health problems, retirement funds and elder care. 'One estimate is that the number of people aged over 65 will more than treble from the current level . . . to 1.5 million in 50 years' time. This will mean a significantly increased dependency ratio (the ratio between the economically active and their younger and older dependents)' (Lalor *et al.* 2007:334).
- According to CSO (2006:16), 'It is the change in the number of persons of working age which has been the main determinant of the shape of the dependency ratio graph. This population sub-group, which has grown from 1.63 million in 1961 to 2.9 million in 2006, has insured that the

dependency ratios have continued to decline during that period.' At present there are more than four workers contributing to the support of every pensioner. This will fall to 2.7 in 2026 and less than 1.5 workers per pensioner in fifty years' time' (O'Brien 2006, cited in Lalor *et al.* 2007:334).

URBANISATION DEFINED

'Urbanisation – the process of living in and depending upon towns' (O'Donnell 2002:230).

According to the Population Reference Bureau (2003), 'Today, about 47 per cent of the world's population is urban, but this figure obscures the difference between industrial and traditional societies (cited in Curry *et al.* 2005:446).

Population increase and industrialisation have been linked to a growth of urban areas of unprecedented size. In 1975 39 per cent of the world's population lived in urban localities; this figure is predicted to be 63 per cent by 2025 (Giddens 2001:573). He believes that urban populations are growing much faster than the world's overall population. Industrialisation fuelled the growth of cities as people left the countryside and moved to cities in search of work. Urbanisation changed the physical environment and transformed many patterns of social life. According to Ferdinand Tonnies (1855–1936), urbanisation changed the basis and nature of social contacts. He noted a 'shift from *Gemeinschaft* or community characterised by close-knit, personal and stable relationships between friends and neighbours to . . . *Gesellschaft* or association based on transitory, instrumental relationship' (cited in Bilton *et al.* 2002:38).

Different types of cities emerged in the twentieth century. These included:

- megacities – cities with a population over 8 million
- megalopolises – urban areas containing a number of cities and their surrounding areas.

In common with many developed countries, Ireland has moved from having a largely rural population to a predominately urban one. The following statistics from the CSO support this:

- Between 1981 and 1991 the population living in urban areas (i.e. in towns with a population of 1,500 or more) was around 1.9 to 2 million.
- In the ten years to 2006 the urban population has increased by 460,000.

- The number of people in urban areas (towns with a population of 1,500 or more) surpassed 2.8 million for the first time in 2001.
- The population of small towns (population of 3,000 or less) had an increase of 33 per cent since 2006, making it the fastest growing category.
- Dublin had 39 per cent of the urban population in 2011. (2012:14)

O'Donnell (2002:241) lists the following as the advantages and disadvantages of urbanisation:

Advantages of urbanisation

1. greater access to educational and professional opportunities for more people
2. greater choice – more shops, pubs, clubs etc.
3. reduced physical isolation
4. easier communications
5. greater cultural diversity.

Disadvantages of urbanisation

1. social isolation due to lack of close-knit, personal relationships
2. higher levels of crime and violence due to reduced common identity, less certainty of detection
3. more pollution, road congestion
4. less homogenous – differences among people create potential for conflict. (2002:241)

HUMAN IMPACT ON THE ENVIRONMENT

'Population affects the quality of our lives, in large part through affecting our society's ecosystem: an interlocking, stable group of plants and animals – including humans – living in their natural habitat' (Curry et al. 2005:439). Human activity has had a harmful impact on the natural world and a growing population puts stress on the environment. Two areas of major concern are:

1. pollution and waste products that are released into the environment, and
2. depletion of renewable resources' (Giddens 2001:573).

According to Miller (1992), 'The members of all high-income societies represent 20 per cent of humanity, but utilise 80 per cent of all energy' (cited in Macionis and Plummer 2005:665).

A document entitled *Making Ireland's Development Sustainable* (2002) recognised the importance of global warming and saw that a national response to climate change was seen as a priority area (Dept. of the Environment and Local Government 2002, cited in Murphy 2006:108).

In 1990 the marketing, sales and distribution of bituminous coals within the city of Dublin was banned by the Irish government and it was seen as 'one of the most significant actions in Irish environment' (*Ibid*.: 110). The number of cars registered in Ireland had increased and this in turn increased carbon emissions. According to the *Statistical Yearbook of Ireland* (2006:407), 'The total number of registered vehicles has increased by 93 per cent over the period 1990–2004. Related CO_2 emissions had increased by 149 per cent in the same period'. Friends of the Earth (2005) 'claim that the average car in Ireland travelled 24,000 km a year, which is 70 per cent higher than Germany, 50 per cent higher than Britain and 30 per cent higher than the USA' (cited in Murphy 2006:113).

The Environmental Protection Agency regulates matters relating to air, noise and water pollution. A report by the EPA entitled *Environment in Focus 2002* reported 'that in the first six months of 2001, local authorities issued 13,453 on-the-spot fines for littering offences and initiated 1,003 prosecutions. Litter hotspots were identified as bus stops, secondary schools, fast food outlets, construction sites, recycling centres and beaches' (Kilcommins *et al.* 2004:96). Waste management is also an area of concern: according to Withers (2004) 'every year this country produces hundreds of thousands of tonnes of rubbish – 2.3 million tonnes in 2001 – yet we recycle only 13 per cent of it. Like Britain, but unlike just about every other European neighbour, we take a "bin, burn and bury" approach to waste management' (cited in Bacik 2004:215). Bacik believes the introduction of a 15-cent levy on plastic bags in 2002 was the most effective initiative by the government to curb the waste problem. 'Dept. of Environment figures show that the levy raised more than €9 million for the Exchequer during its first four months in operation, and reduced the use of plastic bags by 90 per cent in the same period' (Bacik 2004:218).

The EPA continues to highlight factors which put pressures on our environment. Environmental pressures include changes in land use, increased traffic flows and the need for increased infrastructure such as housing, water supply, sewerage and waste management facilities. Key concerns include the following:

1. There has been an increase in one-person households and it has 'been estimated on average, that they consume 38 per cent more products,

generate 42 per cent more packaging waste and use 55 per cent more electricity per person than four-person households' (EPA 2013:1).

2. Ireland is still heavily reliant on the car for its transport needs. Despite a shift to purchasing cars with smaller engines and lower emissions, three-quarters of all journeys are made by private car.

3. Ireland continues to depend on fossil fuels for its energy source. Renewable energy use has increased but still 'only accounted for just 6 per cent of the primary requirement in 2011'. (*Ibid.*:3)

People need to be educated regarding environmental issues. 'In 1998 the Green Schools initiative was launched. This is an international programme which aims to engender responsible attitudes in primary school children towards environmental protection' (Murphy 2006:117).

According to Giddens:

- Since 1960 consumption of fresh water has doubled.
- The burning of fossil fuels has almost quintupled in the past fifty years.
- In the last twenty-five years the consumption of wood is up by 40 per cent.

Organisations such as Greenpeace aim to raise awareness about environmental issues. People are being educated to conserve the earth's resources, to recycle and to keep pollution to a minimum. 'Population is one of today's most pressing concerns. The relationship between the number of people living on the planet and the resources to support their continued existence and welfare is a complex and dynamic one' (Tovey and Share 2003:134).

In conclusion, knowledge of a society's population structure and the changes that have occurred within it are necessary to identify social needs and to ensure services are developed to meet these needs. Updated demographic information and data 'constitute the basis for strategic economic and social planning and development throughout the public, voluntary and private sectors' (Courtney 1995:84).

Bibliography

Abbott, D. (1998) *Culture and Identity*, Hodder and Stoughton, England.

Age Action Ireland (2007) *Positive Ageing Cross-Border Project*, Age Action Ireland, Monaghan.

Age Action Ireland (2012) *Equality Authority's annual report highlights scale of ageism in Ireland* [Internet]. Available from: <www.ageaction.ie/equality-authority%E2%80%99s-annual-report-highlights-scale-ageism-ireland> [accessed August 2013].

Allen, M. (2005) 'Mental Health and Suicide' in Quin, S. and Redmond, B., eds. *Mental Health and Social Policy in Ireland*, UCD Press, Dublin, pp. 88–103.

An Garda Síochána (2006) *Crime Statistics* [Internet]. Available from: <www.cso.ie/releasepublications/documents/crime_justice/current/gardacrimestats.pdf> [accessed 8 October 2008].

Babbie, E. (1988) *The Sociological Spirit*, Wadsworth Publishing Company, California.

Bacik, I. (2004) *Kicking and Screaming: Dragging Ireland into the 21st century*, O'Brien Press, Dublin.

Bacik, I. (2013) *Women in Politics: The statistics* [Internet]. Available from: <www.ivanabacik.com/women-in-politics/women-in-politics-the-statistics> [accessed August 2013].

Barry, A. M. and Yuill C. (2002) *Understanding Health: A sociological introduction*, Sage Publications, London.

Bell, J. (2005) *Doing Your Research Project: A guide for first time researchers in education, health and social science*, 4th edn, Open University Press, England.

Bilton, T., Bonnett, K. and Jones, P. (2002) *Introductory Sociology*, 4th edn, Palgrave Macmillan, Great Britain.

Blane, D. (2000) 'Inequality and Social Class' in Scambler G., ed. *Sociology as Applied to Medicine*, Harcourt Publishers, UK, pp. 103–20.

Blaxter, L., Hughes, C. and Tight, M. (2001) *How to Research*, 2nd edn, Open University Press, England.

Bloom, D., Boersch-Supan, A., McGee, P. and Seike, A. (2011) *Program on the Global Demography of Aging – working series paper* [Internet]. Available from: <www.hsph.harvard.edu/pgda/WorkingPapers/2011/PGDA_WP-71.pdf> [accessed August 2013].

Bowling, A. (2007) *Research Methods in Health: investigating health and health services*, 2nd edn, Open University Press, UK.

Browne, K. (2005) *An Introduction to Sociology*, 3rd edn, Polity Press, Cambridge.

Cairde, (2006) *Assessing the Health and Related Needs of Minority Ethnic Groups in Dublin's North Inner City* [Internet]. Available from: <www.cairde.ie/wp-content/uploads/2009/08/ASSESS1.pdf>

CARDI (2012) *Focus on Loneliness and Physical Health* [Internet]. Available from: <www.cardi.ie/userfiles/May%20Loneliness.pdf> [accessed August 2013].

Carr, J. (2009) *Changing Irish Norms: The smoking ban, Department of Sociology, University of Limerick* [Internet]. Available from: <www.ul.ie/sociology/socheolas/vol 1/1> [accessed July 2013].

CECDE (2004) *A historical overview of our conceptualisation of childhood in Ireland in the twentieth century* [Internet]. Available from: < www.cecde.ie/english/pdf/conference_papers/Our%20Conceptualisation%20Of%20Childhood%20In%20Ireland.pdf> [accessed July 2013].

Census (2002) available from: <www.cso.ie/statistics/population.htm> [accessed October 2005].

Central Statistics Office (2004) *Women and Men in Ireland* [Internet] Central Statistics Office. Available from: <www.cso.ie/releasepublications/documents/otherreleases/2004/womenandmeninireland2004.pdf> [accessed September 2005].

Central Statistics Office (2006) *Census 2006 Prinicpal Demographic Results*, Stationery Office, Dublin.

Central Statistics Office (2006) *Statistical Yearbook of Ireland 2006*, Stationery Office, Dublin.

Centre for Gypsy Research (1993) *The Education of Gypsy and Traveller Children*, University of Hertfordshire Press, England.

Clancy, P. (1999) 'Education Policy' in Quin, S., Kennedy, P., O'Donnell, A. and Kiely, G., eds. *Contemporary Irish Social Policy*, UCD Press, Dublin, pp. 72–107.

Clarke, L., Sachs, B. and Ford-Sumner, S. (2000) *Health and Social Care*, 3rd edn, Stanley Thornes, UK.

Cleary, A. and Treacy, M. (1997) *The Sociology of Health and Illness in Ireland*, UCD Press, Dublin.

Coakley, A. (2004) 'Poverty and Insecurity' in Fanning, B., Kennedy, P., Kiely, G. and Quin, S., eds. *Theorising Irish Social Policy*, UCD Press, Dublin, pp. 112–27.

Cole, T. (1999) *Wealth, Poverty and Welfare*, Hodder and Stoughton, England.

Community Foundation for Ireland (2013) *Economy: Housing* [Internet]. Available from: <www.foundation.ie/index.php/vitalsigns/cat/housing> [accessed July 2013].

Conneely, S. (2005) 'Legal Issues in Social Care' in Share, P. and McElwee, N., eds. *Applied Social Care: An introduction for Irish students*, Gill and Macmillan, Dublin, pp. 127–44.

Considine, M. and Dukelow, F. (2009) *Irish Social Policy: A critical introduction*, Gill and Macmillan, Dublin.

Cormack, D. (2000) *The Research Process in Nursing*, 4th edn, Blackwell Science Ltd, Oxford.

Cotter, A. (1999) 'The Criminal Justice System in Ireland' in Quin, S., Kennedy, P., O'Donnell, A. and Kiely, G., eds. *Contemporary Irish Social Policy*, UCD Press, Dublin, pp. 286–305.

Courtney, D. (1995) 'Demographic Structure and Change in the Republic of Ireland and Northern Ireland' in Clancy, P., Drudy, S., Lynch, K. and O'Dowd, L., eds. *Irish Society: Sociological Perspectives*, Institute of Public Administration, Dublin, pp. 39–89.

Cox, C. (1987) *Sociology*, Butterworth and Co. Ltd, Nolfolk.

Crowley, N. (1999) 'Travellers and Social Policy' in Quin, S., Kennedy, P., O'Donnell, A. and Kiely, G., eds. *Contemporary Irish Social Policy*, UCD Press, Dublin, pp. 243–62.

CSO (2011) *Preliminary Report* [Internet]. Available from: <www.cso.ie/en/census/census2011reports> [accessed July 2013].

CSO (2011) *Women and Men in Ireland*, Stationery Office, Dublin.

CSO (2012) *Statistical Yearbook of Ireland*, Stationery Office, Dublin.

CSO (2012) *This is Ireland – Highlights from Census 2011*, Part 1, Stationery Office, Dublin.

CSO (2013) *Garda Recorded Crime Statistics 2007–2011*, Stationery Office, Dublin.

Curry, T., Jiobu, R. and Schwirian, K. (2005) *Sociology for the Twenty-First Century*, 4th edn, Pearson/Prentice Hall, New Jersey.

Dawson, C. (2009) *Introduction to Research Methods: A practical guide for anyone undertaking a research project*, How to Books Ltd, UK.

Daykin, N. (2001) 'Sociology' in Naidoo, J. and Wills, J., eds. *Health Studies: An introduction*, Palgrave, New York, p. 102.

Denscombe, M. (2002) *Ground Rules for Good Research: A 10-point guide for social researchers*, Open University Press, England.

Denscombe, M. (2007) *The Good Research Guide for Small Scale Social Research Projects*, 3rd edn, Open University Press, England.

Department of Health and Children (2002) *Traveller Health: A national strategy*, Government Publications Office, Dublin.

Department of Health and Children (2013) *Positive Ageing – Starts Now! The National Positive Ageing Strategy* [Internet]. Available from: <www.dohc.ie>publications/pdf/National_Positive_Ageing_Strategy_English.pdf> [accessed September 2013].

Department of Justice, Equality and Law Reform (2009) *Fear of Crime in Ireland and its Impact on Quality of Life*, Stationery Office, Dublin.

Donohoe, J. and Gaynor, F. (1999) *Education and Care in the Early Years*, Gill and Macmillan, Dublin.

Donohoe, J. and Gaynor, F. (2003) *Education and Care in the Early Years*, 2nd edn, Gill and Macmillan, Dublin.

Doorley, P. (1999) 'Health Status' in McAuliffe, E. and Joyce, L., eds. *A Healthier Future? Managing Healthcare in Ireland*, Institute of Public Administration, Dublin.

Drudy, S. (1995) 'Class Society, Inequality and the Declassed' in Clancy, P., Drudy, S., Lynch, K. and O'Dowd, L., eds. *Irish Society: Sociological Perspectives*, Institute of Public Administration, Dublin, pp. 295–323.

Drury, M. (2005) 'Ageing and Mental Health' in Quin, S. and Redmond, B., eds. *Mental Health and Social Policy in Ireland*, UCD Press, Dublin, pp. 115–29.

DTEDG (1992) *Irish Travellers: New Analysis and New Initiatives*, Pavee Point, Dublin.

EC.europa (2013) *The EU and Irish Women* [Internet]. Available from: <http://ec.europa.eu/ireland/ireland_in_the_eu/impact_of_eu_on_irish_women/index_en.htm> [accessed August 2013].

Edmondson, R. (1997) 'Older People and Life Course Construction in Ireland' in Cleary, A. and Treacy, M., eds. *The Sociology of Health and Illness in Ireland*, UCD Press, Dublin, pp. 156–74.

EPA (2012/13) *Environmental Pressures: Households and consumption* [Internet]. Available from: <www.epa.ie/irelandsenvironment/socio-economic> [accessed September 2013].

ESRI (2012) *Perinatal Statistics Report 2011* [Internet]. Available from: <www.esri.ie>News>events>Pressreleases> [accessed September 2013].

European Commission (2012) *Economic and Financial Affairs* [Internet]. Available from: <http://ec.europa.eu/economy_finance/index_en.htm> [accessed August 2013].

Eurostat (2012) *Marriage and Divorce Statistics* [Internet]. Available from: <http://epp.eurostat.eu.europa.eu/statistics_explained> [accessed August 2013].

Fahey, T. (1995) 'Family and Household in Ireland' in Clancy, P., Drudy, S., Lynch, K. and O'Dowd, L., eds. *Irish Society: Sociological Perspectives*, Institute of Public Administration, Dublin, pp. 205–34.

Fahey, T., Hayes, B. and Sinnott, R. (2005) *Conflict and Consensus: A study of values and attitudes in the Republic of Ireland and Northern Ireland*, Institute of Public Administration, Dublin.

Fanning, B. (2004) 'Locating Irish Social Policy' in Fanning, B., Kennedy, P., Kiely, G. and Quin, S., eds. *Theorising Irish Social Policy*, UCD Press, Dublin, pp. 6–22.

Fanning, B. (2006) 'Immigration, Racism and Social Exclusion' in Fanning, B. and Rush, M., eds. *Care and Social Change in the Irish Welfare Economy*, UCD Press, Dublin, pp. 80–92.

Farrell, C., McAvoy, H., Wilde, J. and Combat Poverty Agency (2008) *Tackling Health Inequalities: An all-Ireland approach to social determinants* [Internet]. Available from: <www.publichealth.ie/files/Tackling%20Health%20inequalities pdf> [accessed July 2013].

Feldman, A. (2006) 'Social Research and Immigration' in Fanning, B. and Rush, M., eds. *Care and Social Change in the Irish Welfare Economy*, UCD Press, Dublin, pp. 93–106.

Fine-Davis, M. (2011) *Attitudes to Family Formation in Ireland – findings from the Nationwide Study* (FSA), Trinity College, Dublin.

Fitzgerald, E. (1999) 'Financing Social Services' in Kiely, G., O'Donnell, A., Kennedy, P. and Quin, S., eds. *Irish Social Policy in Context*, UCD Press, Dublin, pp. 269–92.

Gallagher, C. (2005) 'Social Care Work and the Older Person' in Share, P. and McElwee, N., eds. *Applied Social Care: An introduction for Irish students*, Gill and Macmillan, Dublin, pp. 288–301.

Geohive (2013) *Current World Population 2013* [Internet]. Available from: <www.geohive.com./earth/population_now.aspx> [accessed September 2013].

Giddens, A. (2001) *Sociology*, 4th edn, Polity Press, UK.

Giddens, A. (2009) *Sociology*, 6th edn, Polity Press, UK.

Gilmartin, M. (2012) *The Changing Landscape of Irish Migration 2000–2012*, NUI Maynooth, Kildare.

Gould, N. (2005) 'International Trends in Mental Health Policy' in Quin, S. and Redmond, B., eds. *Mental Health and Social Policy in Ireland*, UCD Press, Dublin, pp. 7–22.

Green, S. (2000) *Research Methods in Health, Social and Early Years Care*, Stanley Thornes, UK.

Hall, D. and Hall, I. (1996) *Practical Social Research*, Macmillan Press, London.

Handy, C. (2009) 'Nomads – Will They Change the Family?' in Bohan, H., ed. *Family Life Today*, Veritas Publications, Dublin, pp. 45–60.

Haralambos, M. and Holborn, M. (2000) *Sociology: Themes and Perspectives*, HarperCollins, London.

Haralambos, M. and Holborn, M. (2004) *Sociology: Themes and Perspectives*, 6th edn, HarperCollins, London.

Harvey, L., MacDonald, M. and Hill, J. (2000) *Theories and Methods*, Hodder and Stoughton, England.

Healy, L. (2009) *Capitalism and the Transforming Family Unit* [Internet]. Available from: <www.3/ul/ie/sociology/socheolas/vol2/1/Lisa%20Healy.pdf> [accessed July 2013].

Hennessey, M. (2013) *Gender discrimination is biggest barrier to work promotions for women* [Internet]. Available from: <www.thejournal.ie/gender-discrimination-promotions-819524-Mar2013> [accessed August 2013].

Hogg, M. and Vaughan, G. (2005) *Social Psychology*, Pearson Education Ltd, England.

Holdaway, S. (1988) *Crime and Deviance*, Macmillan Education, London.

HSE (2013) *Policy on Domestic, Sexual and Gender-Based Violence* [Internet]. Available from: <www.hse.ie/eng/services/Publications/services/Children/HSE%

20Policy%20on%20Domestic,%20Sexual%20and%20Gender%20Based%20 Violence.pdf> [accessed August 2013].

Humphreys, J. (2005) '"Irish Population Growth Europe's Highest" Says Report', *The Irish Times*, 15 September, pp. 1, 3.

Hunter, N. (2011) *Life expectancy increasing* [Internet]. Available from: <www. irishhealth.com/article.htm?id.20179> [accessed September 2013].

Hyde, A., Lohan, M. and McDonnell, O. (2004) *Sociology for Health Professionals in Ireland*, Institute of Public Administration, Dublin.

ICT (2011) *Taking Racism Seriously: Migrants' Experiences of Violence, Harassment and Anti-social Behaviour in the Dublin Area* [Internet]. Available from: <http:// emn.ie/files/p_201211220244102011_TakingRacismSeriously_ICI.pdf> [accessed September 2013].

IMO (2012) *Health Inequalities* [Internet]. Available from: <http://www.imo.ie/ news-media/publications/IMO-BMA-NI-Health-Inequalities-Position-Paper. pdf> [accessed September 2013].

IMO (2012) *Position Paper on Health Inequalities* [Internet]. Available from: <www.imo. ie/policy-international-affair/research-policy/imo-position-papers/imo-position- paper-on-hea/IMOPP-Health-Inequalities-(2)-.pdf> [accessed September 2013].

IPRT (2012) *The Vicious Circle of Social Exclusion and Crime : Ireland's disproportionate punishment of the poor* [Internet]. Available from: <www.iprt.ie/files/position_ paper_final_pdf> [accessed August 2013].

Ireland Funds (2004) *Mental Health: Healing the Hurt* [Internet]. Available from <www.irlfunds.org/ireland/news_17.asp> [accessed on 12 October 2005].

Irish Times (2013) *Generation Emigration* [Internet]. Available from: <www. irishtimes.com/blogs/generationemigration/2013/09/27/major-study-reveals- true-picture-of-irish-emigration> [accessed September 2013].

Jackson, A. (2005) 'Ask the Experts: Travellers in Ireland and issues of social care' in Share, P. and McElwee, N., eds. *Applied Social Care: An Introduction for Irish Students*, Gill and Macmillan, Dublin, pp. 253–70.

Kane, E. (1983) *Doing Your Own Research*, Turoe Press, Dublin.

Kelly, A. (2013) *'Modern-day Slavery'* says report, *The Guardian*, 3rd April [Internet]. Available from: <www.theguardian.com/global-development/20> [accessed July 2013].

Kennedy, F. (1997) 'The Course of the Irish Welfare State' in Ó Muircheartaigh, F., ed. *Ireland in the Coming Times*, Institute of Public Administration, Dublin, pp. 129–55.

Kennedy, P. (2004) 'Women, Autonomy and Bodily Integrity' in Fanning, B., Kennedy, P., Kiely, G. and Quin, S., eds. *Theorising Irish Social Policy*, UCD Press, Dublin, pp. 78–94.

Kennedy, P. and Hickey, E. (2005) 'Women and Mental Health' in Quin, S. and Redmond, B., eds. *Mental Health and Social Policy in Ireland*, UCD Press, Dublin, pp. 104–14.

Kilcommins, S., O'Donnell, I., O'Sullivan, E. and Vaughan, B. (2004) *Crime, Punishment and the Search for Order in Ireland*, Institute of Public Administration, Dublin.

Kirby, P. (2004) 'Globalisation' in Fanning, B., Kennedy, P., Kiely, G. and Quin, S., eds. *Theorising Irish Social Policy*, UCD Press, Dublin, pp. 23–41.

Lalor, K., De Róiste, A. and Devlin, M. (2007) *Young People in Contemporary Ireland*, Gill and Macmillan, Dublin.

Lee, D. and Newby, H. (1986) *The Problem of Sociology*, Hutchinson Education, London.

LMU Learning Centre, 'Quote, Unquote' in *The Harvard Style of Referencing Published Material*, Leeds Metropolitan University.

Loyal, S. and Staunton, C. (2001) 'The Dynamics of Political Economy in Ireland: The case of asylum seekers and the right to work', *Irish Journal of Sociology*, Volume 10, No. 2, pp. 33–56.

Lunn, P., Fahey, T. and Hannan, C. (2009) *Family Figures: Family dynamics and family types in Ireland, 1986–2006*, ESRI [Internet]. Available from: <www.fsa.ie/fileadmin/user_upload/Files/Family_Figures.pdf> [accessed July 2013].

Lynch, K. and Morgan, V. (1995) 'Gender and Education: North and South' in Clancy, P., Drudy, S., Lynch, K. and O'Dowd, L., eds. *Irish Society: Sociological Perspectives*, Institute of Public Administration, Dublin, pp. 529–62.

MacGréil, M. (1996) *Prejudice in Ireland Revisited*, St Patrick's College, Maynooth.

MacGréil, M. and Rhatigan, F. (2009) *The Irish Language and the Irish People* [Internet]. Available from: <www.mayococo.ie/en/Services/OifignaGaeilge/Publications/PDFFile,15645,en.pdf> [accessed July 2013].

Macionis, J. and Plummer, K. (1997) *Sociology, a Global Introduction*, Prentice Hall, Europe.

Macionis, J. and Plummer, K. (2002) *Sociology, a Global Introduction*, 2nd edn, Prentice Hall, Europe.

Macionis, J. and Plummer, K. (2005) *Sociology, a Global Introduction*, 3rd edn, Pearson Education Ltd, Essex.

MacLaughlin, J. (1995) *Travellers and Ireland: Whose Country, Whose History?*, Cork University Press, Cork.

Mann, M. (1983) *Macmillan Student Encyclopaedia of Sociology*, The Macmillan Press, London.

Marsh, I. (2000) *Sociology: Making Sense of Society*, 2nd edn, Prentice Hall, England.

Marsh, I. (2002) *Theory and Practice in Sociology*, Pearson Education, England.

Matthewman, C., West-Newman, L. and Curtis, B. (2007) *Being Sociological*, Palgrave Macmillan, New York.

McCullagh, C. (1999) 'Crime and Punishment', *Studies*, Summer, pp. 126–31.

McIntosh, I. and Punch, S. (2005) *Sociology*, Edinburgh University Press, Edinburgh.

McVeigh, T. (2006) 'Education, Life Chances and Disadvantage' in Fanny, B. and Rush, M., eds. *Care and Social Change in the Irish Welfare Economy*, UCD Press, Dublin, pp. 67–79.

Mirkin, B. and Weinberger, M. (2013) *The Demography of Population Ageing* [Internet]. Available from: <www.un.org/esa/population/publications/bulletin42_43/weinbergermirkin.pdf> [accessed August 2013].

Modood, T. and Bethoud, R. (1997) *Ethnic Minorities in Britain: diversity and disadvantage*, Policy Studies Institute, London.

Moffatt, J. (2008) 'What's in a name? The meaning of the Irish language in contemporary Ireland' in Corcoran, M. and Share, P., eds. *Belongings: shaping identity in modern Ireland*, Institute of Public Administration, Dublin, pp. 103–16.

Moffatt, J. (2011) *Paradigms of Irishness for Young People in Dublin*, NUI Maynooth [Internet]. Available from: <http://eprints.nuim.ie/2578/1/Joseph_Moffatt_Paradigms_of_Irishness_for_Young_People_in_Du.pdf> [accessed July 2013].

Moran, J. (2005) 'Mental Health and Ireland's New Communities' in Quin, S. and Redmond, B., eds. *Mental Health and Social Policy in Ireland*, UCD Press, Dublin, pp. 176–88.

Murphy, K. (2006) 'Sustainable Development, Social Policy and the Environment' in Fanning, B. and Rush, M., eds. *Care and Social Change in the Irish Welfare Economy*, UCD Press, Dublin, pp. 107–22.

Naidoo, J. and Wills, J. (2000) *Health Promotion: Foundations for Practice*, 2nd edn, Balliore Tundall, UK.

National Consultative Committee on Racism and Interculturalism (2005) *Traveller and Roma Community* [Internet]. Available from: <www.nccri.com/cdsu-travellers.html> [accessed 6 September 2005].

Naughton, C., Drennan, J., Treacy, M. P., Lafferty, A., Lyons, F., Phelan, A., Quin, S., O'Loughlin, A. and Delaney, L. (2010) *Abuse and Neglect of Older People in Ireland – Report on the National Study of Elder Abuse and Neglect*, UCD, Dublin.

Ní Shuinear, S. (1996) 'Irish Travellers, Ethnicity and the Origins Question' in McCann, M., Ó Síocháin, S. and Ruane, J., eds. *Irish Travellers: Culture and Ethnicity*, Queen's University, Belfast.

Noonan, P. (1996) 'Policy-making and Travellers in Northern Ireland' in McCann, M., Ó Síocháin, S. and Ruane, J., eds. *Irish Travellers: Culture and Ethnicity*, Queen's University, Belfast.

NSOP (2012) *Annual Report* [Internet]. Available from: <www.nosp.ie> [accessed September 2013].

NSRF (2013) *Statistics* [Internet]. Available from: <http:www. nsrf.ie> [accessed September 2013].

NWCI (2012) *Equal but Different: A framework for integrating gender equality in Health Service Executive policy, planning and service delivery* [Internet]. Available from: <www.nwci.ie/download/pdf/equal_but_different_final_report_.pdf> [accessed August 2013].

NWCI (2013) *Leading the Change for Women's Equality Strategic Plan 2013–2015* [Internet]. Available from: <www.nwci.ie> [accessed August 2013].

O'Donnell, G. (2002) *Mastering Sociology*, 4th edn, Palgrave, New York.

O'Donnell, M. (1992) *A New Introduction to Sociology*, Nelson and Sons, Surrey.

OECD (2012) *Spotlight Report Ireland: Equity and Quality in Education: supporting disadvantaged students and schools* [Internet]. Available from: <www.oecd.org/Ireland/49603587.pdf> [accessed July 2013].

O'Loughlin, A. (1999) 'Social Policy and Older People in Ireland' in Quin, S., Kennedy, P., O'Donnell, A. and Kiely, G., eds. *Contemporary Irish Social Policy*, UCD Press, Dublin, pp. 221–42.

O'Mahony, P. (2000) 'Crime in the Republic of Ireland: A suitable case for social analysis', *Irish Journal of Sociology*, Volume 10, pp. 3–26.

O'Neill, B. and Dinh, T. (2013) *Children and the Internet in Ireland: Research and Policy Perspectives*, Dublin Institute of Technology [Internet]. Available from: <http://arrow.dit.ie/cgi/viewcontent.cgi?article=1032&context=aaschmedcon> [accessed November 2013].

Osborne, R. and van Loon, B. (1999) *Introducing Sociology,* Icon Books, Cambridge.

Parish of the Travelling People (2000) *Travellers: Citizens of Ireland*, Parish of the Travelling People, Dublin.

Pierce, M. (2006) 'Older People and Social Care' in Fanning, B. and Rush, M., eds. *Care and Social Change in the Irish Welfare Economy*, UCD Press, Dublin, pp. 190–205.

Pryke, S. (2002) 'The Nature of Social Theory' in Marsh, I., ed. *Theory and Practice in Sociology*, Pearson Education, England, pp. 73–91.

Quin, S. (1999) 'Improving Health Care: Policy in Ireland' in Quin, S., Kennedy, P., O'Donnell, A. and Kiely, G., eds. *Contemporary Irish Social Policy*, UCD Press, Dublin, pp. 27–48.

Quirke, B. (2012) *Selected Key Findings and Recommendations from the All-Ireland Traveller Health Study – Our Geels 2010*, Pavee Point, Dublin.

Rattansi, A. (1992) 'Changing the Subject? Racism, Culture and Education' in Donald, J., and Rattansi, A., eds. *Race, Culture and Difference*, Sage Publications, London, pp. 11–48.

Richardson, V. (1999) 'Children and Social Policy' in Quin, S., Kennedy, P., O'Donnell, A. and Kiely, G., eds. *Contemporary Irish Social Policy*, UCD Press, Dublin, pp. 170–99.

Robson, C. (2002) *Real World Research*, 2nd edn, Blackwell Publishers, UK.

Royal College of Nursing (2012) *Health Inequalities and the Social Determinants of Health* [Internet]. Available from: <www.rcn.org.uk/__data/assets/pdf_file/0007/438838/01.12_Health_inequalities_and_the_social_determinants_of_health.pdf> [accessed August 2013].

Rush, M., (2006) 'The Politics of Care' in Fanning, B. and Rush, M., eds. *Care and Social Change in the Irish Welfare Economy*, UCD Press, Dublin, pp. 46–66.

Rush, M., Richardson, V. and Kiely, G. (2006) 'Family Policy and Reproductive Work' in Fanning, B. and Rush, M., eds. *Care and Social Change in the Irish Welfare Economy*, UCD Press, Dublin, pp. 143–62.

Scambler, G., (2000) 'Deviance, Sick Role and Stigma' in Scambler, G., ed. *Sociology as Applied to Medicine*, 4th edn, Harcourt Publishers, UK, pp. 171–82.

Sclater, S. D. (2000) *Families*, Hodder and Stoughton, England.

Scott, J. and Marshall, G. (2005) *A Dictionary of Sociology*, Oxford University Press, Oxford.

Selfe, P. and Starbuck, M. (1998) *Religion*, Hodder and Stoughton, England.

Shaw, M. (2007) 'The Family' in Matthewman, C., West-Newman, L. and Curtis, B. *Being Sociological*, Palgrave Macmillan, New York, pp. 360–80.

SILC (2013) *Survey on Income and Living Conditions* [Internet]. Available from: <www.cso.ie/en/media/csoie/releasespublications/documents/silc/2010/prelimsilc_2010.pdf> [accessed July 2013].

Silke, D. (1999) 'Housing Policy' in Quin, S., Kennedy, P., O'Donnell, A. and Kiely, G., eds. *Contemporary Irish Social Policy*, UCD Press, Dublin, pp. 49–71.

Smyth, E. and McCoy, S. (2009) *Investing in Education: combating educational disadvantage*, ESRI, Dublin.

'Socialization: From Infancy to Old Age' [Internet]. Available from: <www.usi.edu/liharts/socio/chapter/socialiazation/socialisation.html> [accessed 12 October 2005].

Stratton, D. (2004) *The Housing Needs of Old people*, Age Action Ireland.

Task Force on the Travelling Community (1995) *Report of the Task Force on the Travelling Community*, Stationery Office, Dublin.

Third Age (2013) *Combating Ageism – valuing older people, empowering communities, enriching lives* [Internet]. Available from: <www.thirdageireland.ie/advocacy/14/combating_ageism.html> [accessed August 2013].

Thompson, I. (1986) *Sociology in Focus: Religion*, Longman Group, UK.

TILDA (2011) *Fifty Plus in Ireland: First results from the Irish Longitudinal Study on Ageing*, Trinity College [Internet]. Available from: <www.tcd.ie/tilda> [accessed August 2013].

Tovey, H. and Share, P. (2000) *A Sociology of Ireland*, Gill and Macmillan, Dublin.

Tovey, H. and Share, P. (2003) *A Sociology of Ireland*, 2nd edn, Gill and Macmillan, Dublin.

Tovey, H., Share, P. and Corcoran, M. (2007) *A Sociology of Ireland*, 3rd edn, Gill and Macmillan, Dublin.

Treoir (2013) *Information for Unmarried Parents* [Internet]. Available from: <www.treoir.ie/policy_statistics.pdf> [accessed August 2013].

Turner, C. (2013) *Out of the Shadows: child marriage and slavery* [Internet]. Available from: <www.antislavery.org/english/slavery_today> [accessed July 2013].

United Nations International Labour Organisation (ILO) (2005) *Statistics and Databases* [Internet]. Available from: <www.ilo.org/global statistics-and-databases> [accessed July 2013].

Walliman, N. (2005) *Your Research Project*, 2nd edn, Sage Publications, London.

Walsh, M. (2001) *Research Made Real: A guide for students*, Nelson Thornes, UK.

Webb, R. and Tossell, D. (1999) *Social Issues for Carers: towards positive practice*, 2nd edn, Arnold Publishers, Great Britain.

Women's Aid (2013) *Making Women and Children safe* [Internet]. Available from: <www.womensaid.ie> [accessed August 2013].

Wood, K. and O'Shea, P. (2003) *Divorce in Ireland: Marital Breakdown: Answers and Alternatives*, First Law Ltd, Dublin.

www.boundless.com/sociology/understanding-global-stratification-and-inequality/stratification-systems/caste [accessed July 2013].

www.nyu.edu/classes/persell/reading4htm/P.1 [accessed June 2012].

www.sociology.org.uk/s1.pdf *Basic Concepts – inequality and stratification* [accessed July 2013].

Zinn, M., Stanley-Eitzen, D. and Wells, B. (2011) *Diversity in Families*, 9th edn, Allyn and Bacon, New York.